Object-oriented Programming with C++

A. K. Sharma
Professor and Dean
Department of Computer Science and Engineering
B. S. Anangpuria Institute of Technology and Management
Faridabad, Haryana, India

Pearson

Associate Editor—Acquisitions: Neha Goomer
Editor—Production: M. Balakrishnan

ISBN 978-93-325-1583-3

First Impression, 2014

Published by Pearson India Education Services Pvt. Ltd, CIN: U72200TN2005PTC057128

Head Office: 1st Floor, Berger Tower, Plot No. C-001A/2, Sector 16B, Noida - 201 301, Uttar Pradesh, India.

Registered Office: 6th Floor, Tower A, Unit A and B, International Tech Park, CapitaLand Chennai,
200 Feet Radial Road,Zamin Pallavaram, Old Pallavaram Chennai – 600117, Tamil Nadu, India

Website: in.pearson.com; Email: companysecretary.india@pearson.com

Digitally printed in India by Trinity Academy for Corporate Training Ltd, New Delhi in the year of 2026

Dedicated
to
all the objects around me

CONTENTS

PREFACE

My quest for object-oriented programming (OOP) started at University of Roorkee in November 1989 when my guru Prof. J. P. Gupta asked me the question: "what is object-oriented programming?" I did not have a compelling answer at that time. However, I started looking into the available literature to find the answers. A critical look at the literature revealed that OOP was more of a philosophy than a programming paradigm. In fact, it is nearer to the oriental philosophy which states that the world around us is not absolute but relative to an individual's capacity to perceive the world around him or her. In fact, whatever we perceive through our senses is nothing but an object.

When we look around, we find that we are surrounded by objects only. Everything around us, be it a book, pen, paper, laptop, or even me and you, can all be considered as objects. In fact, any real-world program has to be a collection of objects. For instance, a program about a university has to involve objects such as students, professors, clerks, class rooms, books, chalk and mark sheets. Then, why not write programs using objects, which would be a natural way of creating useful software comprising of interacting objects.

The programming process has evolved through many phases. The journey started with programmers who would write programs which somehow worked, without giving importance to the readability of the program. Languages such as FORTRAN and BASIC neither enforced any discipline nor were they user-centric. The result was the creation of unstructured programs that were susceptible to bugs like the Y2K problem acting as time bombs. The major problem with these programs was that they were not maintainable.

The advent of structured programming techniques did enforce some discipline on the programmers by way of shunning the use of 'goto' statements and encouraging the 'easy to read and difficult to write' style of code statements i.e., choosing long and meaningful names for the variables, functions, procedures, modules etc. The major emphasis was to use block structures in the program. For instance, any code enclosed between a pair of curly braces was termed as a block. Pascal and 'C' supported blocks such as compound statements, loops, functions, procedures, and files. This technique worked well for hardcore programmers, who were able to write large and complex programs using structured programming techniques. The Unix operating system was written using 'C'.

Nevertheless, procedures that helped to solve the problem at hand were emphasized. For a developer, algorithm development consumed more time while data was given least importance. Thus, a program turned out to be a collection of decomposed components i.e., interacting functions or modules exchanging data and data structures among them. Such data, especially the global data, was vulnerable to inadvertent corruption by the fellow programmers.

The above-mentioned drawbacks are remedied by paying more attention to data and trying to create reusable software components. The reusable components can further be combined to get bigger and more powerful software. In our day-to-day life, we create bigger objects from smaller objects. For example, the desktop computer is made up of many smaller objects such as the mother board, RAM, HDD, SMPS, the mouse and the keyboard. We utilize the functions of these objects without being keen to understand how they work or who made them.

OOP is a paradigm shift in programming that defines, creates, and manipulates objects to develop reusable software. C++ is an imperative language developed to support OOP components and features such as classes, objects, abstraction, encapsulation, inheritance, and polymorphism.

I have taught OOP at I.I.I.T.M Gwalior, JMI Delhi, YMCAUST Faridabad, and BSAITM Faridabad. And at these institutions, there has been a consistent demand from my students and fellow teachers to write a book on this subject.

Object-oriented programming with C++ has been written to help the readers look at OOP as a philosophy and think of the problem at hand as a collection of objects. It helps the reader to identify the classes to which the objects belong and also establish the relationship among the classes.

C++ supports the creation and manipulation of OOP components and tools such as classes, objects, abstraction, encapsulation, code reuse, code sharing, and polymorphism. Hence, the book introduces C++ as an object-oriented programming language.

UML is an object-oriented modelling language. An introduction to UML has been given with a view to acquaint the reader with various graphical tools offered by UML to represent OOP components.

This book would not have been possible without the good wishes, comments and suggestions I had received from many significant people. I place on record my thanks to Dr Atul Mishra, Dr Jyoti, Dr Anuradha Pillai, Dr Naresh Chauhan, Dr Rahul Rishi, Dr Divya Jyoti, and Sh. Pawan Bhadana. In fact, Dr. Atul Mishra has already taught his odd-semester class of 2013 using the proofs of this book.

I am indebted to my teachers and research guides Prof. J. P. Gupta, Prof. Padam Kumar, Prof. Moinuddin, and Prof. D. P. Agarwal for their encouragement. I am also thankful to my friends Prof. Ashok De, Prof. Qasim Rafiq, Prof. Rajender Sahu, Prof. N. S. Gill, and Prof. S. S. Tyagi for their support.

I commend the excellent job done by the team at Pearson Education, which made this beautiful book happen.

My parents always encouraged me and gave me all the strength I needed. And not to miss the everlasting companionship of the two most important people in my life, I convey my heartfelt thanks to my wife Suman and daughter Sagun for their support throughout.

While this book has been written with meticulous care, it is possible that some errors might have unwittingly crept in. I shall be grateful if they are brought to my notice. I shall also be happy to acknowledge suggestions for further improvement of this book.

A. K. Sharma

About the Author

A. K. Sharma is currently Professor (CSE) and Dean (PG and Research) at B. S. Anangpuria Institute of Technology and Management. Earlier, he was Professor and Dean, Faculty of Engineering and Technology, YMCA University of Science and Technology, Faridabad.

A member of the board of studies and academic council of several renowned universities, Dr Sharma has guided more than twenty students in doctoral programs leading to their Ph.D. degrees. He has published more than 250 research papers in national and international journals of repute and made presentations in numerous academic conferences. He heads a group of researchers actively working on the design of Web crawlers.

INTRODUCTION TO C++

1

1.1 INTRODUCTION

The 'C' programming language was created as a structured programming tool for writing large and complex system programs such as operating systems. No wonder that in 1973, Unix operating system was developed using 'C'. The software developers liked 'C' because of its characteristics such as speed, compactness, and ability to harness the power of the hardware through low-level features.

Niklaus Wirth has defined that a program is composed of two components Algorithms and Data structures, as given below:

```
Algorithms + Data Structures = Programs
```

Thus, there can be two approaches towards the development of software, i.e. to develop programs either centered around *functions* or with an emphasis given to *data*. The structured/top-down/modular programming was focussed on functions, with less importance given to the associated data. On the contrary, *object oriented paradigm of programming*, developed in 1960s, focused on *data* instead of functions.

Simula 67 was the first Object Oriented Programming language developed in 1960s. It was followed by Smalltalk in 1970s.

In 1980s the computing world grew at a tremendous rate and the need for thousands of system programmers was felt. Whereas the number of hard core 'C' programmers who could write and manage large and complex programs was hopelessly less. It was found that the structured programming itself had flaws and limitations, as there was no inherent support for code reusability, sharing, and extensibility. Therefore, it became necessary to develop a new programming language that could support fast development of extremely large, complex, and extendable software.

In 1983, Bjarne Stroustrup created C++ on the principles of object-oriented programming. It supported much-required features such as code reusability, extensibility, sharing and variety of polymorphism. Obviously, it was quickly adapted by programmers mainly because of its support for inheritance.

A comparison of various programming paradigms is provided in Chapter 2.

It may be noted that in addition to the Object Oriented Programming features, almost all the procedural programming features are available in C++. For instance, C++ supports basic data types (int, float, char, etc.), control structures, pointers, files, etc. Therefore, to start with, non-object oriented features of C++ are discussed in the following sections.

1.2 CHARACTERS USED IN C++

The set of characters allowed in C++ consists of alphabets, digits, and special characters as listed below:

1. *Letters*: both lower case and upper case letters of English:

   A, B, C, … X, Y, Z.

   a, b, c, …, x, y, z.

2. Decimal digits:

   0,1, 2, …, 7, 8, 9.

3. Special characters:

   !, *, +, \, ", <, #, (, =, {, >, %,), ~, :, }, /, ^, –, [, &,], ?, ', ., blank.

1.3 BASIC DATA TYPES

Every program specifies a set of operations to be carried out on some data in a particular sequence. The data can be of many types such as numbers, characters, Boolean, etc. In fact a data type defines the range of values and the set of operations that could be applied on that type of data. The range of values allowed for a data type depends upon the number of bytes allocated for its storage by the system. For example, one byte of allocation allows values ranging from −128 to +127 and two bytes allow values ranging from −32,768 to +32,767.

The basic data types supported by C++ are integer, floating point, and character types. A brief discussion on these types is given below:

1. **Integer (int).** An integer is an integral whole number without a decimal point. These numbers are used for counting. Examples of some valid integers are 525, 28, −24, 571, 209, −9.

   C++ supports two types of integers: **'int'** and **'long'**. These types are used for normal and extremely large values of counting numbers, respectively. The range of values that can be held in these data types is given in Table 1.1.

2. **Floating point (float).** A floating point number has a decimal point. Even if it has an integral value, it must include a decimal point at the end. These numbers are used for measuring quantities. Examples of some valid floating point numbers are 435.21, −987.1, 123., 0.435.

   C++ supports three types of floating points: **'float'**, **'double'**, **'long double'**. They can hold values in the increasing order of precision as given in Table1.1

3. **Character (char).** It is a non-numeric data type consisting of a single alphanumeric character. Examples of some valid characters are 'X', '9', 'r', 'V', '&', etc.

   It may be noted that the data items: '9' and 9 are of different types. The former is of type char and later of type int.

4. **void.** It is a special type that represents an empty set of different data types. No object can be defined of type void. At this moment, it is not worthwhile to discuss more on this data type. We shall discuss more on this type later in the book especially when we reach a stage where it can be used.

1.3.1 Data Types Modifiers

The range of values supported by a particular data type can be very large. A data type modifier can be used by programmer to refer to different sub-ranges of the values supported by a data type. The various data modifiers, their associated data types, range of values, and memory size occupied in bytes are tabulated in Table 1.1.

Table 1.1 Data Type Modifiers and Range of Values

Data Type	Modifier	Range of Values	Memory Size (bytes)
Integer	short	–32,768 to 32,767	2
	signed short	–32,768 to 32,767	2
	unsigned short	0–65,535	2
	int	Same as short	2
	unsigned int	Same as unsigned short	2
	signed int	Same as signed short	2
	long	–2,147,438,648 to 2,147,438,647	4
Floating point	float	$3.4 * 10^{-38}$ to $3.4 * 10^{38}$	4
	double	$1.7 * 10^{-308}$ to $1.7 * 10^{308}$	8
	long double	$3.4 * 10^{-4932}$ to $3.4 * 10^{4932}$	10
Character	char	–128 to 127	1
	signed char	–128 to 127	1
	unsigned char	0 to 255	1

1.4 C++ TOKENS

A token is a group of characters that belong together. It is the lowest level of semantic unit of C++. Therefore, any sentence or statement written in C++ must contain tokens such as *if*, +, *1008*, *for*, *while*, etc. C++ supports the following types of tokens:

- Identifiers
- Keywords
- Constants
- Operators

1.4.1 Identifiers

An identifier is a symbolic name that is used to identify and refer to data items or objects used by a programmer in his/her program. For example, if it is desired to store a value (say 27) in a memory location then the programmer must choose a symbolic name (say Num) and perform the following assignment:

```
Num = 27;
```

The symbol '=' is an *assignment operator* that stores the value '27' into a memory location called 'Num' as shown in Fig. 1.1. The character ';' marks the end of a statement and therefore it is called a *statement terminator*.

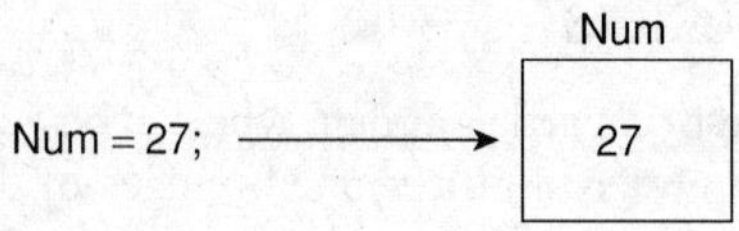

Figure 1.1 *Identifier 'Num' is being assigned the value '27'*

As defined earlier, an identifier is a token, i.e. a sequence of characters taken from C++ character set. The rules of formation of C++ identifiers are given below:

1. An identifier can consist of alphabets, digits, and/or underscore. However special characters such as space, comma etc., are not allowed to be included in an identifier name.
2. It must not start with a digit.
3. C++ is case sensitive language, i.e. upper case and lower case letters are considered different from each other. However, the identifier name can be a combination of uppercase and lower case letters.
4. An identifier name can start with an underscore.

   Examples of some acceptable identifiers are:

```
salary
basicPay
_bit
age_of_student
sri1008
```

   Examples of some unacceptable identifiers are:

```
Salary          (blank not allowed)
Basic,Pay       (special characters such as ',' not allowed)
345bit          (first character cannot be a digit)
```

   It may be noted that *salary* and *Salary* are two different identifiers.

1.4.2 Keywords

A keyword is a reserved word of C++. This cannot be used as an identifier in a program. The set of C++ keywords is given in Appendix.

1.4.3 Constants

A symbolic name or identifier, which does not change its contents during execution of a program is known as a constant. Any attempt to change the contents of a constant will result in an error message. The C++ constant can be of any basic data types, i.e. integer constants, floating point constants, and character constants.

const qualifier can be used to declare a constant as shown below:

```
const float Pi = 3.1415;
```

The above declaration means that identifier 'Pi' is a floating point constant having a fixed value equal to 3.1415.

Examples of some valid constant declarations are:

```
const int rate = 50;
const float Pi = 3.1415;
const char ch = 'A';
```

It may be noted that a character sequence enclosed within double quotes is called as a *string literal*. For instance the character sequence, "saiRam" is a *string literal*. When a string literal is assigned to an identifier, declared as a constant, then it is known as a *string constant*.

1.4.4 Variables

A variable is an identifier. It is the most fundamental aspect of any computer language. It is a location in the memory whose contents can change. It is given a symbolic name for easy reference. To understand this concept, let us have a look at the following statements:

1. total = 500.25;
2. net = total – 100;

In statement number (1) a value 500.25 is being assigned to a variable called *total*. The variable *total* is used in statement number (2) wherein the result of the expression on right-hand side (total – 100) is being assigned to another variable called *net*, appearing on the left-hand side of '=', the assignment operator. *The point worth noting is that the variable 'total' is being referred by its name in statement (2) but not by its content*. In fact, all variables are referred to by their names and not by their contents. This important feature of variables makes them a powerful tool in the hands of a programmer.

However, a variable needs to be defined of a particular type before it is used in a program. This activity enables the compiler to make available the appropriate amount of memory for the given type of the variable asked by the programmer. The definition of variable has the following format:

```
<data type> <variable name>;
```

where <data type> is the type of data to be stored and <variable name> is the user defined name of the variable.

For example, a variable called 'roll' of type integer can be defined as:

```
int roll;
```

Similarly, a variable called 'salary' of type float can be defined as:

```
float salary;
```

Examples of some valid variable declarations are:

1. `char ch;`
2. `int i, j, k;`

3. **float** payMonth;
4. **int** rollStudent;
5. **long** num;

C++ also allows initialization of a variable with a value at the time of declaration. For example, the variable called 'sum' of type int can be initialized to a value 100 as shown below:

```
int sum = 100;
```

1.5 INPUT–OUTPUT STATEMENTS

Input–output statements are program instructions used for interaction of data and messages with the user of the program and/or input-output devices. Input statements are used to provide data to the program. Output statements are used to display data on the screen. These statements can also be used to store the data on auxiliary devices such as hard disk, pen-Ram, etc.

In hills, the villagers bring an input stream of water underneath their houses from a river as shown in Fig. 1.2. The water for the kitchen is taken from the input stream and the waste water is let out into the output stream.

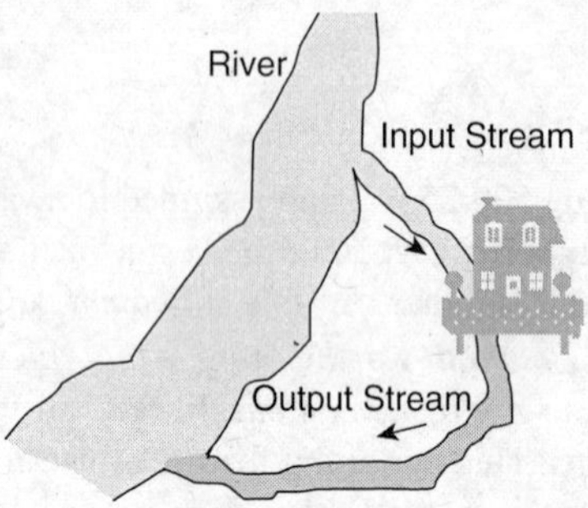

Figure 1.2 *Input and output streams of water for houses in hills*

Likewise, C++ also maintains input and output streams. The input and output devices are attached to the input and output streams, respectively, as shown in Fig. 1.3.

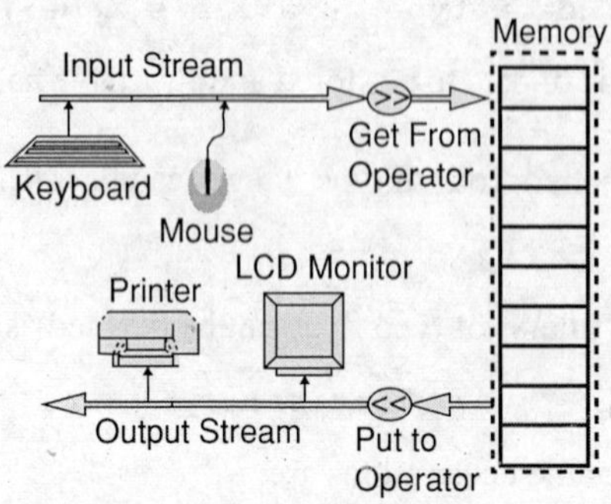

Figure 1.3 *Input–output streams in C++*

cin is the standard input stream (keyboard) and it can be used to input a value entered by the user from the keyboard. However, cin uses a *get from operator* (i.e. >>) to get the typed value from keyboard. The value is stored at a designated location of a variable in the main memory. Let us consider the following program segment:

```
int marks;
cin >> marks;
```

In the above segment, the user has defined a variable called marks of integer type in the first statement and in the second statement he/she is asking to read a value from the keyboard into marks. Once this set of statements is obeyed by the computer, whatever is typed on the keyboard (say 98) is received by the input stream cin which then hands over the received value to (get from operator) >>. The operator stores the value in the corresponding memory location called marks as shown in Fig. 1.4.

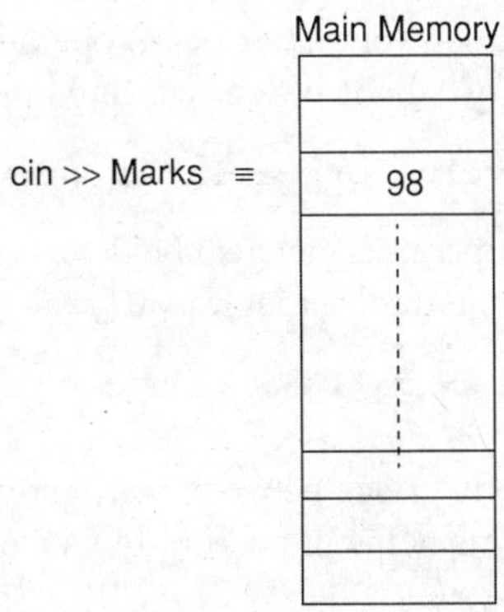

Figure 1.4 *Value inputted to a variable marks through cin*

cout is the standard output stream (visual display unit) and it can be used to display a value stored in a variable onto a display device such as an LCD display. Similar to cin, cout also uses a *put to* operator (i.e. <<) to extract the value from the variable. The value is then sent to the LCD display.

The contents of the variable (marks) can be displayed on the screen by the statement given below:

```
cout << marks;
```

The output of the above statement will be displayed on the screen as:

```
98
```

A message can be displayed on the screen as text enclosed within parentheses. Let us consider a situation where a user desires to display a message "My first attempt" on the screen. This can be achieved through the following statement:

```
cout << "My first attempt";
```

Once the above statement is executed by the computer, the following message will appear on the screen.

```
My first attempt
```

Similarly, the following program segment defines a variable *some* of integer type, initializes it to a value 500 and displays the contents of the variable on the screen

```
        :
int some;
some = 500;
cout << "The value of variable some =";
cout << some;
        :
```

Once the above program segment is executed by the computer, the following output is displayed on the screen:

```
The value of variable some = 500
```

In fact, we can also use more than one output or *put to* operators within the same output statement as shown below. This activity is known as **cascading** of operators:

```
cout << "The value of variable some = " << some;
```

Similarly, cascading of *get from* operators can also be done with a cin statement. For example, the following statement would input three variables val1, val2, and val3 from the keyboard.

```
cin >> val1 >> val2 >> val3;
```

Note: A stream acts as an interface between the Input/Output (I/O) system of the operating system and the program. This helps in making I/O statements independent of the actual physical devices attached to the system.

1.6 STRUCTURE OF A C++ PROGRAM

Every program written in C++ must follow the format or structure specified by the language. The general structure of a C++ program is given below:

```
# include <header file>
  main( )
  {
     ..........;
     ..........;
     ..........;
  }
```

It may be observed that the C++ program starts with a function called main( ). The body of the function is enclosed between curly braces. These braces are equivalent to Pascal's BEGIN and END keywords. The program statements are written within the braces. Each statement must end by a semicolon (the statement terminator).

A C++ program may contain as many functions as required. However, when the program is loaded in the memory, the control is handed over to function main( ) and it is the first function to be executed.

Let us now write our first program:

```
#include <iostream.h>
void main( )
  {
   cout << "My first attempt";
  }
```

When the above program is executed the following output is displayed on the visual display unit (VDU) screen.

```
My first attempt
```

It may be noted here that the statement **# include <iostream.h>,** has been placed at the top of the program. This is one of the header files defined by C++. It contains declarations for standard library functions for stream I/O.

1.6.1 Comments

A comment can be added to the program by enclosing the text between the pair: /* ... */, i.e. /* indicates the beginning of the comment and */marks the end of it. For example, the following line is a comment:

```
/* This is my first program */
```

A single line comment can be added in a C++ program by using double slash sequence (//) as shown in the following program:

```
// This is my first program
#include <iostream.h>
void main( )
  {
    cout << "My first attempt";
  }
```

It may be noted here that *a comment is a non-executable statement* in the program.

1.7 ESCAPE SEQUENCE (BACKSLASH CHARACTER CONSTANTS)

'C++' has some special character constants called *backslash character constants*. These are unprintable ASCII characters that can perform special functions in the output statements. A back slash character constant is nothing but a back slash ('\') character followed by another character.

For example, "\n" can be used in a cout statement to send the next output to the beginning of the next line.

Consider the following program:

```
#include <iostream.h>
void main( )
```

```
   {
    cout << "Our body has five Koshas as given below:";
    cout << "Anna, Prana, Mann, Gyan, and Anand";
   }
```

The output of this program would be:

Our body has five Koshas as given below: Anna, Prana, Mann, Gyan, and Anand

It may be noted that though two separate cout statements were written in the above program, the output has been displayed on the same line.

In order to display the text in two lines, the "\n" character constant should be placed either at the end of the text in the first cout statement or at the beginning of the text in the second cout statement.

Consider the following modified program:

```
#include <iostream.h>
void main( )
   {
    cout << "Our body has five Koshas as given below:";
    cout << "\n Anna, Prana, Mann, Gyan, and Anand";
   }
```

The character constant "\n" has been placed at the beginning of the text of the second cout statement and therefore the output of the program would be:

```
Our body has five Koshas as given below:
Anna, Prana, Mann, Gyan, and Anand
```

Some important backslash constants are listed below:

Backslash Character Constant	Meaning
\t	Tab
\b	Backspace
\a	Bell (alert)
\n	Newline character

Note: The backslash characters are also known as escape sequences. Such characters can be used within apostrophes or within double quotes.

A brief discussion on these backslash characters follows:

1. **'\t' (Tab):** this character is called as a tab character. Wherever it is inserted in an output statement, the display moves over to the next present tab stop. Generally a tab is of 8 blank spaces on the screen. An example of usage of character '\t' is given below:

```
#include <iostream.h>
void main( )
```

```
{
   cout << "\n \tAnna \tPrana \tMann \tGyan \tAnand";
}
```

The output of the above statement would be on the new line with spacing as shown below:

```
Anna     Prana     Mann     Gyan     Anand
```

2. **'\b' (Backspace):** this character is also called as backspace character. It is equivalent to the backspace key symbol (←) available on the computer or typewriter. It moves one column backward and positions the cursor on the character displayed on that column. An example of usage of character '\b' is given below:

```
#include <iostream.h>
void main( )
  {
   cout << "\n ASHOKA\b?";
  }
```

The output of the above statement would be:

```
ASHOK?
```

We can see that the trailing letter 'A' has been overwritten by the character '?' at the end of the string constant <ASHOKA> the reason being: '\b' moved the cursor one column backward, i.e. at 'A' and the *cout* statement printed the character '?' on that column position.

3. **'\a' (Alert):** this character is also called as alert or bell character. Whenever it is inserted in an output statement, it sounds a bell which can be heard by the user sitting on computer terminal. It can be used in a situation where the programmer wants to catch the attention of the user of this program. An example of usage of '\a' character is given below:

```
#include <iostream.h>
void main( )
  {
   cout << "\n Error in data \a";
  }
```

The output of the above statement would be the following message on the screen and thereafter sounding of a bell on the system speaker.

```
Error in data
```

4. **'\n' (new line):** as discussed earlier, this character is called as newline character. Wherever it appears in the output statement, the immediate next output is taken to the beginning of the next new line on the screen. Consider the program given below:

```
#include <iostream.h>
void main( )
  {
   cout << "\n This is \n a test";
  }
```

The output of this program would be:

```
This is
a test
```

1.8 OPERATORS AND EXPRESSIONS

An **operator** is a symbol or letter used to indicate a specific operation to be carried out on variables in a program. For example, the symbol '+' is an add operator that adds two data items called operands.

An **expression** is a combination of operands (i.e. constants, variables, numbers, etc.) connected by operators and parenthesis. For example, in the expression given below, A and B are operands and '+' is an operator.

```
A + B
```

C++ supports three basic types of operators: *arithmetic*, *relational*, and *logical*. An expression that involves arithmetic operators is known as an arithmetic expression. The computed result of an arithmetic expression is always a numerical value. The expression which involves relational and/or logical operators is called a Boolean expression or logical expression. The computed result of such an expression is a logical value, i.e. either 1 (True) or 0 (False).

The rules for formation of an expression are:

1. A signed or unsigned constant or variable is an expression.
2. An expression connected by an operator to a variable or a constant is an expression.
3. Two expressions connected by an operator is also an expression.
4. Two operators should not occur in continuation.

1.8.1 Arithmetic Operators

The valid arithmetic operators supported by C++ are given in Table 1.2.

Table 1.2 Arithmetic Operators

Symbol	Stands For	Example
+	Addition	x + y
–	Subtraction	x – y
*	Multiplication	x*y
/	Division	x/y
%	Modulus or remainder	x%y
––	Decrement	––x x––
++	Increment	++x x++

1.8.1.1 Unary Arithmetic Operators

A unary operator requires only one operand or data item. The unary arithmetic operators supported by C++ are, unary minus ('–'), increment ('++'), and decrement ('––'). As compared to binary operators, the unary operators are right associative in the sense that they evaluate from right to left.

The unary minus operator is written before a numerical value, variable or an expression. Examples of usage of unary minus operator are given below:

```
(i) -57; (ii) -2.923; (iii) -x; (iv) -(a * b); (v) 8 * (-(a + b))
```

It may be noted here that the result of application of unary minus on an operand is the negation of its operand.

The operators '++' and '––' are unique to C and C++. These are called increment and decrement operators, respectively. The increment operator ++ adds 1 to its operand. Therefore, we can say that, the following expressions are equivalent.

$$i = i + 1 \equiv ++i;$$

For example, if the initial value of i is 10 then the expression $++i$ will increment the contents of i to 11. Similarly, the decrement operator –– subtracts 1 from its operand. We can say that, the following expressions are equivalent:

$$j = j - 1 \equiv --j;$$

For example, if the initial value of j is 5 then the expression $--j$ will decrement the contents of j to 4.

The increment and decrement operators can be used both as a prefix and postfix to a variable as shown below:

$$++x \text{ or } x++$$
$$--y \text{ or } y--$$

As long as the increment or decrement operator is not used as part of an expression, the prefix and postfix forms of these operators do not make any difference. For example, $++x$ and $x++$ would produce the same result. However, if such an operator is part of an expression then the prefix and postfix forms would produce entirely different results.

In the prefix form the operand is incremented or decremented before the operand is used in the program.

1.8.2 Relational and Logical Operators

A relational operator is used to compare two values and the result of such an operation is always logical, i.e. either true or false. The valid relational operators supported by C++ are given in Table 1.3.

Table 1.3 Relational Operators

Symbol	Stands For	Example
>	Greater than	x > y
>=	Greater than equal to	x >= y
<	Less than	x < y
<=	Less than equal to	x <= y
==	Equal to	x == y
!=	Not equal to	x != y

A logical operator is used to connect two relational expressions or logical expressions. The result of such an operation is always logical, i.e. either true or false. The valid logical operators supported by C++ are given in Table 1.4.

Table 1.4 Logical Operators

Symbol	Stands For	Example
&&	Logical AND	x && y
||	Logical OR	x || y
!	Logical NOT	!x

Rules of logical operators:

1. The output of a logical AND operation is true if its both the operands are true. For all other combinations the result is false.
2. The output of logical OR operation is false if both of its operands are false. For all other combinations the result is true.
3. The logical NOT is a unary operator. It negates the value of the operand.

For initial value of $x = 5$ and $y = 7$, consider the following expression

```
(x < 6) && (y > 6)
```

The operand $x < 6$ is true and the operand $y > 6$ is also true. Thus, the result of above given logical expression is also true. However, the result of following expression is false because one of the operands is false:

```
(x < 6) && (y > 7)
```

Similarly, consider the following expression:

```
(x < 6) || (y > 7)
```

The operand $x < 6$ is true whereas the operand $y > 7$ is false. Since these operands are connected by logical OR, the result of this expression is true (Rule 2). However, the result of following expression becomes false (negation of true).

```
!(x < 6) || (y > 7)
```

Note: The expression on the right-hand side of logical operators && and ||, does not get evaluated in case the left-hand side determines the outcome.

Consider the expression given below:

```
x && y
```

If *x* evaluates to false (zero) then the outcome of above expression is bound to be false irrespective of *y* evaluating to any logical value. Therefore, there is no need to evaluate the term *y* in the above expression.

Similarly, in the following expression, if *x* evaluates to true (non-zero) then the outcome is bound to be true. Thus, *y* will not be evaluated.

```
x || y
```

1.8.3 Conditional Operator

C++ provides a conditional operator (? :) which can help the programmers in performing simple conditional operations. It is represented by the symbols '?' and ':'. For example, if one desires to assign the bigger of two variables *x* and *y* to a third variable *z* the conditional operator is an excellent tool. The general form of this operation is:

```
E1 ? E2 : E3
```

where E1, E2 and E3 are expressions.

In the conditional operation, the expression E1 is tested, if E1 is true then E2 is evaluated otherwise the expression E3 is evaluated as shown in Fig. 1.5.

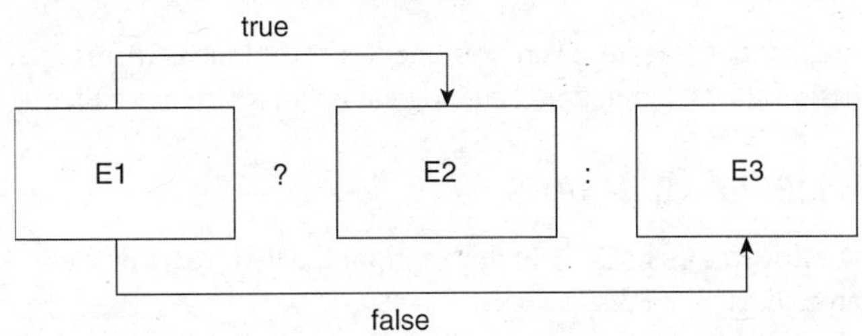

Figure 1.5 *Conditional operation*

Consider the following conditional expression:

```
z = (x > y) ? x : y;
```

The expression $x > y$ is evaluated. If *x* is greater than *y*, then *z* is assigned *x* otherwise *z* gets *y*.

Examples of valid conditional expressions are:

(i) $y = (x >= 10)\ ?\ 0 : 10;$

(ii) $\text{Res} = (i < j)\ ?\ \text{sum} + i : \text{sum} + j;$

(iii) $q = (a == 0)\ ?\ 0 : (x/y);$

It may be noted here that the conditional operator (? :) is also known as a **ternary** operator because it operates on three values.

1.8.4 Order of Evaluation of Expressions

A number of logical and relational expressions can be linked together with the help of logical operators as shown below:

```
(x < y) || (x > 20) && !(z) || ((x < y) && (z > 5))
```

For the above complex expression, it becomes difficult to make out as to in what order the evaluation of sub-expressions would take place.

In C++, the order of evaluation of an expression is carried out according to the operator precedence given in Table 1.5.

Table 1.5 Operator Precedence

Operators	Priority	Associativity
– ++ –– !	Highest	Right to left
* / %	↓	Left to right
+ –		Left to right
< <= > >=		Left to right
== !=		Left to right
&&		Left to right
||	Lowest	Left to right

It may be noted here that in C++, false is represented as zero. True is represented as any non-zero value. Thus, expressions that use relational and logical operators return either 0 (false) or 1 (true).

1.8.5 Some Special Operators

There are many other operators in C++. In this section, the two frequently used operators: sizeof and comma operators have been discussed.

1.8.5.1 sizeof( ) Operator

C++ provides a compile time unary operator called sizeof. When applied on an operand, it returns the number of bytes the operand occupies in the main memory. The operand could be a variable, a constant or a data type. For example, the following expressions:

```
a = sizeof("sum");
b = sizeof(char);
c = sizeof(123L);
```

would return the sizes occupied by arguments: sum, data type char and constant '123L' on your machine. It may be noted that

(i) The parentheses used with sizeof are required when the operand is a data type. With variables or constants, the parentheses are not necessary.

(ii) sizeof( ) operator has the same precedence as prefix increment/decrement operators.

Example 1. *Write a program that illustrates the usage of sizeof( ) operator.*

Solution: We would print the values of *a*, *b*, and *c* which contain the size of arguments: "sum", data type char and constant '123L' respectively. The required program is given below:

```
// The usage of sizeof operator

# include<iostream.h>
void main( )
 {
   int a, b, c;
   a = sizeof ("sum");
   b = sizeof (char);
   c = sizeof (123L);
       cout << "\n size of string : 'sum' = "<< a <<" bytes";
       cout << "\n size of data type : char = "<< b <<" bytes";
       cout << "\n size of number : 123L= "<< c <<" bytes";
 }
```

The output of the program is given below:

```
size of the string : 'sum' =4 bytes
size of the data type :char =1 bytes
size of number : 123L=4 bytes_
```

1.8.5.2 Comma Operator

The comma operator is used to string together a number of expressions which are performed in a sequence from left to right.

For example, the following statement

```
a = (x = 5, x + 2);
```

executes in the following order

(i) value 5 is assigned to variable x;

(ii) x is incremented by 2;

(iii) the value of expression $x + 2$ (i.e. 7) is assigned to the variable a.

The following points may be noted regarding comma operators:

1. A comma-separated list of expressions is always evaluated from left to right.

2. The final data type of a comma-separated list of expressions is always same as the data type of the rightmost expression in the list.
3. The comma operator has the lowest precedence among all C++ operators.

1.8.5.3 Assignment Operator

Statements are the smallest executable units of a C++ program and each statement is terminated with a semicolon. An assignment statement assigns the value of the expression on the right-hand side to a variable on the left-hand side of the assignment operator (=). Its general form is given below:

```
<variable name> = <expression>;
```

The expression on the right-hand side could be a constant, a variable or an arithmetic, relational, or logical expression. Some examples of assignment statements are given below:

```
a = 10;
a = b;
a = b * c;
```

(i) The assignment operator is a kind of a store statement, i.e. the computed value of the expression on the right-hand side is stored in the variable appearing on the left-hand side of the assignment operator. The variable on the left-hand side of the assignment operator is also called ***lvalue*** and is an accessible address in the memory. Expressions and constants on the right-hand side of the assignment operator are called ***rvalue***.

(ii) The assignment statement overwrites the original value contained in the variable on the left-hand side with the new value of the right-hand side.

(iii) Also the same variable name can appear on both the sides of the assignment operator as shown below:

```
count = count +1;
```

(iv) Multiple assignments in a single statement can be used specially when same value is to be assigned to a number of variables.

```
a = b = c = 30;
```

These multiple assignment statements work from right to left and at the end all variables have the same value. The above statement assigns the value (i.e. 30) to all variables *c*, *b*, and *a*. However, the variables must be of same type.

(v) A point worth nothing is that C++ converts the type of value on the right-hand side to the data type on the left.

1.9 FLOW OF CONTROL

A statement is the smallest executable unit of a C++ program. It is terminated with a semicolon. It is an instruction given to the computer to perform a particular task like reading input, displaying output, evaluating an expression, etc.

A single statement is also called as a simple statement. Some examples of simple statements are given below:

(i) `int a = 100;`

(ii) `S = S + a;`

(iii) `count ++;`

A statement can also be an empty or null statement as shown below:

```
;
```

The high-level languages such as Pascal, C, and C++ have been designed for computers based on Von-Neumann architecture. Since this architecture supports only sequential processing, the normal flow of execution of statements in a high-level language program is also sequential, i.e. each statement is executed in the order of its appearance in the program. For example in the following C++ program segment, the order of execution is sequential from top to bottom:

```
x = 10;   |
y = 20;   |        Order of execution
z = x + y; ↓
:
```

The first statement to be executed is '$x = 10$', and the second statement is '$y = 20$;'. The execution of statement '$z = x + y$' will take place only after the execution of the statement '$y = 20$'. Thus, the processing is strictly sequential. Moreover, every statement is executed one and only once.

Depending upon the requirements of a problem, it is often needed to alter the normal sequence of execution in the program. This means that we may desire to selectively and/or repetitively execute a program segment. A number of 'C++' control structures, are available for controlling the flow of processing. These structures are discussed in the following sections.

1.9.1 The Compound Statement

A compound statement is a group of statements separated from each other by a semicolon. The group of statements, also called a block of code, is enclosed between a pair of curly braces, i.e. '{' and '}'. The significance of a block is that the sequence of statements enclosed in it, is treated as a single unit. For example, the following group of statements is a block.

```
/* a block of code */
{
   cin >> a >> b;
   c = a + b;
   cout << c;
}
```

One compound statement can be embedded in another as shown below:

```
{
   :
   {
      :
   }
   :
}
```

In fact, the function of curly braces '{' and '}' in a C or C++ program is same as the function of Begin and End, the reserved words in Pascal. C and C++ call these braces as delimiters.

1.9.2 Selective Execution (Conditional Statements)

In some cases, it is desired that a selected segment of a program be executed on the basis of a test, i.e. depending upon the state of a particular condition being true or false. In C++, '*if statement*' is used for selective execution of a program segment.

1.9.2.1 The if Statement

This statement helps us in the selection of one out of two alternative courses of action. The general form of if statement is given below:

```
if (expression)
{
    statement sequence
}
```

where '**if**' is a reserved word; expression is a Boolean expression enclosed within a set of parentheses. These parentheses are necessary even if there is a single variable in the expression. Statement sequence is either a simple statement or a block. However, it cannot be a declaration.

Examples of acceptable if statements are:

```
(i) if (A > B) A = B;
(ii) if (total < 100) {
    total = total + val;
    count = count + 1;
    }
(iii) if ((Net > 7000) && (I_tex == 500)) {
    :
    }
```

1.9.2.2 The if–else Statement

It may be observed from the above examples that the simple if statement does nothing when the expression is false. An if–else statement takes care of this aspect.

The general form of this construct is given below:

```
if (expression)
    {
            statement sequence1
    }
else
    {
          statement sequence2
    }
```

where '*if*' is a reserved word; expression is a Boolean expression, written within parentheses; statement sequence1 can be a simple or a compound statement; '*else*' is a reserved word; statement sequence2 can be a simple or a compound statement.

Examples of if–else statements are:

(i)
```
if (A > B) C = A;
else C = B;
```

(ii)
```
if (x == 100)
cout << "Equal to 100";
else
cout "\n Not Equal to 100";
```

It may be noted here that both the if and else parts are terminated by semicolons.

Example 2. *Write a program that reads a year and determine whether it is a leap year or not.*

Solution: We know that a year is leap if it is evenly divisible by 4 or 400. However, a century year such as 1900 is not a leap year. Thus, it should not be divisible by 100. The program for this problem is given below:

```
//This program determines whether an input
  //year is a leap year or not

  #include <iostream.h>
  # include <conio.h>
  void main( )
   {
     int leapyear;
     clrscr( );
     cout << "Enter the year =";
     cin >> leapyear;
       //check if it is divisible by 4 & not divisible by 100
       // or divisible by 400
     if ((leapyear % 4 == 0)&&(leapyear % 100 != 0)
            || (leapyear % 400 == 0))
       cout << leapyear << "is a leap year\n";
     else
       cout << leapyear << "is not a leap year \n";
   }
```

Sample outputs are given below:

```
Enter the year =2000
2000 is a leap year
```

```
Enter the year =2006
2006 is not a leap year
```

1.9.2.3 Nested if Statements (if–else–if ladder)

The statement sequence of if or if–else may contain another if statement, i.e. the if–else statements can be nested within one another as shown below:

```
if (exp1)
 if (exp2)
    {
    :
    }
else
 if (exp3)
    {
       :
    }
 else
    {
       :
    }
```

It may be noted here that sometimes the nesting may become complex in the sense that it becomes difficult to decide "which if does the else match". This is called as "*dangling else problem*". The 'C++' compiler follows the following rule in this regard:

Rule: each else matches to its nearest unmatched preceding if.

Consider the following nested if:

```
if (x < 50) if (y > 5) Net = x + y; else Net = x - y;
```

In the above statement, the else part matches the second if (i.e. if ($y > 5$)) because it is the nearest preceding if. It is suggested that the nested ifs should be written with proper indentation. The else(s) should be lined up with their matching if(s). Nested if(s) written in this fashion are also called **if–else–if ladder**. For example, the nested if given above should be written as:

```
if (x < 50)
if (y > 5)
   Net = x + y;
else
   Net = x - y;
```

However, if one desires to match the else with the first if, then the braces should be used as shown below:

```
if (x < 50) {
if (y > 5)
   Net = x + y;
}
else
   Net = x - y;
```

The evaluation of if–else–if ladder is carried out from top to bottom. Each conditional expression is tested and if found true only then its corresponding statement is executed. The remaining ladder is, therefore, bypassed. In a situation where none of the nested conditions is found true then the final else part is executed.

1.9.2.4 Switch Statement (Selection of One Out of Many Alternatives)

If it is required in a program to select one out of several different courses of action then the switch statement of C++ can be used. In fact, it is a multi-branch selection statement that makes the control to jump to one of the several statements based on the value of an integer variable or expression. The general form of this statement is given below:

```
switch (expression)
   {
   case constant 1:      statement;  break;
   case constant 2:      statement;  break;
          :
   default  :   statement;
   }
```

where **switch** is a reserved word; expression must evaluate to an integer or character value; **case** is a reserved word; **constant** must be an int or char compatible value; **statement** is a simple or compound statement; **default** is a reserved word and is an optional entry; **break** is a reserved word that stops the execution within the switch and the control comes out of the switch construct.

The switch statement works according to the following rules:

1. The value of the expression is matched with the random case constants of the switch construct.
2. If a match is found then its corresponding statements are executed and when break is encountered, the flow of control jumps out of the switch statement. If break statement is not encountered then the control continues across other statements. In fact, switch is the only statement in 'C++' which is error prone. The reason being that is if the control is in a particular case then it keeps running through all the cases in the absence of a proper break statement. Thus, absence of a break statement is a common error. This phenomenon is called as "***fall-through***".
3. If no match is found and if a default label is present then the statement corresponding to default is executed.
4. The values of the various case constants must be unique.
5. There can be only one default statement in a switch statement.

Examples of acceptable switch statements are:

(i)
```
switch (BP)
     {
          case 1 : total + = 100;
                   break;
          case 2 : total + = 150;
```

```
            break;
        case 3 : total + = 250;
    }
```

(ii)
```
switch (code)
    {
        case 101 : Rate = 50; break;
        case 102 : Rate = 70; break;
        case 103 : Rate = 100; break;
        default : Rate = 95;
    }
```

From the statement (ii) it may be observed that depending on the value of the code one out of the four instructions is selected and obeyed. For example, for the code 103, the third instruction (i.e. Rate = 100;) would be selected. On the other hand, if the code evaluates to 101 then the first instruction (i.e. Rate = 50) would be selected.

Example 3. *Write a program that determines in which quadrant an angle lies.*

Solution: The program for this problem is given below:

```
// This program determines the quadrant for a given angle. It checks
for the value of angle
// between the range 0 to 360

# include <iostream.h>
void main( )
  {
  float val_angle;
  int term;
  cout << "Enter the angle in degrees 0-360";
  cin >> val_angle;
  if ((val_angle > 0) && (val_angle <= 360))
  {
  term = (int) val_angle/90;
    switch (term)
       {
       case 0 : cout << "\n Ist quadrant"; break;
       case 1 : cout << "\n 2nd quadrant"; break;
       case 2 : cout << "\n 3rd quadrant"; break;
       case 3 : cout << "\n 4th quadrant";
       }
  }
    else
       cout << "\n Error in data";
}
```

1.9.3 Repetitive Execution (Iterative Statements)

Some problems require that a set of statements be executed a number of times, each time changing the values of one or more variables, so that every new execution is different from the previous one. This kind of repetitive execution of a set of statements in a program is known as a *Loop*.

We can categorize loop structures into two categories: *non-deterministic* loops and *deterministic* loops. When the number of times the loop is to be executed is not known then the loop is called as non-deterministic loop, otherwise it is called a deterministic loop.

C++ supports while, do–while, and 'for' loop constructs to help repetitive execution of a compound statement in a program. The 'while' and 'do–while' loops are non-deterministic loops and the 'for' loop is a deterministic loop.

1.9.3.1 The while Loop

It is the fundamental conditional repetitive control structure in C and C++. The general form of this construct is given below:

```
while <cond> statement;
```

where **while** is a reserved word of C++; **<cond>** is a Boolean expression; **statement** can be a simple or compound statement.

The sequence of operation in a while loop is as follows:

1. Test the condition.
2. If the condition is true then execute the statement and repeat step 1.
3. If the condition is false, leave the loop and go on with the rest of the program.

Thus, it performs a **pre-test** before the body of the loop is allowed to execute.

Example 4. *Write a program that computes the factorial of a number* N.

```
N! = N * (N - 1) * (N -2) * ··· * 3 * 2 * 1
```

Solution: We would use the while loop for the iterations required in the computation of the factorial.

```
// This program computes the factorial of a number N

  # include <iostream.h>
  # include <conio.h>
  void main( )
   {
     int N;
     int fact;
     clrscr( );
     cout << "Enter the Number =";
     cin >> N;
```

```
            // initialize fact
    fact = N;
            // accumulate factorial in fact
    while (N > 1)
      {
        N = N - 1;
        fact = fact * N;
      }
            // print factorial
    cout << "\n The factorial of" << N << "is =" << fact;
     }
```

It may be noted here that the variables used in the <cond> or Boolean expression must be suitably initialized somewhere before the while statement is encountered otherwise the loop may not execute even once.

1.9.3.2 The do–while Loop

It is another conditional repetitive control structure provided by C and C++. The syntax of this construct is given below:

```
do
  {
     statement;
  }
while <cond>;
```

where **do** is a reserved word; **statement** can be a simple or a compound statement; **while** is a reserved word; **<cond>** is a Boolean expression.

The sequence of operations in a do–while loop is as follows:

1. Execute the statement.
2. Test the condition.
3. If the condition is true then repeat steps 1–2.
4. If the condition is false, leave the loop and go on with the rest of the program.

Thus, it performs a **post-test** in the sense that the condition is not tested until the body of the loop is executed at least once. Therefore, it is suitable for constructing "Menus".

Example 5. *Write a program that displays the following "Menu" to the user and asks for his/her choice. Thereafter, appropriate messages are displayed.*

Menu: mode of travel

Travel by air   1

Travel by train 2
Travel by bus 3
Travel by taxi 4
Quit 5
Enter your choice:

Solution: We would use the do–while loop to display the menu and switch statement to pick the choice entered by the user. The required program is given below:

```
// This program displays a Menu to the user

  #include <iostream.h>
  # include <conio.h>
  void main( )
   {
     int choice;
     clrscr( );
   do
   { clrscr( );     //display Menu
     cout << "\n \tMenu:mode of travel";
     cout << "\n";
     cout << "\n \tTravel by Air 1";
     cout << "\n \tTravel by Train 2";
     cout << "\n \tTravel by Bus 3";
     cout << "\n \tTravel by Taxi 4";
     cout << "\n \tQuit 5";
     cout << "\n";
     cout << "\n Enter your choice:";
                   // Get the choice
     cin >> choice;
      switch (choice)
       {
         case 1 : cout << "\n Fast and Risky";
                 break;
         case 2 : cout << "\n Comfortable and Safe";
                 break;
         case 3 : cout << "\n Slow and Jerky";
                 break;
         case 4 : cout << "\n Quick and costly";
        }
       getch( ); // wait for a key
      }
      while (choice !=5);
   }
```

1.9.3.3 The for Loop

It is a count-controlled loop in the sense that the program knows in advance how many times the loop is to be executed. The general form of this construct is given below:

```
for (initialization; expression; increment)
   {
      statement
   }
```

where **for** is a reserved word; **initialization** is usually an assignment expression wherein a **loop control variable** is initialized; **expression** is a conditional expression required to determine whether the loop should continue or be terminated; **increment** modifies the value of the loop control variable by a certain amount; statement can be a simple or a compound statement.

The loop is executed with the loop control variable at initial value, final value and the values in between.

We can increase the power of for-loop with the help of the comma operator. This operator allows the inclusion of more than one expressions in place of a single expression in the for statement as shown below:

```
for (exp1a, exp1b; exp2; exp3a, exp3b;) statement;
```

Example 6. *Write a program that computes x^y where x and y are integers.*

$$x^y = x * x * x * \cdots * x$$

Solution: We would iteratively multiply x to itself y times as shown below:

$$6^4 = 6 * 6 * 6 * 6$$

The required program is given below:

```
// This program computes x to the power y

   #include <iostream.h>
   # include <conio.h>
   void main( )
    {
      int x, y, pow;
      int i;
      clrscr( );
      cout << "\n Enter the values for x and y";
      cin >> x >> y;
        // initialize
      pow = x;
      for (i = 2; i <= y; i++)
       {
        pow = pow * x;
       }
      cout << x << "^" << y << "=" << pow;
```

```
    }
```

A sample output is given below:

```
Enter the values for X and y 6 4
6^4=1296
```

Consider the following program segment:

```
            :
    for (i = 1, j = 10; i < = 10; i ++, j --)
  {
   :
  }
```

The variables *i* and *j* have been initialized to values 1 and 10, respectively. Please note that these initialization expressions are separated by a 'comma'. However, the required semicolon remains as such. During the execution of the loop, *i* increases from 1 to 10 whereas simultaneously *j* decreases from 10 to 1. Similarly the increment and decrement operations have been separated by a 'comma' in the for statement.

Though the power of the loop can be increased by including more than one initialization and increment expressions separated with the comma operator but there can be only one test expression which could be simple or complex.

1.9.3.4 The 'break' and 'continue' Statements

The *break* statement can be used in a loop to terminate its execution. We have already seen that it is used to exit from a switch statement. In fact, whenever the break statement is encountered in a loop, the control is transferred out of the loop. This is used in a situation where some error is found in the program inside the loop or it becomes unnecessary to continue with the rest of the execution of the loop.

Consider the following program segment:

```
         :
   while (val != 0)
  {
     cin >> val;
     cout << "val =" << val;
     if (val < 0){
            cout << "\n Error in input";
            break;
        }
    :
  }
```

Whenever the value read in variable val is negative, the message: 'Error in input', would be displayed and because of the break statement the loop will be terminated.

A *continue* statement can also be used in loop to bypass the rest of the code segment of the current iteration of the loop. The loop, however, is not terminated. The execution of the loop resumes with the next iteration. For example, the following loop computes the sum of positive numbers in a list of 50 numbers:

```
:
sum = 0;
for (i = 0; i < 50; i ++)
  {
     cout << val;
       if (val < = 0) continue;
       sum = sum + val;
  }
:
```

It may be noted here that continue statement has no relevance as far as switch statement is concerned. Therefore, it cannot be used in a switch statement.

1.9.3.5 The exit( ) Function

In the event of encountering a fatal error, the programmer may desire to terminate the program itself. For such a situation, C++ supports a function called exit( ) which can be invoked by the programmer to exit from the program. This function can be called from anywhere inside the body of the program. For normal termination, the programmer can include an argument 0 while invoking this library function as shown below:

```
#include <iostream.h>
#include <process.h>
 void main( )
    {
             :
             if (error) exit (0);
             :
    }
```

It may be noted here that the file process.h has to be included as header file because it contains the function prototype of the library function exit( ).

1.9.4 Nested Loops

It is possible to nest one loop construct inside the body of another. The inner and outer loops need not be of the same construct.

```
while <cond>
  {
    do
    {
    } while <cond>;
    for (init; exp; inc)
         {
```

```
        :
        }
        :
}
```

The rules for the formation of nested loops are:

1. An outer for loop and an inner for loop cannot have the same control variable.
2. The inner loop must be completely nested inside the body of the outer loop.

1.10 ARRAYS

An *array* is a data structure with the help of which a programmer can refer to and perform operations on a collection of similar data types such as simple *lists* or *tables* of information. For example, a list of names of '*N*' number of students of a class can be grouped under a common name (say studList). This list can be easily represented by an array called studList for '*N* = 45' students as shown in Fig. 1.6.

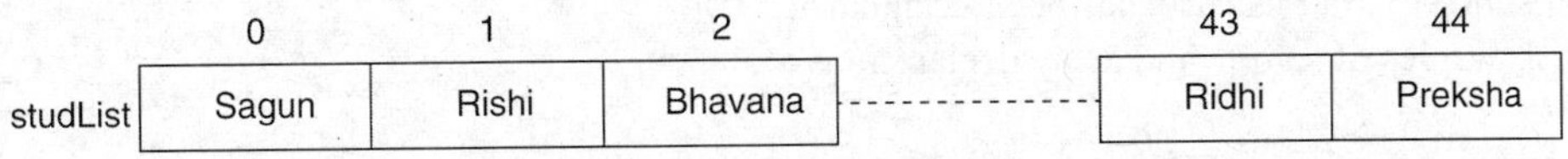

Figure 1.6 *Schematic representation of an array*

In fact, the studList shown in Fig. 1.6 can be looked upon by the following two points of views:

1. It is a linear list of 45 names stored in contiguous locations – an abstract view of a list having finite number of homogeneous elements (i.e. 45 names) .
2. It is a set of 0–44 memory locations sharing a common name called studList – it is an array data structure in which 45 names have been stored.

It may be noted that all the elements in the array are of same type, i.e. *string of char* in this case. The individual elements within the array can be designated by an index. The individual elements are randomly accessible by integers, called the index.

For instance, the 0th element (Sagun) in the list can be referred to as studList [0] and the 43rd element (Ridhi) as studList [43], where 0 and 43 are the indices and an index has to be of type integer.

An index is also called as a **subscript**. Therefore, individual elements of an array are called as **subscripted variables**. For instance, studList [0] and studList [43] are subscripted variables.

From the above discussion, we can arrive at the following definition:

Array: a finite ordered collection of items of same type. It is a set of *index*, *value* pairs.

An array is a built-in data structure in every programming language. Arrays are designed to have a fixed size. Some languages provide *0-based* indexing whereas other languages provide *1-based* indexing. 'C++' is an example of *0-based indexing* language because the index of its arrays starts from 0. Pascal is the example of *1-based addressing* because the index of its arrays starts from 1.

An array whose elements are specified by a single subscript is known as *one-dimensional array*. The array whose elements are specified by two or more than two subscripts is called as multi-dimensional array.

1.10.1 One-dimensional Arrays

One-dimensional arrays are suitable for processing lists of items of identical types. They are very useful for problems that require the same operation to be performed on a group of data. For example, an array called list of 50 locations of integer type can be declared as shown below:

```
int LIST [50];
```

The above declaration means that LIST is an array of 50 memory locations, each of which is of integer type. Once this declaration is obeyed, we get a group of 50 locations of integer type in the memory of the computer as shown in Fig. 1.7.

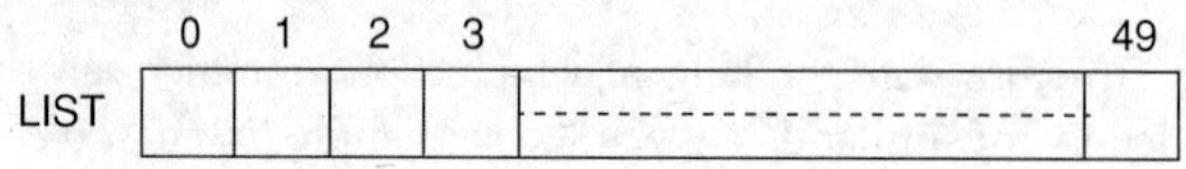

Figure 1.7 *A one-dimensional array of 50 locations*

It may be noted here that in C and C++ the first array element has the subscript 0. Therefore, the last subscript, in this case, has been designated as 49.

Examples of some valid array declarations are:

(i) `int series [100];`

(ii) `char names [20];`

(iii) `float sal [50];`

Generally, arrays are manipulated in a fashion of component-by-component processing. In simple words, we can say that similar operations are performed on some or all the components of the array.

Example 7. *Write a program which finds the largest number and its position in a list of N numbers.*

Solution: The basic solution is that if the list contains only one element then that element is the largest. Therefore, we would consider the zeroth number as the largest. The program is given below:

```
// This program finds the largest number in a list and its position
  # include <iostream.h>
  main( )
   {
      int set [100];
      int lar, pos, i;
      int N; // Size of the list
      cout << "\n Enter the size of the list";
      cin >> N;
      cout << "\n Enter the list \n";
         for (i = 0; i <= N - 1; i++)
```

```
        cin >> set [i];
        pos = 0;
        lar = set [0]; // Set the first value equal to large
        for (i = 1; i <= N - 1; i++)
            {
                if (set [i] > lar)
                    {
                        lar = set[i];
                        pos = i;
                    }
            }
        pos ++;
        cout << "\n The largest =" << lar << " " << "pos =" << pos;
}
```

A sample output is given below:

```
Enter the size of the list 5
Enter the list
12 5 67 52 31
The largest =67 Pos =3
```

1.10.2 Multi-dimensional Arrays

An array having more than one subscript is known as a multi-dimensional array. A two-dimensional array (having two subscripts) is suitable for table processing or matrix manipulations. For this purpose, we use two subscripts enclosed in square brackets. The first subscript designates the number of rows and the second subscript designates the number of columns. For example, a two-dimensional array of 5 rows and 4 columns (i.e. total 5 * 4 = 20 locations) of integer type can be declared as given below. Let us assume that the name of the array is mat.

```
int mat [5][4];
```

The above declaration means that mat is a two-dimensional array having 5 rows and 4 columns, i.e. totally 20 locations with each location of integer type as shown in Fig. 1.8.

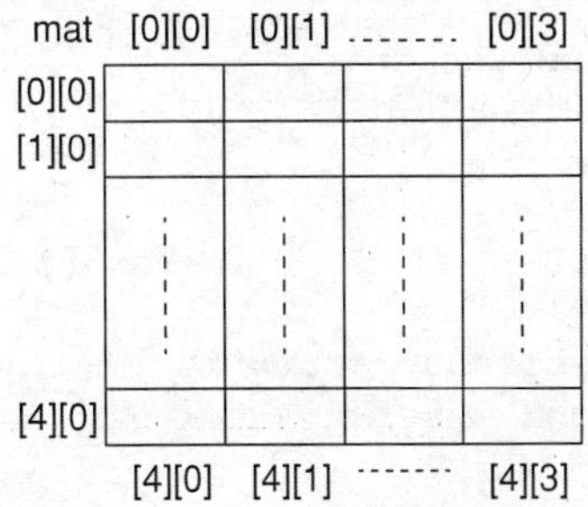

Figure 1.8 *A two-dimensional array*

An individual element of the array can be referred to by two subscripts, i.e. row and column subscripts. For example, a memory location at 4th row and 2nd column can be designated as mat [4] [2].

Example 8. *Given two matrices A and B of order m × n. Compute the sum of the two matrices such that:*

$$C(I, J) = A(I, J) + B(I, J), I = 1, \ldots, m \text{ and } J = 1, \ldots, n$$

Solution: The solution for this problem involves two-dimensional arrays. We would employ two nested loops, the outer for row traversal and the inner for column traversal. The required program is given below:

```
/* This program adds two matrices. The matrices are stored in
the 2-dimensional array MATA and MATB. The result of computation
is stored in a third two-dimensional array MATC */

# include <iostream.h>
# include <conio.h>
void main( )
{
   int MATA [10][10], MATB [10][10], MATC [10][10];   int i, j; //
Indexes of nested loops
   int m, n; //Order of matrices
     cout << "\n Enter the order of matrices \n";
     cin >> m >> n;
     cout << "\n Enter the elements of matrix A \n";
      for (i = 0; i < m; i++)
     {
      for (j = 0; j < n; j++)
         cin >> MATA [i][j];
     }
     cout << "\n Enter the elements of matrix B \n";
     for (i = 0; i < m; i++)
     {
      for (j = 0; j < n; j ++)
         cin >> MATB [i][j];
     }
             // Compute the sum
   for (i = 0; i < m; i++)
   {
     for (j = 0; j < n; j++)
      MATC [i][j] = MATA [i][j]+ MATB [i][j];
   }
   cout << "\n The resultant matrix is ... \n";
     for (i = 0; i < m; i++)
     {
      for  (j = 0; j < n; j++)
```

```
        cout << MATC [i][j] << ' ';
            cout << '\n';
            }
    }
```

1.10.3 Array Initialization

A programmer can initialize an array even at the time of its declaration. This is done by specifying the values of some or all its elements. For example, the string "SCHOOL" can be initialized in an array called '*texts*' in the following two ways:

```
char texts [7] = {"SCHOOL"};
char texts [7] = {'S', 'C', 'H', 'O', 'O', 'L', '\0'};
```

In the first case the string "SCHOOL" has been moved to the array text of size 7 where 6 locations have been used for the characters in the string and 7th for the null character '\0'. In the first case, the null character gets automatically attached at the end. However in second case, the string "SCHOOL" is being moved character by character. Therefore, it is necessary to provide the null character '\0' at the end of the string.

During initialization of arrays, one need not specify the dimension of the array as shown below:

```
int rol [ ] = {101, 105, 210, 319, 570};
```

The C++ compiler automatically calculates the dimensions of the un-sized initialized arrays. This type of un-sized array initialization is also possible for strings in C++. For example, the following array initialization is a valid initialization:

```
char text [ ] = {"SCHOOL"};
```

In this case also, the C++ compiler automatically computes the dimensions of the array. The multi-dimensional arrays can also be initialized in the similar fashion. Consider the matrix of order 4 * 3 given below:

$$A = \begin{pmatrix} 5 & 2 & 7 \\ 3 & 2 & 9 \\ 8 & 2 & 5 \\ 1 & 2 & 6 \end{pmatrix}$$

This matrix can be initialized in a two-dimensional array as shown below:

```
int A [4][3] = {5, 2, 7,
                3, 2, 9,
                8, 2, 5,
                1, 2, 6};
```

Note: The initialization of arrays at the time of declaration is possible only outside a function. Inside the function the initialized array has to be declared as static.

1.11 STRUCTURES

Arrays are very useful for list and table processing. However, the elements of an array must be of the same data type. In certain situation, we require a construct that can store data items of mixed data types. C and C++ support structures for this purpose. The basic concept of a structure comes from day to day life. We observe that certain items are made up of components or sub-items of different types. For example, a date is composed of three parts: day, month, and year as shown in Fig. 1.9.

Day	Month	Year
17	Aug	2012

Figure 1.9 *Date*

Similarly, the information about a student is composed of many components such as Name, Age, Roll No., and Class; each of them belonging to different types.

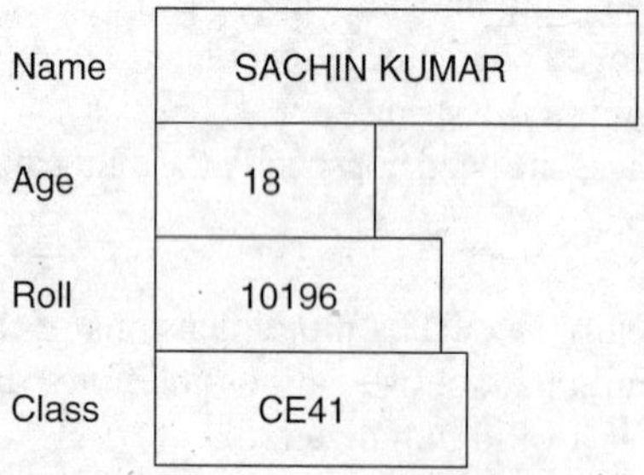

Figure 1.10 *Student*

The collective information about the student as shown in Fig. 1.10 is called a structure. It is similar to a record construct supported by other programming languages. Similarly, the date is also a structure. The term **structure** can be precisely defined as *a group of related data items of arbitrary types*. Each member of a structure is, in fact, a variable that can be referred to through the name of the structure.

1.11.1 Defining a Structure in 'C++'

A structure can be defined by the keyword *struct* followed by its name and a body enclosed in curly braces. The body of the structure contains the definition of its members and each member must have a name. The declaration ends by a semicolon. The general format of structure declaration is given below:

```
struct <name> {
   member 1
   member 2
   :
```

```
member n
};
```

where **struct** is the keyword; **<name>** is the name of the structure; **member** 1, 2, …, *n* are the individual member declarations.

Let us now define the C++ structure to describe the information about the student given in Fig. 1.10.

```
struct student
{
    char Name [20];
    int age;
    int roll;
    char class[5];
};
```

The above declaration means that the student is a structure consisting of data members: name, age, roll, and class. A variable of this type can be declared as given below :

```
student stud;
```

Once the above declaration is obeyed, we get a variable stud of type student in the computer memory which can be visualized as shown in Fig. 1.11.

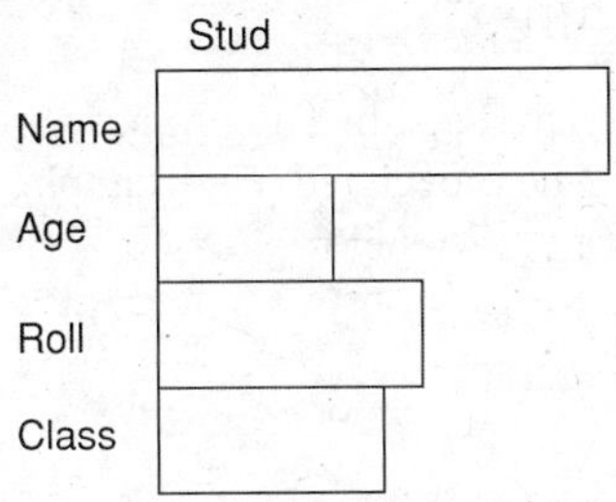

Figure 1.11 *Memory space allocated to variable stud of type student*

The programmer is also allowed to declare one or more structure variables along with the structure declaration as shown below:

```
struct student
{
    char name [20];
    int age;
    int roll;
    char class [5];
}
stud1, stud2;
```

In the above declaration the structure declaration and the variable declaration of the structure type have been clubbed, i.e. the structure declaration is followed by two variable names stud1 and stud2 and the semicolon.

1.11.1.1 Referencing Structure Elements

The structure variable stud has four members: name, age, roll, and class. These members can be designated as stud.name, stud.age, stud.roll, and stud.class, respectively. In this notation, an individual member of the structure is designated or qualified by the structure variable name followed by a period and the member name. The **period** is called as *structure member operator* or simply a dot operator.

However, the information of a student (Fig. 1.10) can be stored in structure variable stud in either of the following ways:

1. Initialize the elements of the structure

```
strcpy (stud.name , "SACHIN KUMAR");
stud.age = 18;
stud.roll = 10196;
strcpy (stud.class, "CE41");
```

2. The variable stud can be read in a C++ program by the I/O statements as shown below:

```
cin >> stud.name;
cin >> stud.age;
cin >> stud.roll;
cin >> stud.class;
```

1.11.2 Arrays of Structures

An array of structures can be declared just like an ordinary array. However, the structure has to be defined before an array of its type is declared. For example, 50-element array of type student, called stud_list, can be defined as shown below:

```
struct student {
    char name [20];
    int roll;
    int sub1, sub2, sub3, sub4;
    int total;
    };
student stud_list [50]; /* declaration of an array of structures */
```

1.11.3 Initializing Structures

When a structure variable is declared, its data members are not initialized and therefore contain undefined values. Similar to arrays, the structure variables can also be initialized. For instance, the structure shown in Fig. 1.10 can be declared and initialized as shown below:

```
struct student
    {
    char name[20];
    int age;
    int roll;
    char class[5];
    };
```

```
// Initialize variable of type student
struct student stud1 = {"SACHIN KUMAR",18,10196,"CE41"};
```

Please note that the values are enclosed within curly braces. The values are assigned to the members of the structure in the order of their appearance, i.e. first value is assigned to the first member, second to second, and so on.

1.11.4 Assignment of Complete Structures

It has been appreciated that the individual fields of a structure can be treated as simple variables. The main benefit of a structure, however, is that it can be treated as a single entity. For example, if two structure variables stud1 and stud2 have been declared as shown below:

```
student stud1, stud2;
```

then the following assignment statement is perfectly valid.

```
stud1 = stud2;
```

This statement will perform the necessary internal assignments.

1.11.5 Nested Structures

Nested structures are structures as member of another structure. For instance, the date of birth (DOB) is a structure within the structure of a student shown in Fig.1.12. These types of structures are known as nested structures.

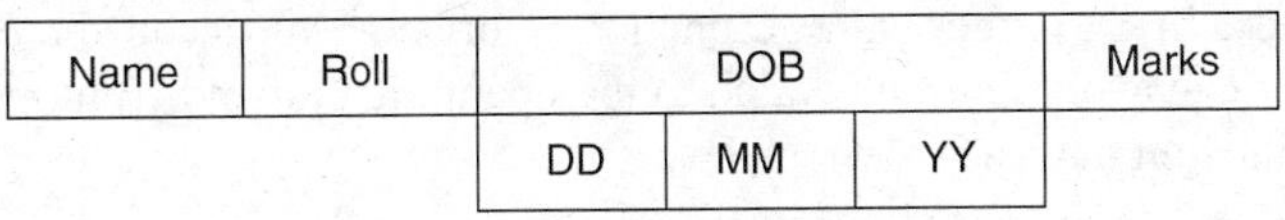

Figure 1.12 *Nested structures*

The nested structure shown in Fig. 1.12 can be declared in a program as shown below:

```
// Nested structures
struct date
   {
        int dd;
        int mm;
        int yy;
   };
struct student
   {
        char name[20];
        int roll;
        struct date dob;
        int marks;
   };
```

It may be noted here that the member of a nested structure is referenced from the outermost to innermost with the help of dot operators. Let us declare a variable stud of type student:

```
student stud;
```

The following statement illustrates the assignment of value 10 to the member mm of this nested structure stud

```
stud.dob.dd = 10;
```

The above statement means store value 10 in dd member of a structure dob which by itself is a member of structure variable called stud.

1.12 FUNCTIONS

A function is a sub-program that can be defined by the user in his/her program. It is a complete program by itself in the sense that its structure is similar to main( ) function except that the name 'main' is replaced by the name of the function. The general form of a function is given below:

```
<type> <name> (arguments)
```

where <type> is the type of value to be returned by the function. If no value is returned then keyword void should be used; <name> is a user defined name of the function. A function can be called from another function by its name; arguments is a list of parameters (parameter is the data that the function may receive when called from another function).

The program segment enclosed within the opening brace and closing brace is known as the function body. In C++, the main( ) function returns an integer to the operating system. The programmer can avoid returning value to the operating system by putting void before the declaration of function main as shown below

```
void main( )
   {

   }
```

Let us write a function *add( )* which receives two parameters *x* and *y* of type integer from the calling function and returns the sum of *x* and *y*.

```
int add (int x, int y)
    {
     int temp;
     temp = x + y;
     return temp;
     }
```

In the above function, we have used a local variable temp to obtain the sum of *x* and *y*. The value contained in temp is returned back through a return statement. In fact, variable temp has been used to only enhance the readability of the function otherwise it is unnecessary. The function can be optimised as shown below:

```
ind add (int x, int y)
    {
    return (x.+ y);
    }
```

Thus, a function has following four elements:

1. A name;
2. A body;
3. A return type; and
4. An argument list.

The name of the function has to be unique so that compiler can identify it. The body of the function contains valid C++ statements which define the task performed by the function. The return type is the type of value that the function is able to return to the calling function. The argument or parameter list contains the list of values of variables required from outside by the function to perform the given task. For example, the function given above has a name add. It has a body enclosed between the curly braces. It can return a value of type int. The argument list is *x* and *y*.

1.12.1 Function Prototypes

Similar to variables, all functions must be declared before they are used in a program. 'C++' allows the declaration of a function in the calling program with the help of a function prototype. The general form of a function prototype in the calling program is given below:

```
<type> <name> (arguments);
```

where **<type>** is the type of value to be returned by the function; **<name>** is a user-defined name of the function; and **arguments** is a list of parameters. The semicolon at the end of the comment is necessary.

For example, the prototype declarations for the functions add( ) can be written as shown below:

```
int add(int x, int y);
```

It may be noted that a function prototype ends with a semicolon. In fact, a function prototype is required for those functions which are intended to be called before they are defined. In the absence of a prototype, the compiler stops at a *function call* because, it cannot do the type checking of the arguments being sent to the function. In simple words, we can say that the main purpose of function prototype is to help the compiler in static type checking of the data requirement of a function.

1.12.2 Calling a Function

A function can be called or invoked from another function by using its name. The function name must be followed by a set of actual parameters, enclosed in parentheses separated by commas. A function call to function add( ) from the main program can be written as:

```
int val1 = 30, val2 = 45, result;
result = add (val1, val2);
```

This statement will transfer the control to function add( ) and the value returned by the function would be stored into result, the variable written on the left of the assignment operator.

1.12.3 Parameter Passing in Functions

We know that the two-way communication between the various functions can be achieved through parameters and return statement. The set of parameters defined in a function are called *formal* or *dummy* parameters whereas the set of corresponding parameters sent by the calling function are called *actual* parameters. For instance the variables *x* and *y* in the argument list of function add are formal parameters. The parameters included in the function call, i.e. val1 and val2 of main( ) are actual parameters.

The actual parameters can be passed to a function in one of the following two ways:

1. Call by value.
2. Call by reference.

1.12.3.1 Call by Value

For better understanding of the concept of parameter passing, let us consider the function **big( )** given below. It receives two values as dummy arguments *x* and *y* and returns back the bigger of the two through a return statement.

```
    // This function compares two variables and returns the bigger of
the two int big(int x, int y)
        {
        if (x > y)
        return x;
        else
        return y;
        }
```

The function big( ) can be called from the function main( ) by including the variables *a* and *b* as the actual arguments of the function call as shown below:

```
void main( )
  {
    int a = 30;
    int b = 45;
    int c;
    c = big (a, b);
   cout << "\n The bigger = " << c;
  }
```

The output of the above program would be:

```
The bigger = 45
```

Let us now write a program which reads the values of two variables *a* and *b*. The values of *a* and *b* are sent as parameters to a function exchange( ). The function exchanges the contents of the parameters with the help of a variable temp. The changed values of *a* and *b* are printed.

```
// This program sends the parameters to a function called exchange( )

# include <iostream.h>
# include <conio.h>
void exchange(int x, int y);

void main( )
  {
    int a, b;
    clrscr( ); /* clear screen    */
    cout << "\n Enter two values";
    cin >> a >> b;
    exchange(a, b);
    // print the exchanged contents
    cout << "\n The exchanged contents are: " << a << " and " << b;
  }

void exchange(int x, int y)
    {
        int temp;
        temp = x;
        x = y;
        y = temp;
    }
```

A sample output of the above program is given below:

```
Enter two values 34 56

The exchanged contenents are: 34 and 56
```

The above program seems to be wonderful but it fails badly because the contents of the variables *a* and *b* have not been exchanged. The reason for this behaviour is that at the time of function call, the values of actual parameters *a* and *b* get copied into the memory locations of the formal parameters *x* and *y* of the function exchange( ) as shown in Fig. 1.13.

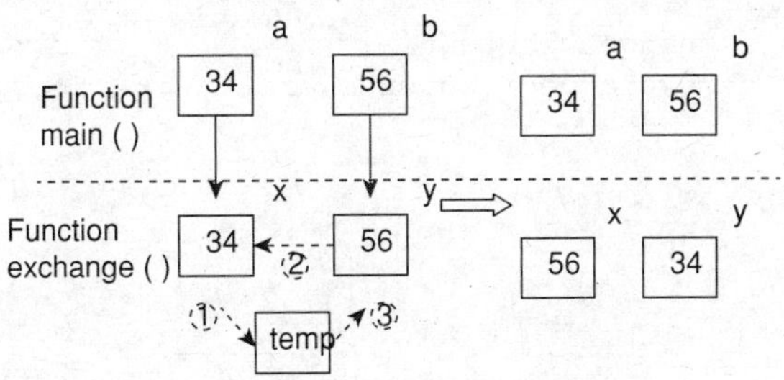

Figure 1.13 *Call by value*

It may be noted that the variables *x* and *y* have entirely different memory locations from variables *a* and *b*. Therefore, any changes done to the contents of *x* and *y* are not reflected back to the variables *a* and *b*. Thus, the original data remains unaltered. In fact, this type of behaviour is desirable from a pure function.

Since in this type of parameter passing, only the values are passed from the calling function to the called function, the technique is called as **call by value.**

1.12.3.2 Call by Reference

If the programmer desires that the changes made to the formal parameter be reflected back to the corresponding actual parameters then he/she should use call by reference method of parameter passing. This technique passes the addresses or references of the actual parameters to the called function. Thus, the actual and formal parameters share the same memory locations. This is achieved by applying an address operator (&) to the formal parameters in the function definition.

Let us rewrite the function exchange.

```
void exchange(int &x, int &y)
{
   int temp;
   temp = x;
   x = y;
   y = temp;
}
```

The complete program is given below:

```
// This program sends the parameters by reference to a function

# include <iostream.h>
# include <conio.h>
void exchange(int &x, int &y);
void main( )
 {
   int a, b;
   clrscr( ); /* clear screen   */
   cout << "\n Enter two values";
   cin >> a >> b;
   exchange(a, b);
   // print the exchanged contents
   cout << "\n The exchanged contents are: " << a << " and " << b;
 }

void exchange(int &x, int &y)
   {
      int temp;
      temp = x;
      x = y;
      y = temp;
   }
```

A sample output of the above program is given below:

```
Enter two values 34 56
The exchanged contenents are: 56 and 34
```

Now we can see that the program has worked correctly in the sense that changes made to formal parameters in the function exchange are available to corresponding actual parameters *a* and *b* in the function main( ). Thus, the address operator & has done the required task. In fact, the same memory locations are being looked upon as *a* and *b* by function main( ) and as *x* and *y* by the function exchange( ) as shown in Fig. 1.14.

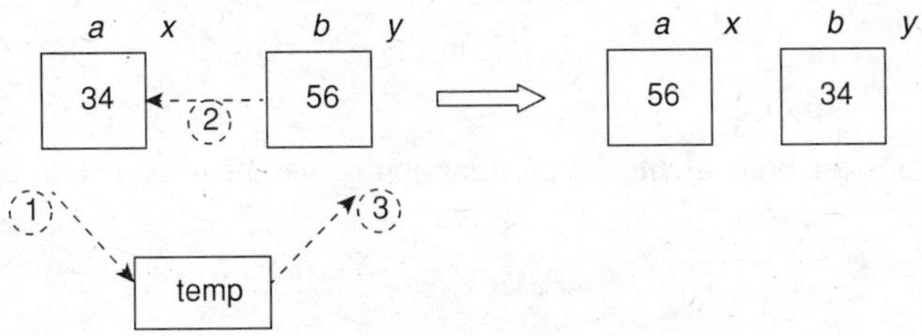

Figure 1.14 *Call by reference*

It may be noted that similar to variables, the *structures* can also be passed to other functions as arguments both by value and by reference.

1.12.3.3 Array Parameters

Arrays can also be passed as parameters to functions. This is always done through call by reference method. In C++, the name of the array represents the address of the first element of the array and, therefore, during the function call only the name of the array is passed from the calling function. For example, if an array *xyz* of size 100 is to be passed to a function some( ) then the function call will be as given below:

```
some(xyz);
```

The formal parameters can be declared in the called function in three ways. The following different ways are illustrated with the help of a function some( ) that receives an array *xyz* of size 100 of integer type.

First Method. In this method, the array is declared without subscript, i.e. of an unknown size as shown below:

```
void some(int xyz [ ])
   {


   }
```

The C++ compiler automatically computes the size of the array based on the actual parameter sent by the calling function.

Second Method. In this method, an array of specified size and type is declared as shown below:

```
void some(int xyz [100])
    {

    }
```

Third Method. In this method, the operator * is applied on the name of the array indicating that it is a pointer.

```
void some(int *xyz)
    {
    }
```

All the three methods are equivalent and the function some( ) can be called by the following statement.

```
some(xyz);
```

Note:

1. The arrays are never passed by value and cannot be used as the return type of a function.
2. In C and C++, the name of the array represents the address of the first element or the zeroth element of the array. So when an array is used as an argument to a function only the address of the array gets passed and not the copy of the entire array. Hence, any changes made to the array inside the called function are automatically reflected in the calling function. You do not have to use ampersand (&) with array name even though it is a call by reference method. The '&' operator is implied in case of arrays.

1.12.4 Returning Values from Functions

Earlier in this chapter we have used functions which either return no value or integer values. The functions that return no value are declared as void. We have been prefixing int to functions which return integer values. This is valid but unnecessary because the default return value of a function in C++ is of type int. Thus, the following two declarations are equivalent in the sense that we need not prefix int to a function which returns an integer value.

```
int add (int a, int b);
    add (int a, int b);
```

On the other hand, whenever a function returns non-integer values, the function must be prefixed with the appropriate type. For example, a function myFunc( ) that returns a value of type float can be declared as shown below:

```
float myFunc(...)
{    float a;
     :
     return a;
}
```

Similarly, a function yourfunc( ) that returns a value of type char can be declared as shown below:

```
char yourFunc(...)
{    char ch;
     :
     return ch;
}
```

It may be noted that similar to variables, the structures can also be returned from a function.

Example 9. *Write a program that generates the nth term of Fibonacci sequence as given below:*

0, 1, 1, 2, 3, 5, 8, 13, ...

Solution: From the sequence, it may be observed that except 1st and 2nd terms, an *n*th term is equal to the sum of its immediate previous two terms, i.e. $(n-1)$th and $(n-2)$th terms. The recursive definition of a term of this sequence is given below:

$$\text{term}(n) = \begin{cases} 0, & \text{if } n = 0 \\ 1, & \text{if } n = 1 \\ \text{term}(n-1) + \text{term}(n-2), & \text{if } n >= 2 \end{cases}$$

We would use a function called genTerm( ) to generate a Fibonacci term. The program is given below:

```
// This program generates a Fibonacci term using a function genTerm( )

# include <iostream.h>
# include <conio.h>
int genTerm(int n);
void main( )
{
  int N, nthTerm;
  cout << "\n Enter the number of terms (N):";
  cin >> N;
  nthTerm = genTerm(N);
  cout << "\n The <<" N << "th Term of the Fibonacci series =" <<
  nthTerm;
}
int genTerm(int n)
  {
    int i,term1 = 0, term2 = 1, term3;
    if (n == 0) return term1;
    if (n == 1) return term2;

   for (i = 3; i <= n; i++)
```

```
    {
term3 = term1 + term2;
term1 = term2;
term2 = term3;
    }
   return term3;
}
```

1.13 I/O FUNCTIONS

In addition to iostream functions: cin and cout, C++ supports following functions also which allow the input and output of character type data from standard I/O devices.

1. getchar( )
2. putchar( )
3. gets( )
4. puts( )

The C++ environment assumes keyboard as standard input device and VDU as standard output device. In order to use the above functions, the programmer should include the stdio.h header file at the beginning of his/her program as shown below:

```
# include <stdio.h>
```

1.13.1 getchar( ) and putchar( ) Functions

These functions are character-based input and output functions. The getchar( ) function reads a single character from the standard input device. For example, if it is desired to read a character from keyboard in a character variable called 'ch' then the following set of statements can be used.

```
char ch;
ch = getchar( );
:
```

It may be noted here that the function getchar( ) is buffered in the sense that the character typed by the user is stored in a buffer and not passed to the variable ch until the user hits the enter or return key, i.e. ↵.

Since the getchar( ) function is buffered, it is suggested that after an input operation from the standard input device (i.e. keyboard) the input buffer should be cleared. This operation is required to avoid interference with subsequent input operations. The function provided for this activity is fflush(stdin). The usage is shown below:

```
:
char ch;
ch = getchar( );
```

```
fflush(stdin);
:
```

The function putchar( ) is used to send a single character to the standard output device. The character to be displayed on the VDU screen is included as an argument to the putchar( ) function as shown below:

```
ch = 'A';
putchar(ch);
:
```

Once the above program segment is executed, the character A has to be displayed on the screen. The putchar( ) function is also buffered. The output buffer is cleared only when a new line character '\n' is used. The function call for this activity is fflush(stdout).

Example 10. *Write a program that prints the following output on the screen.*

A
AB
ABC
ABCD
ABCDE

Solution: It can be observed that there are five rows to be printed on the screen. Each row contains columns equal to the number of the rows, i.e. in row number 3, there are three columns to be displayed. Therefore, this is a case of nested loops. We will initialize a variable (say ch) with the character 'A' at the beginning of each row and print it. Subsequent increments of variable ch will generate the next character (column) required in the row. At the end of each row, the character '\n' will be printed to go to the next line.

The required program is given below:

```
/* This program illustrates the usage of getchar( ) and putchar( )
functions. It generates a pattern on the screen */

  # include <iostream.h>
  # include <stdio.h>
  main( )
  {
   char ch;
   int i, j;
   for (i = 1; i < = 5; i++)
   {
      ch = 'A';
      for (j = 1; j <= i; j++)
      {      putchar(ch);
             ch++;
      }
```

```
        putchar('\n');
        fflush(stdout);
    }
}
```

1.13.2 getc( ) and putc( ) Functions

The getc( ) and putc( ) functions are also character based functions. They have been basically designed to work with the files. However, these functions can also be used to read and write data from standard input and output devices by specifying stdin and stdout as input and output files, respectively.

For example, the function getc(stdin) is equivalent to the function *getchar*( ). Both will get a character from the standard input device (keyboard). Where the function getchar( ) by default reads from keyboard, the argument stdin of function *getc*(*stdin*) makes it read from a file represented by the standard input device which is nothing but the keyboard. Similarly, the function *putc*(*ch, stdout*) is equivalent to the function *putchar(ch)*. Both the functions send the character ch to the standard output device, i.e. VDU screen.

1.13.3 gets( ) and puts( ) Functions

These functions are string-based input–output functions. The function gets( ) reads a string from the standard input device (keyboard). It is also buffered and therefore the return or enter key (symbol ↵) has to be typed to terminate the input. The fflush( ) function should also be used after each gets( ) to avoid interference within the succeeding inputs. The program segment given below reads a string in a variable (name) from keyboard:

```
name = gets( );
fflush(stdin);
        :
```

Similarly the function puts( ) is used to send a string to the standard output device. The string to be displayed on the VDU screen is included as an argument to the puts( ) function as shown below:

```
city = "New Delhi";
  puts(city);
        :
```

Once this program segment is executed, the following text will be displayed on the screen:

```
New Delhi
```

Example 11. *Write a program that accepts a character from the keyboard and determines if it is a vowel or not. If yes then it prints the vowel otherwise gives the message:*

It is not a vowel

Solution: In this program we will use puts( ) function to print the messages and getchar( ) function to read the character from the keyboard. However, a switch construct will be employed to check if the input character is a vowel. The required program is given below:

```
// This program determines if an input character is a vowel

# include <iostream.h>
# include <stdio.h>
void main( )
{
  char ch;
  puts("Enter a lower case character");
  ch = getchar( ); //read character
  fflush(stdin); //clear input buffer
  switch (ch)
  {
   case 'a' : puts("The vowel is a");
         break;
   case 'e' : puts("The vowel is e");
         break;
   case 'i' : puts("The vowel is i");
         break;
   case 'o' : puts("The vowel is o");
         break;
   case 'u' : puts("The vowel is u");
         break;
   default: puts("It is not a vowel");
  }
}
```

1.14 STRINGS

We know that a sequence of characters is called as *string*. For example, the character sequence: *"India is an ancient civilization"*, is a string. 'C++' does not provide a built-in data type for strings. In previous section, it has been discussed that a string can be represented by an array of characters terminated by the null character '\0'.

However, 'C++' provides a stream called 'string.h' that provides variety of useful functions for manipulation of strings. Some of the important functions supported by the stream 'string.h' are discussed below:

1. **strcpy( ):** this function copies one string to another. The general form of this function is given below:

   ```
   strcpy(dest, source);
   ```

   It copies the 'source' string into the 'dest' string. The copying process stops after the null character '\0' of 'source' is copied to the 'dest' string.

The following program reads a string called 'source' and copies it to another string called 'dest'. The contents of 'dest' are displayed.

```
// This program illustrates the usage of function strcpy( )

# include <iostream.h>
# include <stdio.h>
# include <string.h>
void main( )
{
 char source[25], dest[25];
 puts("\ Enter source string");
 gets(source);
 strcpy(dest, source);
 puts("\n The destination string is…");
 puts(dest);
}
```

A sample output is given below:

```
 Enter source string
Help ever Hurt never

 The destination string is...
Help ever Hurt Never
```

2. **strcat( ):** this function appends one string to the end of another. The general form of this function is given below:

```
strcat(dest, source);
```

It appends the 'source' string to the end of the 'dest' string such that the size of the 'dest' string becomes equal to the total of both the strings.

The following program reads a string called 'source' and appends it to another string called 'dest'. The contents of 'dest' are displayed.

```
// This program illustrates the usage of function strcat( )

# include <iostream.h>
# include <stdio.h>
# include <string.h>
void main( )
  {
   char source[30], dest[15];
   puts("\n Enter destination string");
   gets(dest);
   puts("\n Enter source string");
   gets(source);
   strcat(dest, source);
   puts("\n The destination string is…");
   puts(dest);
   }
```

A sample output is given below:

```
Enter source string
Mangal pandey
Enter source string
- The revolutionary
The revolution string is...
Mangal pandey- The revoiutionary
```

3. **strlen( ):** it calculates the length of a given string. The general format of this function is given below:

```
strlen( string);
```

The following program reads a string called 'text' and gets its length computed through the function strlen( ) and displays the length.

```
// This program illustrates the usage of function strlen( )

# include <iostream.h>
# include <stdio.h>
# include <string.h>
void main( )
  {
   char text[30];
   int lenth;
   puts("\n Enter a text");
   gets(text);
   lenth = strlen(text);
   puts("\n The length of text string is…");
   cout << lenth;
  }
```

The sample output is given below:

```
Enter a text
C++ is object oriented langage
The length of text string is...
31
```

4. **strcmp(string1, string2):** this function compares two strings 'string1' and 'string2'. The comparison begins with the first character of both the strings and continuous with the subsequent characters until the end of the strings is reached or the compared characters do not match with each other. This function returns a value as per the following criteria:

```
                              ┌< 0 if (string1 < string2)
strcmp (string1, string2) =  ─┤= 0 if (string1 = string2
                              └> 0 if (string1 > string2
```

The flowing program compares two strings and gives messages: equal or not equal as per the types of string provided by the user.

```
// This program illustrates the usage of function strcmp( )

# include <iostream.h>
# include <stdio.h>
# include <string.h>
void main( )
 {
   char string1[20], string2[20];
   puts("\n Enter a string1");
   gets(string1);
   puts("\n Enter a string2");
   gets(string2);
   if (!strcmp (string1, string2))
   puts("\n The strings are equal");
   else
   puts("\n The strings are not equal");
}
```

A sample output is given below:

```
Enter a string1
Bharat

Enter a string2
Bharat

The strings are equal
```

1.15 SUMMARY

C++ is a superset of ‘C’ language. Built-in data types of ‘C++’ are int, float, and char. Built-in data structures of C++ are arrays, structures, files, and pointers. A semicolon (;) acts as a statement terminator. The ‘++’ and ‘—’ are called increment and decrement operators, respectively. The **while** construct, is a pre-test iteration loop. The **do–while** is a post-test iteration loop. The **for** construct is a count-controlled loop. Arrays are manipulated on a component-by-component basis. A function prototype ends with a semicolon.

MULTIPLE CHOICE QUESTIONS

1. Consider the following declaration

   `int list [5] = {2, 4, 0,6,1};`

   What will be the values assigned to list[0] and list[3]

   (a) 4, 6 (b) 2, 6
   (c) 2, 0 (d) 0, 4

2. Consider the following declaration

```
int val = 50;
```

Which option would print: half

```
(a) if (val < 50) && (val == 50 ) cout << "half";
(b) if (val < 50) && (val != 50 ) cout << "half";
(c) if (val < 50) || (val > 50 )  cout << "half";
(d) if (val < 50) || (val == 50 ) cout << "half";
```

3. A function call that sends the copy of its actual parameters to a function is called as:
   (a) call by value (b) call by reference
   (c) call by pointer (d) none of the above
4. A break statement causes the program control to exit:
   (a) from innermost to outermost loop or switch statement
   (b) from innermost to penultimate loop or switch statement
   (c) from all nested loops or switches
   (d) none of the above
5. A exit ( ) causes the program control to exit:
   (a) from innermost to outermost loop or switch statement
   (b) from the block in which it is encountered.
   (c) from all the loops
   (d) from the program itself
6. What would be the output of the following code?

```
int val1, val2, val3;
val2 = val3 = 50;
val1  = ( val3 = = val2);
cout << val1;
```

   (a) 100 (b) 50
   (c) 0 (d) 1
7. A 'for-loop' is:
   (a) pre-test loop (b) a post-test loop
   (c) count-controlled loop (d) none
8. A comment is:
   (a) an executable statement (b) a necessary statement in a program
   (c) a non-executable statement (d) none of the above
9. The variable on the left-hand side of an assignment operator is called
   (a) rvalue (b) lvalue
   (c) realvalue (d) none
10. The "fall through" phenomenon happens in context of a
   (a) for loop (b) switch statement
   (c) if–else construct (d) function

ANSWERS

1. b **2.** d **3.** a **4.** d **5.** d **6.** d **7.** c **8.** c **9.** b **10.** b

EXERCISES

1. Differentiate among the following
   (a) Identifier and keyword
   (b) Constant and variable
   (c) cin and cout
   (d) '\n' and '\t'
2. Write a program in C++ that displays the following message on the screen:

   " C++ is an Object Oriented Programming Language"
3. How comments can be added to a C++ program?
4. Given the following declarations:

```
char ch;
int i, j ,k;
const char c = 'X';
float val;
```

   which of the following assignment is illegal
   (i) *j* = val; (ii) *c* = ch; (iii) ch = *c*; (iv) *i* = *j* = 40; (v) val = 67.34
5. What is the output of the following program?

```
# include <iostream.h>
void main( )
  {
    int val;
    cout << "\n val = " << val;
}
```

   (i) An error (ii) 0 (iii) unpredictable
6. What is the output of the following program?

```
# include <iostream.h>
void main( )
 {
   int val;
   val = 12 > 13 ? 40 : 50;
   cout << val;
 }
```

7. What is the output of the following program?

```
# include <iostream.h>
void main( )
  {
```

```
int val = 20;
val = ++val == 21;
cout << val;
}
```

8. What is the output of the following program?

```
# include <iostream.h>
void main( )
  {
   int val = 20;
   val = val++ == 21;
   cout << val;
  }
```

9. What is meant by a nested if statement? Explain if–else–if ladder in brief.
10. Write a program that generates the following pattern on the screen

1 2 3 4 5
1 2 3 4
1 2 3
1 2
1

11. What would be the output of the following program?

```
# include <iostream.h>
void main( )
  {
    int i;
    for (i = 1; i <= 10; i++);
    cout << "Aloha";
  }
```

12. Write a program that removes duplicates from a list, stored in an array.
13. Write a program that computes the sum of diagonal elements of a square matrix.
14. What would be the output of the following program?

```
# include <iostream.h>
void main( )
  {
    char Text[6] ={'1', '2', '3', '4', '\0', '5'};
    cout << Text;
  }
```

15. A date comprises of three components as given below:

dd	
mm	
yy	

Write a program that uses above structure to read a date and checks for its validity.

16. The record of a player has following components:

Name			Age	Game	Address			
First Name	Middle Name	Last Name			H.No.	Street	City	State

Give a suitable C++ structure declaration for the above given record.

17. A perfect number is that number that equals the sum of all the numbers that divides it evenly. For example, 1, 2, and 3 divide evenly the number 6 and their sum is also 6. Write a function called **ifPerfect(int num)** function which determines whether **num** is perfect or not and accordingly returns 1 or 0, respectively.
18. Write a complete program that uses the function ifPerfect( ) given in Q.17 to print all perfect numbers between 1 and 100.
19. Write function **find(int List[], int X)** that searches the number X in a list called List. If the search is successful, it returns 1 else 0.
20. Write a program that counts the number of non-zero elements present in a two-dimensional array **MAT[][]** ***m*** * ***n*** of type integers.
21. How is it possible to have multiple inputs and outputs in a single *cin* and *cout* statements?

ANSWERS

4. (iii) **5.** (iii) **6.** 50 **7.** 1 **8.** 1 **11.** Aloha **14.** 1234

POINTERS

2

2.1 INTRODUCTION

Pointers are one of the most important features of C++. The beginners of C and C++ find pointers hard to understand and manipulate, though the treatment of pointers in C++ is comparatively simpler than in C. In an attempt to unveil the mystery behind this aspect, the basics of pointers that generally remain in background are being discussed in the following sections.

2.1.1 The & Operator

When a variable x is declared in a program, a storage location in the main memory is made available by the compiler. For example, Fig. 2.1 shows the declaration of x as an integer variable and its storage location in the main memory.

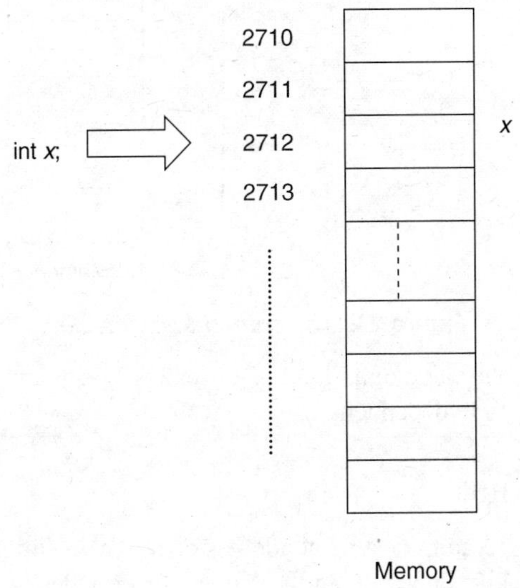

Figure 2.1 *The variable x and its equivalent representation in memory*

From Fig. 2.1, it may be observed that x is the name associated by the compiler to a location in the memory of the computer. Let us assume that, at the time of execution, the physical address of this memory location (called x) is 2712. Now, a point worth noting is that this memory location is viewed by the programmer as variable x and by the operating system as an address 2712.

The address of the variable *x* can be obtained by '&', an address of the operator. This operator when applied to a variable, gives the physical memory address of the variable. Thus, &*x* will provide the address 2712. Consider the following program segment:

```
x = 15;
cout << "\n Value of x = << x;
cout << "\n Address of x = "<< &x;
```

The output of the above program segment would be as shown below:

```
Value of x =15
Address of x = 2712          (assumed value)
```

The contents of variable *x* (memory location 2712) are shown in Fig. 2.2.

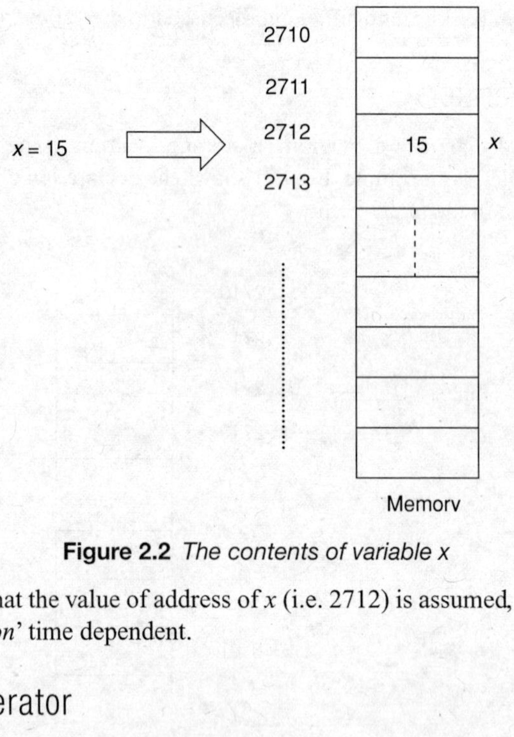

Figure 2.2 *The contents of variable x*

It may be noted here that the value of address of *x* (i.e. 2712) is assumed, and the actual value is '*machine and execution*' time dependent.

2.1.2 The * Operator

The * is an indirection operator or value at address operator. In simple words, we can say that if the address of a variable is known, then the * operator provides the contents of the variable. Consider the following program segment:

```
# include <iostream.h>
void main()
  {
    int x =15;
    cout <<"\n Value of x" << x;
```

```
    cout <<"\n Address of x" << &x;
    cout <<"\n Value at address" << &x << "is =" << *(&x);
}
```

The output of the above program segment would be as shown below:

```
Value of x = 15
Address of x = 2712                (assumed address as per Fig. 2.2)
Value at address 2712 = 15
```

Consider the following program:

```
# include <iostream.h>
main()
  {
    int a;
    *& a = 50;
    cout << a;
  }
```

The output would be 50 because * and & operators complement each other; therefore the 50 is stored in the variable called *a*.

2.2 POINTER VARIABLES

An address of a variable can be stored in a special variable called **pointer** variable. A pointer variable contains the address of another variable. Let us assume that *y* is such a variable. Now, the address of variable *x* can be assigned to *y* by the statement: *y* = &*x*. The effect of this statement is shown in Fig. 2.3.

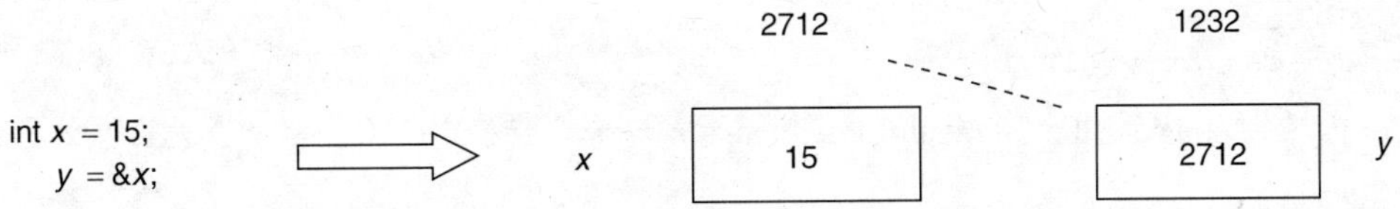

Figure 2.3 *The address of x is being stored in pointer variable* y

From Fig. 2.3, it is clear that *y* is the variable that contains the address (i.e. 2712) of another variable *x*, whereas, the address of *y* itself is 1232 (assumed value). In other words, we can say that *y* is a pointer to variable *x*. See Fig. 2.4.

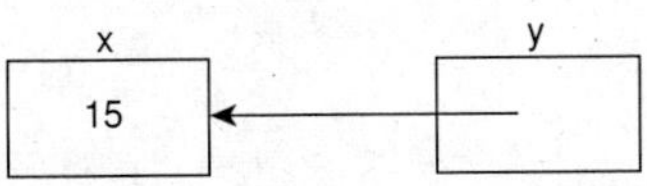

Figure 2.4 y *is a pointer to* x

A pointer variable *y* can be declared in C++ as shown below:

```
int *y;
```

The above declaration means that *y* is a pointer to a variable of type int. Similarly, consider the following declaration:

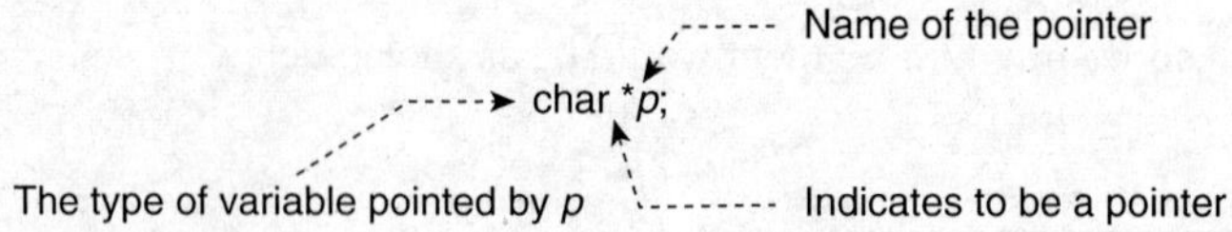

The above declaration means that *p* is a pointer to a variable of type char.

Consider the following program segment:

```
# include <iostream.h>
void main()
  {
    int x =15;
    int *y;
    y = &x;
    cout <<"\n Value of x=  " << x;
    cout <<"\n Address of x=  " << &x;
    cout <<"\n Value of x=  " << *y;
    cout <<"\n Address of x=" << y;
    cout <<"\n Address of y=" << &y;
  }
```

The output of the above program segment would be as shown below. We have shown only the assumed addresses as per Fig. 2.3.

```
Value of x =15
Address of x =2712
Value of x =15
Address of x =2712
Address of y =1232
```

Let us now, consider the following statements:

```
float val = 35.67;
float *pt;
```

The first statement declares val to be a variable of type float and initializes it by value 35.67. The second statement declares pt to be pointer to a variable of type float. Please notice that pt can point to a variable of type float, but it is currently not pointing to any variable as shown in Fig. 2.5.

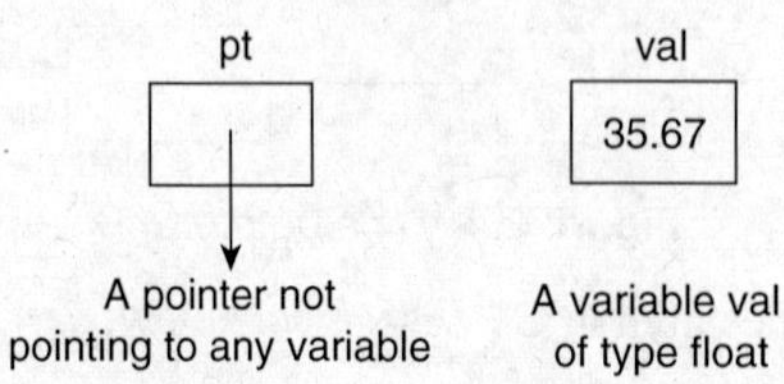

Figure 2.5 *The pointer pt is not pointing to any variable*

The pointer pt can point to the variable val by assigning the address of val to pt as shown below.

```
pt = &val;
```

Once the above statement is executed, the pointer pt gets the address of val, and we can say that logically pt points to the variable val as shown in Fig. 2.6.

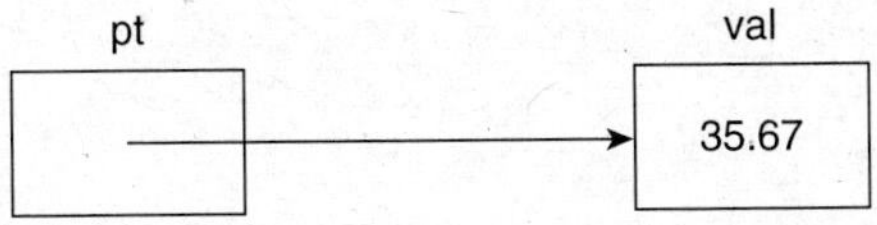

Figure 2.6 *The pointer pt pointing to variable val*

However, one must keep in mind that the arrow is for illustration sake. Actually, the pointer pt contains the address of val. The address is an integer that is not a simple value but a reference to a location in the memory.

Examples of some valid pointer declarations are:

(i) int *p;

(ii) char *i, *k;

(iii) float *pt;

(iv) int **ptr;

The example (iv) means the ptr is a pointer to a location which itself is a pointer to a variable of type integer.

It may be noted here that a pointer can also be incremented to point to an immediately next location of its type. For example, if the contents of a pointer p of type integer are 5224, then the content of p++ will be 5226 instead of 5225 (see Fig. 2.7). The reason being an int is always of 2 bytes size and therefore stored in two memory locations as shown in Fig. 2.7. The amount of storage taken by the various types of data is tabulated in Table 2.1.

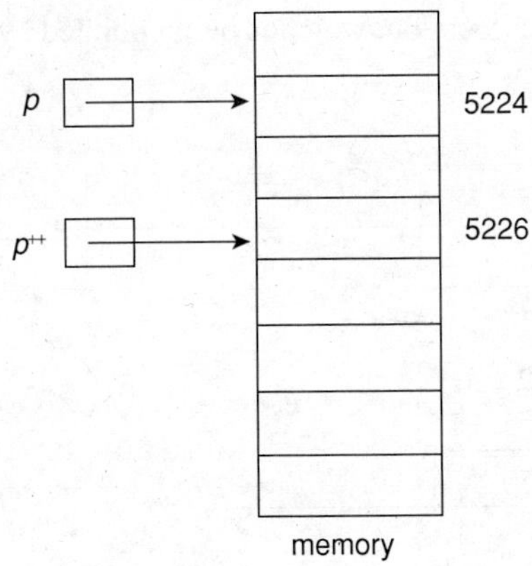

Figure 2.7 *The variable of type int occupies two bytes*

Table 2.1 Amount of Storage Taken by Data Types

Data Type	Amount of Storage
character	1 byte
integer	2 byte
Float	4 byte
Long	4 byte
Double	8 byte

Thus, a pointer of float type will point to an address of 4 bytes of locations, and therefore an increment to this pointer will increment its contents by 4 locations. It may be further noted that more than one pointer can point to the same location. Consider the following program segment:

```
int x = 37
int * p1, * p2;
```

The following statement

```
p1=& x;
```

makes the pointer *p*1 to point to variable *x* as shown in Fig. 2.8.

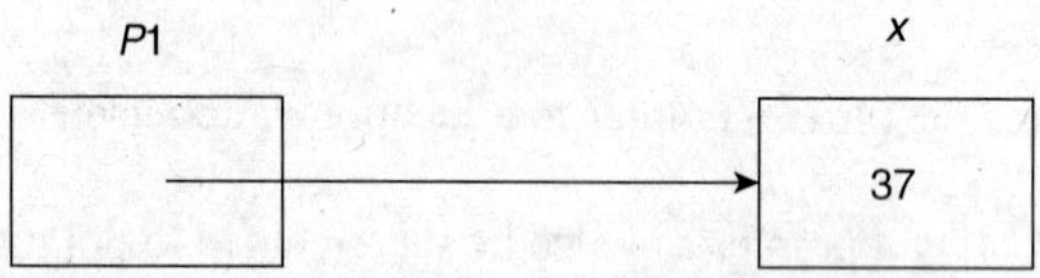

Figure 2.8 *Pointer p1 points to variable x*

The following statement

```
p2 = p1
```

makes *p*2 to point to the same location, which is being pointed by *p*1 as shown in Fig. 2.9.

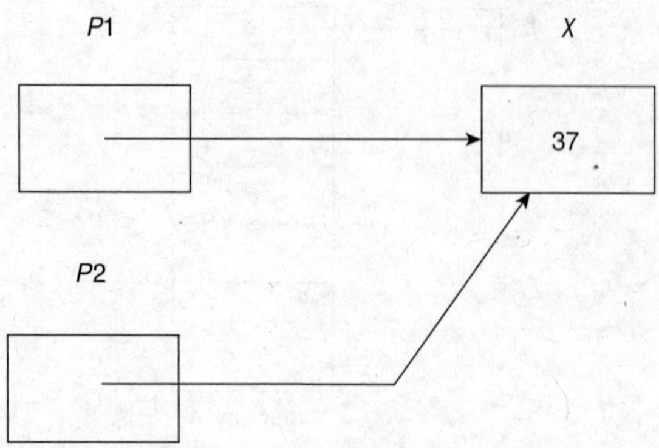

Figure 2.9 *Pointer p1 and p2 pointing to x*

The contents of variable x are now reachable by both the pointers $p1$ and $p2$. Thus, two or more entities can cooperatively share a single memory structure with the help of pointers. In fact, this technique can be used to provide efficient communication between different parts of a program.

The pointers can be used for a variety of purposes in a program. Some of them are given below.

1. To pass address of variables from one function to another
2. To return more than one value from a function to the calling function
3. For the creation of linked structures such as linked lists and trees.

Consider the following program:

```
# include <iostream.h>
main()
  {
   int i = 50;
   int *j = &i;
   cout <<"\n" << ++ *(j);
  }
```

The output would be 51 because the contents pointed by pointer j are being incremented before the display.

Example 1. *Write a program that reads from keyboard two variables x and y of type integer. It prints the exchanged contents of these variables with the help of pointers without altering the variables.*

Solution: We will use two pointers $p1$ and $p2$ for variables x and y. A third pointer $p3$ will be used as a temporary pointer for the exchange of pointers $p1$ and $p2$. The scheme is shown in Fig. 2.10.

The program is given below:

```
// This program illustrates the usage of pointers to
exchange the contents of two variables//

   # include <iostream.h>
   void main()
     {
       int x,y;
       int *p1, *p2, *p3; // pointers to integers
       cout << "\n Enter two integer values";
       cin >> x >> y;
    // Assign the addresses x and y to p1 and p2
       p1 = &x;
       p2 = &y;
    // Exchange the pointers
       p3 = p1;
       p1 = p2;
```

```
    p2 = p3;
  // Print the contents through exchanged contents
    cout <<"\n The exchanged contents are ";
    cout <<  *p1 << " and " <<  *p2;
  }
```

A sample output is given below:

```
Enter two interger values 25 34
The exchanged contents are 34 and 25
```

Note: The output shows the exchanged values because of exchange of pointers (see Fig. 2.10), whereas the contents of *x* and *y* have remained unaltered.

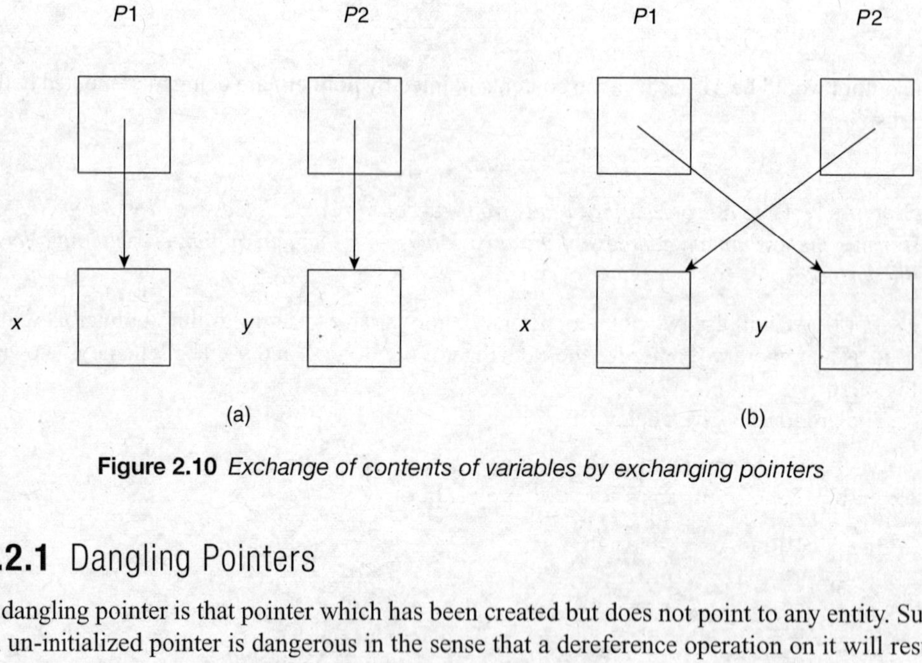

Figure 2.10 *Exchange of contents of variables by exchanging pointers*

2.2.1 Dangling Pointers

A dangling pointer is that pointer which has been created but does not point to any entity. Such an un-initialized pointer is dangerous in the sense that a dereference operation on it will result in an unpredictable operation or may result in a runtime error.

Consider the following code:

```
int * ptr;
*ptr = 50;
```

The first statement declares the pointer called ptr. At runtime it will be created as shown in Fig. 2.11. It may be noted that currently ptr is a dangling pointer. The second statement is trying to load a value (i.e. 50) to a location that is pointed by ptr. Obviously, this is a dangerous situation because the results will be unpredictable. The C++ compiler does not consider it as an error though some compilers may give a warning.

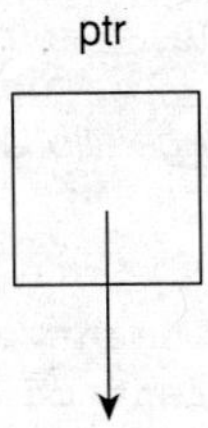

Figure 2.11 *The dangling pointer*

Therefore, if pointers are being used, the following steps must be followed:

Step 1. Declare the pointer.

Step 2. Allocate the variable or entity to which the pointer is to be pointed.

Step 3. Point the pointer to the entity.

Let us assume that it is desired that the pointer ptr should point to a variable val of type int. The correct code in that case would be as given below:

```
int * ptr;
int val;
ptr = &val;
* ptr = 50;
```

The result of above program segment is shown in Fig. 2.12.

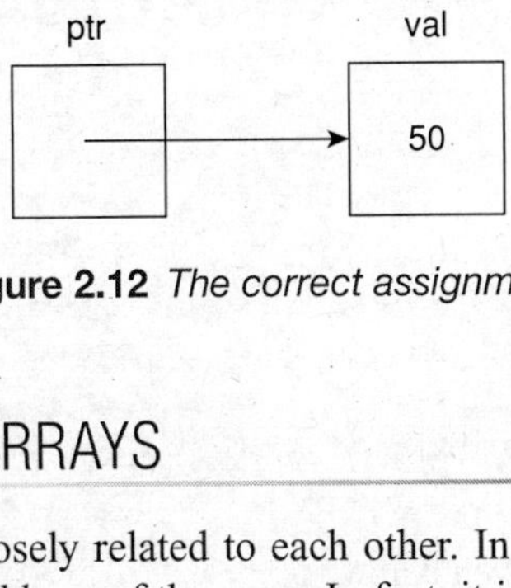

Figure 2.12 *The correct assignment*

2.3 POINTERS AND ARRAYS

Pointers and arrays are very closely related to each other. In C++, the name of an array is a pointer that contains the base address of the array. In fact, it is a pointer to the first element of the array. Consider the array declaration given below:

```
int list[] = { 20, 30, 35, 36, 39 };
```

This array will be stored in the contiguous locations of the main memory with starting address equal to 1001(assumed value), as shown in Fig. 2.13. Since the array list is of integer type, each element of this array occupies two bytes. The name of the array contains the starting address of the array, i.e. 1001

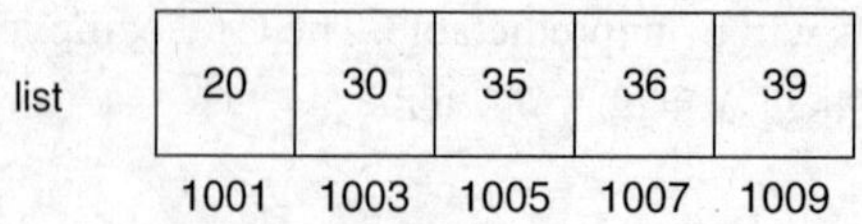

Figure 2.13 *The contiguous storage allocation with starting address = 1001*

Consider the following program segment:

```
cout << "\n Address of zeroth element of array list"<<  list;
cout << "\n value of zeroth element of array list" << *list;
```

Once the above program segment is executed, the output would be as shown below:

```
Address of zeroth element of array list = 1001
Value of zeroth element of array list = 20
```

We could have achieved the same output also by the following program segment:

```
cout << "\n Address of zeroth element of list" << & list [0];
cout << "\n value of zeroth element of list" <<  list [0];
```

Both the above given approaches are equivalent because of the following equivalence relations:

`list ≡ &list [0]`—both denote the address of zeroth element of the array list

`*list ≡ list[0]`—both denote the value of zeroth element of the array list

The left-side approach is known as pointer method and right side as array indexing method. Let us now write a program that prints out a list by array indexing method.

```
// Array indexing method
#include <iostream.h>
void main()
  {
     static int list [] = { 20,30,35,36,39};
     int i;
     cout << "\n The list is ...";
     for ( i = 0; i < 5; i++)
     cout << "\n "<< list[i];
  }
```

The output of this program is given below:

```
The list is ___
20
30
35
36
39_
```

The above program can also be written by pointer method as shown below:

```
/* pointer method of processing an array */

#include <iostream.h>
void main()
  {
     static int list [] = { 20,30,35,36,39};
     int i;
     cout << "\n The list is ...";
     for ( i = 0; i < 5; i++)
     cout << "\n "<< *(list+i);
  }
```

It may be noted in the above program that we have used the term * (list + *i*) to print an *i*th element of the array. Let us analyze this term. Since the list designates the address of zeroth element of the array, we can access its value through value at address operator, i.e. *. The following terms are equivalent:

```
*list ≡ *(list + 0) ≡ list [0]
*(list + 1) ≡ list [1]      and so on
```

Thus, we can refer to the *i*th element of array list by either of the following ways:

```
*(list + i) or *(i + list) or list [i]
```

So far, we have used the name of an array to get its base address and manipulate. However, there is a small difference between an ordinary pointer and the name of an array. The difference is that the array name is a **pointer constant** and its contents cannot be changed. Thus, the following operations on list are illegal because they try to change the contents of list, a pointer constant.

```
List = NULL; // Not allowed
List = & Val; // Not allowed
list++        // Not allowed
list--        // Not allowed
```

Consider the following program:

```
# include <iostream.h>
void main()
{
  char text[6] ="Helpme";
  char *p ="Helpme";
  cout << "\n"<< text[3];
  cout << "\n"<< p[3];
}
```

The output of above program would be:

```
p
p
```

From the above program, it looks as if the following declarations are equivalent as text [3] and *p*[3] behave in identical manner.

```
char text [6];
char *p;
```

It may be noted that the above declarations are not at all equivalent, though the behaviour may be same. In fact, the array declaration 'text [6]' asks from the complier for six locations of char type whereas the pointer declaration char **p* asks for a pointer that can point to any variable of following types:

(i) char—a character

(ii) string—a string of characters

(iii) Null—nowhere

Consider the following declarations:

```
int list = {20,30,35,36,39};
int *p;        // pointer variable p
p = list;      // assign the starting address of array list to pointer p
```

Since *p* is a pointer variable and has been assigned the starting address of array list, the following operations become perfectly valid on this pointer:

```
p++, p-- etc.
```

Let us now write a third version of the program that prints out the array. We will use pointer variable *p* in this program.

```
// pointer variable method of processing an array

# include <iostream.h>
void main()
  {
     static int list [] = { 20,30,35,36,39};
     int *p;
     int i =0;
     p = list; // Assign the starting address of the list
     cout << "\n The list is ...";
       while (i < 5)
       {
     cout << "\n"<< *p;
     i++;
     p++;  //increment pointer
       }
  }
```

The output of above program is given below:

```
The list is ...
20
30
35
36
39_
```

From our discussion on arrays, we know that the strings are stored and manipulated as array of characters, with last character being a null character (i.e. \0).

For example, the string ENGINEERING can be stored in an array (say text) as shown in Fig. 2.14.

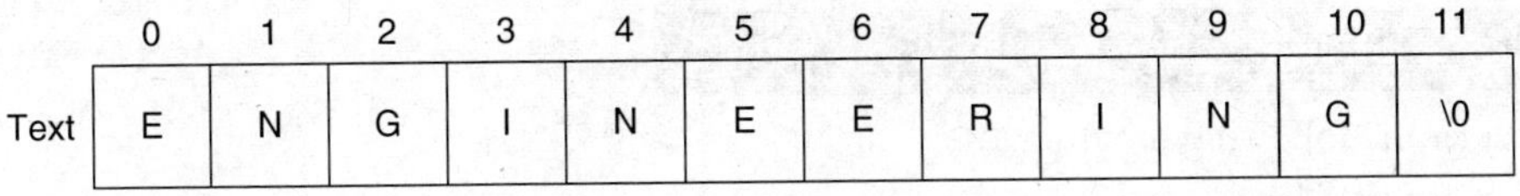

Figure 2.14 *The array called 'Text'*

We can declare this string as a normal array by the following array declaration:

```
char text [11];
```

Consider the following declaration:

```
char *p;
p=text;
```

In the above set of statements, we have declared a pointer *p* that can point to a character or string of characters. The next statement assigns the starting address of character string 'text' to the variable pointer *p* (see Fig. 2.15).

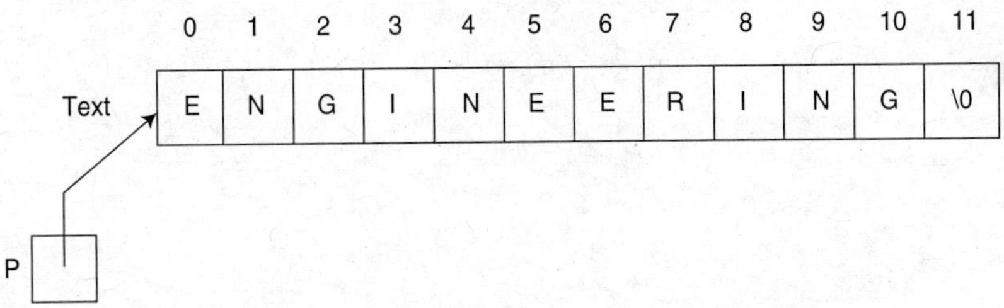

Figure 2.15 *Pointer p points to the array called 'Text'*

Since text is a pointer constant, its contents cannot be changed. On the contrary, *p* is a pointer variable and can be manipulated like any other pointer as shown in the program given below.

```
// This program illustrates the usage of pointer to a string

# include <iostream.h>
void main()
  {
    char text[] = "ENGINEERING";// The string
    char *p;                     // The pointer

    p = text;               // Assign the starting address of string to p

    cout <<"\n The string..";    // Print the string
    while ( *p != '\0')
      { cout <<" "<< *p;
```

```
    p++ ;
    }
  }
```

The output of the program is given below:

```
| The string__ E N G I N E E R I N G
```

Consider the following program:

```
# include <iostream.h>
  main()
    {
     int tab [3][4] = { 5,6,7,8,
                     1,2,3,4,
                     9,10,0,11 };
     cout << "\n " << *tab[0] + 1 <<  "—" <<  *(tab[0] + 1);
     cout << "\n " << *(* (tab + 0) + 1);
     }
```

The output would be

```
6 -6
6
```

Example 2. *What would be the output of the following?*

```
# include <iostream.h>
void main()
{
  char *ptr;
  ptr = "Nice";
  cout << "\n"<< * & ptr [1];
}
```

Solution: The output would be *i*.

Example 3. *What would be the output of the following?*

```
# include <iostream.h>
void main ( )
{
  int list [5] ={ 2, 5, 6, 0, 9};
  3[list] = 4[list] + 6;
  cout << "\n"<< * (list + 3);
}
```

Solution: The output would be 15.

2.4 ARRAY OF POINTERS

Like any other array, we can also have an array of pointers. Each element of such an array can point to a data item such as variable, array etc. For example, consider the declaration given below:

```
float *x [20];
```

This declaration means that x is an array of 20 elements, and each element is a pointer to a variable of type float. Let us now construct an array of pointers to strings.

```
char *item [ ]{ Chair,
                Table,
                Stool,
                Desk,
              };
```

The above declaration gives an array of pointers called item. Each element of item points to a string as shown in Fig. 2.16.

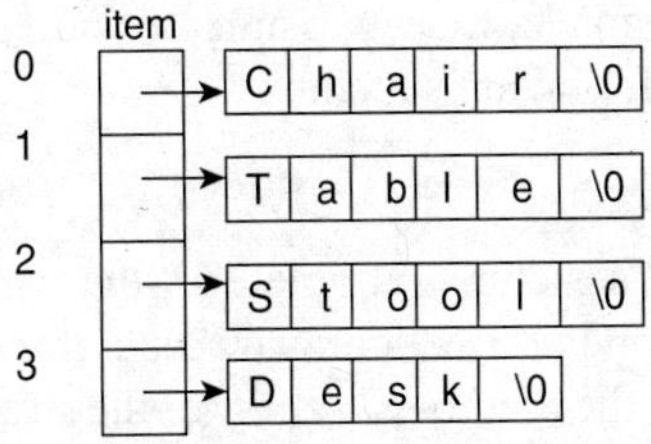

Figure 2.16 *Array of pointers to strings*

The advantage of having an array of pointer to strings is that manipulation of strings becomes convenient. For example, the string-containing table can be copied into a pointer ptr without using strcpy( ) function by the following set of statements.

```
char *ptr;             // declare a pointer to a string
ptr = item [1];        // assign the appropriate pointer to ptr
```

It may be noted that once the above set of statements are executed, both the pointers item[1] and ptr will point to the same string table as shown in Fig. 2.17.

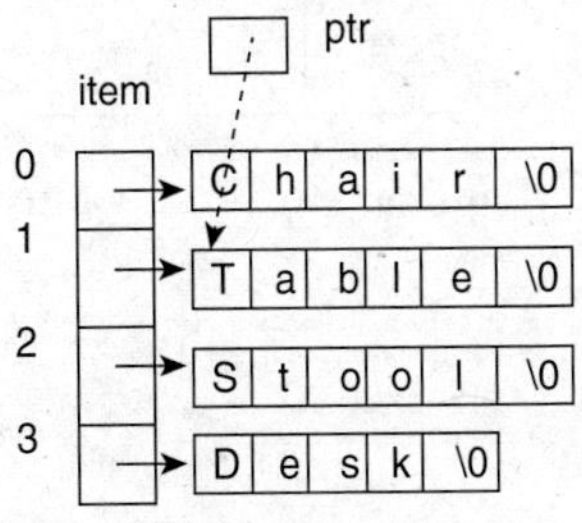

Figure 2.17 *Effect of statement ptr = item[1]*

However, the changes made by the pointer ptr to the string table will definitely disturb the contents of the string pointed by the pointer item [1] and vice versa. Therefore, utmost care should be taken by the programmer while manipulating pointers pointing to same memory locations.

2.5 POINTERS AND STRUCTURES

Similar to the other types of pointers, we can have a pointer to a structure, i.e. we can also point a pointer to a structure. A pointer to a structure variable can be declared by prefixing the variable name by a *. Consider the following declaration:

```
struct xyz {          /* structure declaration */
   int a;
   float y;
};
struct xyz abc; /* declare a variable of type xyz */
struct xyz *ptr; /* declare a pointer ptr to a variable of type xyz */
```

Once the above declarations are made, we can assign the address of the structure variable abc to the structure pointer ptr by the following statement:

```
ptr = &abc;
```

Since ptr is a pointer to the structure variable abc, the members of the structure can also be accessed through a special operator called arrow operator i.e. → (minus sign followed by greater than sign). For example, the members *a* and *y* of the structure variable abc pointed by ptr can be assigned values 30 and 50.9 respectively by the following statement:

```
ptr→a = 30;
ptr→y = 50.9;
```

The arrow operator '→' is also known as a **pointer-to-member** operator.

Example 4. *Write a program that defines a structure called item for the record structure given below. It reads the data of the record through dot operator and prints the record by arrow operator. Use suitable data types for the members of the structure Item.*

Item	*Code*	*quantity*	*Cost*

Solution: We will use a pointer ptr to point to the structure called Item. The required program is given below.

```
// This program demonstrates the usage of an arrow operator

# include <iostream.h>
void main()
  {
    struct item  {
```

```
        char code[5];
        int Qty;
        float cost;
       };
       struct item item_rec; // define a variable of struct type
       struct item *ptr;     // define a pointer of type struct
                             // Read data through dot operator
        cout <<"\n Enter the data for an item";
        cout <<"\nCode:"; cin >>item_rec.code;
        cout <<"\nQty :"; cin >> item_rec.Qty;
        cout <<"\nCost :"; cin >>item_rec.cost;
           // Assign the address of item_rec
        ptr = &item_rec;
          // print data through arrow operator
        cout <<"\n The data for the item...";
        cout <<"\nCode: " << ptr->code;
        cout <<"\nQty :  " << ptr->Qty;
        cout <<"\nCost : " << ptr->cost;
   }
```

From the above program, we can see that the members of a static structure can be accessed by both dot and arrow operators. However, dot operator is used for simple variable whereas the arrow operator for pointer variables.

Example 5. *What is the output of the following program?*

```
#include <iostream.h>
void main()
  {
    struct point
      {
        int x,y;
        } polygon[]= { {1,2},{1,4},{2,4},{2,2}};

     struct point *ptr;
     ptr = polygon;

     ptr++;
     ptr->x++;
     cout << ptr->x;
  }
```

Solution: From the above program, it can be observed that ptr is a pointer to an array of structures called polygon. The statement ptr++ moves the pointer from the zeroth location (i.e {1, 2}) to first location (i.e. {1, 4}). Now, the statement *x*++ has incremented the field *x* of the structure by one (i.e. 1 has incremented to 2).

The output would be 2.

2.6 DYNAMIC ALLOCATION

We know that in a program when a variable *x* is declared, a storage location is made available to the program as shown below.

This memory location remains available, even if it is not needed, to the program as long as the program is being executed (Fig. 2.18). Therefore, the variable *x* is known as a static variable. Dynamic variables, on the other hand, can be allocated from or returned to the system according to the needs of a running program. However, a dynamic variable does not have a name and can be referenced only through a pointer.

Consider the declaration given below.

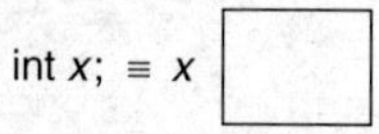

Figure 2.18 *Memory allocation to variable x*

The above declaration gives us a dangling pointer p that points to nowhere (see Fig. 2.19). Now, we can connect this dangling pointer either to a static variable or to a dynamic variable. In our previous discussion on pointers, we have always used pointers with static variables. Let us now see how the pointer can be connected to a dynamic variable.

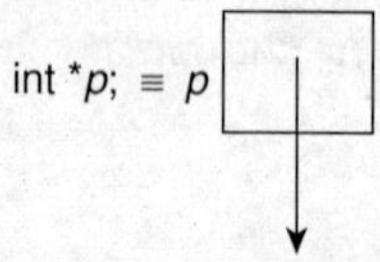

Figure 2.19 *The dangling pointer p*

In C++, dynamic memory can be allocated by an operator called 'new'. The format of dynamic allocation is given below.

```
<pointer> = new  <varType>
```

where <**pointer**>: is a pointer to a variable of type varType

```
new      : is a reserved word indicating that memory allocation is
           to be done.
.varType : is type of dynamic variable required
```

Consider the following declaration

```
int * p;
p = new int
```

The above set of statements are executed in the following manner:

1. The pointer *p* is created. It is dangling, i.e. not connected anywhere (see Fig. 2.20(a))
2. A dynamic variable of type integer is taken through new operator and the dangling pointer *p* is connected to the variable (see Fig. 2.20(b))

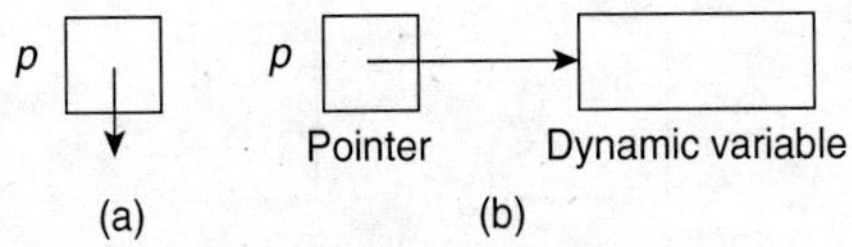

Figure 2.20 *The effect of new operator*

It may noted from Fig. 2.20(b) that a dynamic variable is anonymous in the sense that it has no name, and therefore it can be referenced only through the pointer p. For example, a value (say 50) can be assigned to the dynamic variable by the following statement:

```
*p = 50;
```

The above statement means that it is desired to store a value 50 in a memory location pointed to by the pointer *p*. The effect of this statement is shown in Fig. 2.21.

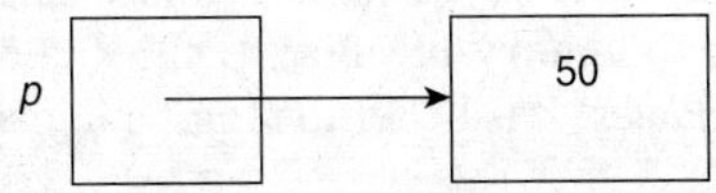

Figure 2.21 *The effect of assignment of *p = 50*

It may observed that *p* is simply a pointer or an address and **p* gives the access to the memory location or the variable where it is pointing to. It is very important to learn the difference between the pointer and its associated dynamic variable. Let us consider the following program segment.

```
int *Aptr, *Bptr;                // declare pointers
Apt   =  new int;                // allocate dynamic memory
Bptr =  new int;
*Aptr   = 15;
*Bptr   = 70;
```

The outcome of the above program segment would be as shown in Fig. 2.22.

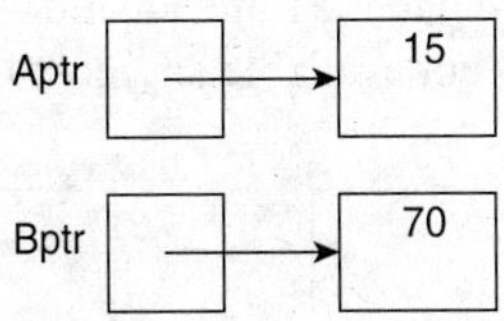

Figure 2.22 *Value assignment through pointers*

Let us now see the effect of the following assignment statement on the memory allocated to the pointers Aptr and Bptr.

```
Aptr = Bptr;
```

The above assignment makes Aptr to point to the same location or variable, which is already being pointed by Bptr as shown in Fig. 2.23. Thus, both Aptr and Bptr are now pointing to the same memory location.

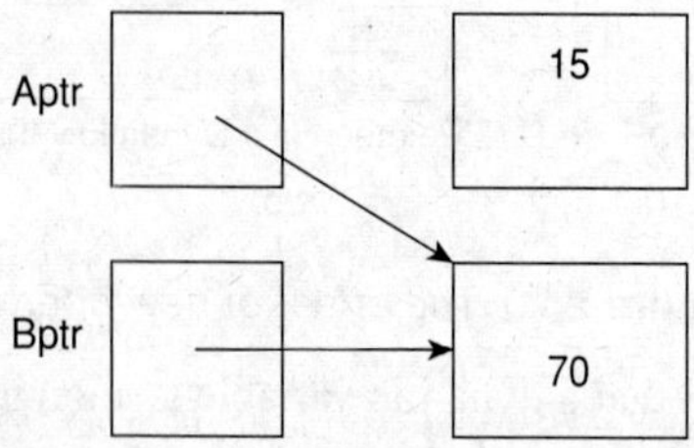

Figure 2.23 *Both pointers pointing to the same location*

A close observation would reveal that the dynamic variable containing value 15 is now lost in the sense that it is neither available to Aptr anymore and nor it is available to the system. The reason being that the system gave it to the pointer Aptr and now Aptr is pointing to some other location. This dynamic variable being anonymous (i.e. without name) is no more accessible. Even if we want to reverse the process, we cannot simply do it. This phenomenon of losing dynamic variables is known as **memory bleeding**. Thus, utmost care should be taken while manipulating the dynamic variables. It is better to return a dynamic variable whenever it is not required in the program.

A dynamic variable can be returned to the system by function called delete. The general form of usage of this operator is given below.

```
delete <pointer>;
```

where **delete:** is a reserved word.

<**pointer**>: is the pointer to the dynamic variable to be returned to the system

Let us consider pointers shown in Fig. 2.23. If it is desired to return the dynamic variable pointed by pointer Bptr, we can do so by the following statement:

```
delete Bptr;
```

Once the above statement is executed, the dynamic variable is returned back to the system, and we are left with two dangling pointers Bptr and Aptr as shown in Fig. 2.24. The reason for this is obvious because both were pointing to the same location. However, the dynamic variable containing value 15 is anonymous and not available anymore and hence a total waste of memory.

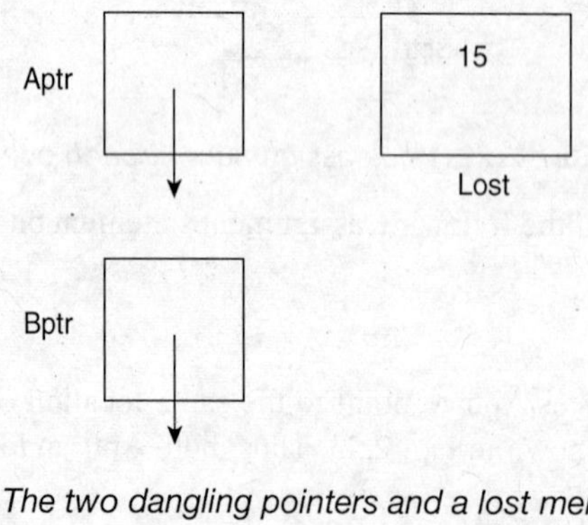

Figure 2.24 *The two dangling pointers and a lost memory variable*

Example 6. *Write a program that dynamically allocates an integer. It initializes the integer with a value, increments it and prints the incremented value.*

Solution: The required program is given below:

```
# include <iostream.h>
void main()
  {
    int *p;             //  A pointer to an int
                       //   allocate a dynamic of size int pointed by p
    p = new int;
    cout << "\n Enter a value :";
    cin >> *p;
    *p = *p +1;
          //      print the incremented value
    cout << "\n The Value =" << *p;
    delete (p);
  }
```

A sample output is given below:

```
Enter a value :240
The incremental Value =241_
```

Example 7. *Write a program that dynamically allocates a structure whose structure diagram is given below. It reads the various members of the structure and prints them.*

Student	*Name*	*Age*	*Roll*

Solution: We will use the following steps to write the required program

1. Declare a structure called student.
2. Declare a pointer ptr to the structure student.
3. Ask for dynamic memory of type student pointed by the pointer ptr.
4. Read the data of the various elements using arrow operator.
5. Print the data.
6. Return the dynamic memory pointed by ptr.

The required program is given below.

```
# include <iostream.h>
# include <stdio.h>

void main()
```

```
{
  struct student {              //     Declare the structure
   char name[15];
   int age;
   int roll;
   };
   struct student *ptr;
           //     Ask for dynamic memory of type student
   ptr = new student;
   cout <<    "\n Enter the data of the student";
   cout <<    "\nName :";  fflush(stdin);  gets(ptr->name);
   cout <<    "\nAge :"; cin >>  ptr->age;
   cout <<    "\nRoll :"; cin >> ptr->roll;
   cout <<    "\n The data is...";
   cout <<    "\nName :"; puts(ptr->name);
   cout <<    "\nAge :"<< ptr->age;
   cout <<    "\nRoll :" << ptr->roll;
   delete (ptr);
 }
```

A sample output is given below:

```
Enter the data of the student
Name :Hasan
Age :19
Roll :103
 The data is _ _ _
Name :Hasan
Age :19
Roll :103
```

An array can also be dynamically allocated as demonstrated in the following example program.

Example 8. *Write a program that dynamically allocates an array of integers. A list of integers are read from the keyboard and stored in the array. The program determines the smallest in the list and prints its location in the list.*

Solution: The solution to this problem is trivial and the required program is given below.

```
//     This program illustrates the usage of dynamically allocated
array

# include <iostream.h>
```

```
void main()
  {
    int i,min, pos;
    int *list;
    int Sz, N;
    cout << "\n Enter the size of the list :";
    cin >> N;
           //      Allocate dynamic array size N
    list = new [N];
    cout << "\n Enter the list";
         //     Read the list
    for (i = 0; i < N; i++)
       {
         cout << "\n Enter Number :";
         cin >> *(list + i);
       }
    pos = 0;                //      Assume that the zeroth element is min
    min = *(list + 0);
         //     Find the minimum
    for ( i = 1; i < N; i++)
       {
          if ( min > *(list + i))
            { min = *(list + i);
              pos = i;
            }
       }                     //      Print the minimum and its location
    cout << "\n The minimum is" << min <<" at position = " << pos;
     delete (list);
  }
```

A sample output is given below:

```
Enter the size of the list :5
Enter the list
Enter Number :23
Enter Number :12
Enter Number :41
Enter Number :56
Enter Number :11
The minimum is 11 at position = 4_
```

From the above example, it can be observed that the size of a dynamically allocated array can be specified even at the run time and the required amount of memory is allocated. This is in sharp contrast to static arrays for whom the size has to be declared at the compile time.

2.6.1 Self Referential Structures

When a member of a structure is declared as a pointer to the structure itself, then the structure is called as **self referential structure**. Consider the following declaration.

```
struct chain {
  int val;
  chain *p;
};
```

The structure chain consists of two members—val and *p*. The member val is a variable of type int, whereas the member *p* is a pointer to a structure of type chain. Thus, the structure chain has a member that can point to a structure of type chain or may be itself. This type of self referencing structure can be viewed as shown in Fig. 2.25.

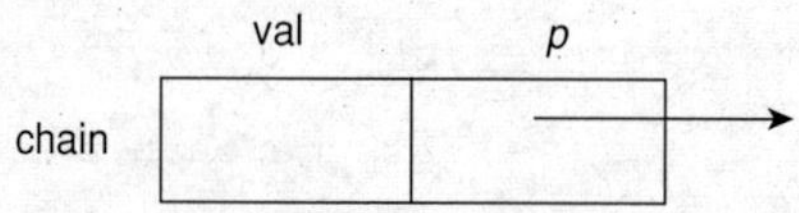

Figure 2.25 *Self referential structure chain*

Since pointer *p* can point to a structure variable of type chain, we can connect two such structure variables A and B to obtain a linked structure as shown in Fig. 2.26.

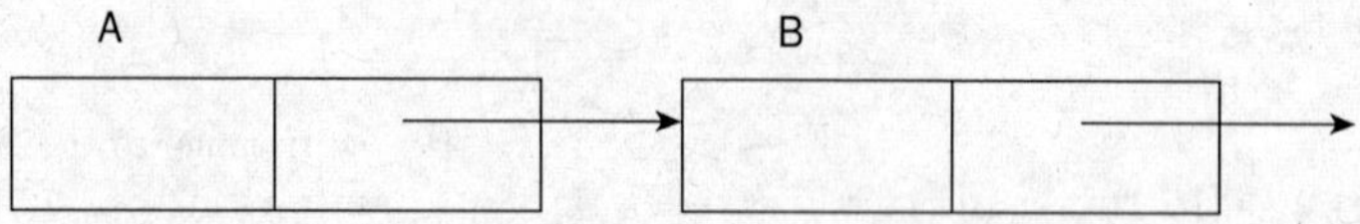

Figure 2.26 *Linked structure*

The linked structure given in Fig. 2.26 can be obtained by the following steps:

1. Declare structure chain.
2. Declare variables A and B of type chain
3. Assign the address of structure B to member p of structure A.

These above steps have been coded in the program segment given below.

```
struct chain {          // declare structure chain
  int val;
  chain *p;
};
chain A, B; // declare structure variables A and B
A.p=&B;                // connect A to B
```

From Fig. 2.26 and the above program segment, we observe that the pointer p of structure variable *B* is dangling, i.e. it is pointing to nowhere. Such pointer can be assigned to NULL, a constant indicating that there is no valid address in this pointer. The following statement will do the desired operation:

```
B.p=NULL;
```

The data elements in this linked structure can be assigned by the following statements:

```
A.val=50;
B.val=60;
```

The linked structure now looks like as shown in Fig. 2.27.

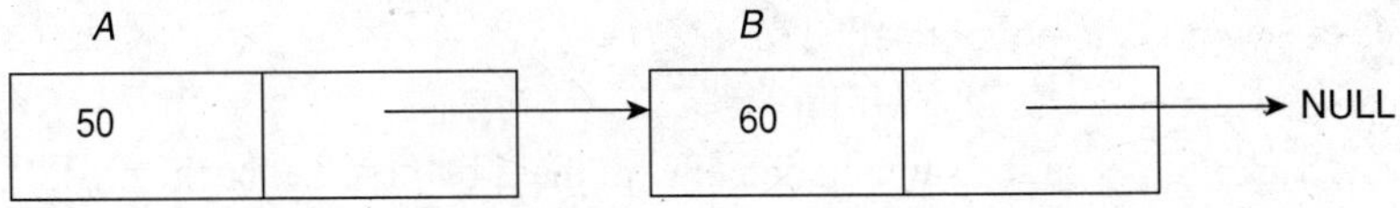

Figure 2.27 *Value assignment to data elements*

We can see that the members of structure *B* can be reached to by two methods:

1. From its variable name *B* through dot operator.
2. From the pointer *p* of variable *A* because it is also pointing to the structure *B*. However, in this case, the arrow operator is needed.

Consider the statements given below:

```
cout << "\n the contents of member val of B =" << B.val;
cout << "\n the contents of member val of B =" << A.p→val;
```

Once the above statements are executed, the output would be:

```
The contents of member val of B = 60
The contents of member val of B = 60
```

The linked structures have great potential and can be used in numerous programming situations such as lists, trees etc.

Example 9. *Write a program that uses self referential structures to create a linked list of dynamic nodes of following structure. While creating the linked list, the student data is read. The list is also travelled to print the data.*

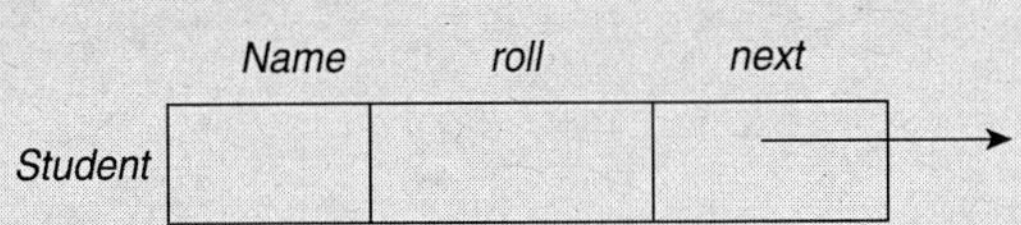

Solution: We will use the following self referential structure for the purpose of creating a node of the linked list.

```
struct stud{
   char name [15];
   int roll;
```

```
stud next;
};
```

The required linked list would be created by using three pointers (Fig. 2.28). First far and back. The following algorithm would be employed to create the list.

Steps:

1. Take a new node in pointer called first.
2. Read first→ name and first →roll.
3. Point back pointer to the same node being pointed by first, i.e. back =first.
4. Bring a new node in the pointer called far.
5. Read far→name and far→roll.
6. Connect next of back to for, i.e. back→next =far.
7. Take back to far, i.e. back = far.
8. Repeat steps 4 to 7 till whole of the list is constructed.
9. Point next of far to NULL, i.e. far→ next=NULL.
10. Stop.

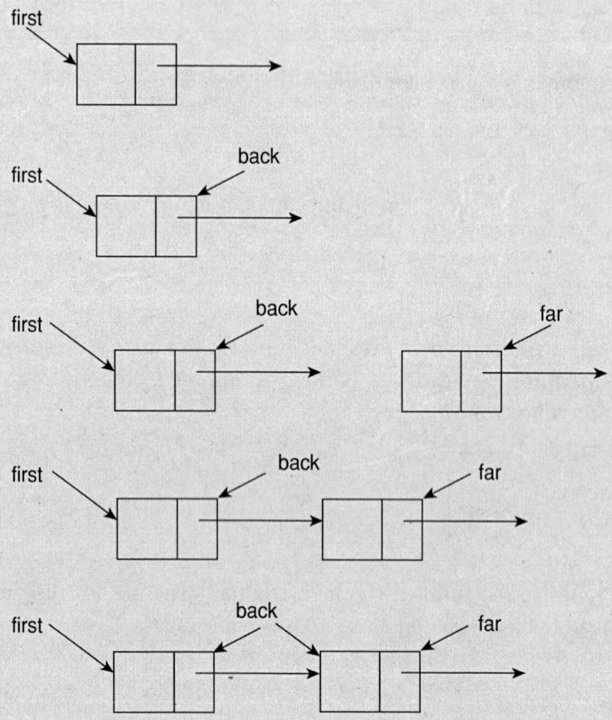

Figure 2.28 *Creation of a linked list*

The required program is given below:

```
# include <iostream.h>
# include <stdio.h>

void main()
  {
   struct student {
        char name [15];
        int roll;
        student *next;
        };
   student *First, *Far, *back;
   int N,i;
   cout << "\n Enter the number of students in the class";
   cin >> N;
        // Take first node
   First = new student;
        // Read the data of the first student

   cout << "\n Enter the data";
   cout << "\n Name : "; fflush(stdin); gets(First->name);
   cout << "\n Roll : "; cin >> First->roll;
        // point back where First points
    back = First;

    for (i =2; i <=N; i++)
      {                 // Bring a new node in Far
        Far =  new student;
              // Read Data of next student
        cout << "\n Name : "; fflush(stdin); gets(Far->name);
        cout << "\n Roll : "; cin >> Far->roll;
              // Connect Back to Far
        back->next = Far;
              // point back where Far points
        back = Far;
       }                  // reapeat the process
        Far->next = NULL;

              // Print the created linked list
        Far = First;    // Point to the first node

        cout <<"\n The Data is ....";
       while (Far != NULL)
    {
        cout << "\n Name = " <<Far->name << " Roll = " << Far->roll;
              // Point to the next node
        Far = Far->next;
    }
   }
```

Example 10. *Modify the program developed in Example 9 such that:*

1. *Assume that the number of students in the list is not known.*
2. *The list of students is split into the two sublists pointed by two pointers: front_half and back_half. The front_half points to the front half of the list and the back_half to the back half. If the number of students is odd, the extra student should go in the front list.*

Solution: The list of students would be created in the same fashion as done in Problem 1. The following steps would be followed to split the list in the desired manner.

1. Travel the list to count the number of students.
2. Compute the middle of the list.
3. Point the pointer called front_half to first and travel the list again starting from the first and reach to the middle.
4. Point back-half to the node that succeeds the middle of the list.
5. Attach NULL to the next pointer of the middle node.
6. Print the two lists, i.e. pointed by front-half and back-half.

The required program is given below:

```
# include <iostream.h>
# include <stdio.h>
void main()
  {
   struct student {
        char name [15];
        int roll;
        student *next;
        };
   student *First, *Far, *back;
   student *front_half, *back_half;
   int N,i,count, middle;
   cout << "\n Enter the number of students in the class";
   cin >> N;
         // Take first node
   First = new student;
         // Read the data of the first student

   cout << "\n Enter the data";
   cout << "\n Name : "; fflush(stdin); gets(First->name);
   cout << "\n Roll : "; cin >> First->roll;
   First->next =NULL;
         // Point back where First points
    back = First;

    for (i =2; i <=N; i++)
      {                 // Bring a new node in Far
```

```
      Far = new student;
              // Read Data of next student
      cout << "\n Name :" ; fflush(stdin); gets(Far->name);
      cout << "\n Roll :"; cin >> Far->roll;
              // Connect Back to Far
      back->next = Far;
              // Point back where Far points
      back = Far;
     }        // Repeat the process
      Far->next = NULL;
              // Count the number of nodes

  Far = First;          // Point to the first node
  count = 0;
     while (Far != NULL)
  {
    count ++;
    Far = Far->next;
   }                // Split the list
 if ( count == 1 )
     {
      cout << "\n The list cannot be split ";
      front_half = First;
     }
  else
  {
       // Compute the middle
 if ( (count % 2) == 0)  middle = count/2;
 else middle = count / 2 + 1;
       // Travel the list and split it
 front_half = First;
 Far = First;

 for (i =1; i <= middle; i++)
    {
     back =Far;
     Far = Far->next;
    }
  back_half = Far;
  back->next = NULL;
 }
     /* Print the two lists           */
  Far = front_half;
  cout << "\n The Front Half...: ";
  for (i =1; i <=2; i++)
    {
     while (Far != NULL)
       {
```

```
        cout << "Name:" << Far->name << " Roll : " << Far->roll;
        Far = Far->next;
      }
     if (count == 1 || i == 2) break;
     cout << "\n The Back Half...: ";
     Far = back_half;
   }
 }
```

Example 11. *Give the output of the following program:*

```
# include <iostream.h>
void main()
  { int i, j;
    char *str = "CALIFORNIA";
    for ( i = 0; str[i]; i++)
      {
        for ( j = 0; j <= i; j++)
        cout << str[j];
        cout <<"\n";
      }
  }
```

Solution: The output would be

```
C
CA
CAL
CALI
CALIF
CALIFO
CALIFOR
CALIFORN
CALIFORNI
CALIFORNIA
```

2.7 SUMMARY

A pointer is a variable that can only store the address of another variable. If a programmer assigns a new pointer, already poing to a new dynamic variable, the earlier dynamic variable is lost. This is also known as memory bleeding. Pointers always contain integers because a pointer can only contain an address, an integer quantity. A pointer can also be incremented to point to an immediately next location of its type. An un-initialized pointer is a dangling pointer that may contain any erroneous address. A NULL pointer does not point to any address location.

MULTIPLE CHOICE QUESTIONS

1. What happens to the dynamic variable if the pointer pointing to it is deleted?
   (a) It is lost
   (b) It is returned to system
   (c) It can be pointed by a new pointer
   (d) None of these
2. Are the expressions (*p)++ and ++*p equivalent?
   (a) Yes
   (b) No
   (c) Cannot be compared
   (d) None of these
3. What does the term ***j* means?
   (a) It is double pointer
   (b) *j* points to two addresses
   (c) *j* is a pointer to a pointer
   (d) None of these
4. The address of a variable can be obtained by
   (a) New operator
   (b) * operator
   (c) = Operator
   (d) & operator
5. The content at address is the
   (a) * operator
   (b) & operator
   (c) = operator
   (d) New operator
6. A pointer contains the
   (a) Name of a variable
   (b) Type of a variable
   (c) Size of a variable
   (d) Address of a variable
7. The increment of a pointer pointing to a float variable will increment its contents by
   (a) 1 location
   (b) 2 locations
   (c) 4 locations
   (d) 8 locations
8. A dangling pointer is:
   (a) Un-instantiated pointer
   (b) Un-initialized pointer
   (c) Points to NULL
   (d) Un-defined pointer
9. The name of an array is a
   (a) Constant pointer
   (b) Pointer variable
   (c) Pointer to a pointer
   (d) None of these
10. A dynamic variable is a
    (a) Anonymous variable
    (b) Is a lost variable
    (c) Is a deleted variable
    (d) A NULL entity

ANSWERS

1. b **2.** a **3.** c **4.** d **5.** a **6.** d **7.** c **8.** b **9.** a **10.** a

EXERCISES

1. Explain '&' and '*' operators in detail with suitable examples.
2. Find the errors in the following program segments

(a)
```
int val=10
int * p;
p=val;
```
(b)
```
char list [10];
char p;
list=p;
```
3. (i) What will be the output of the following programs:
```
# include <iostream.h>
main()
  {
  int val=10;
  int *p, **k;
  p=&val;
  k=&p;
  cout <<"\n " << p << " " <<*p, << " " << *k << " " << **k;
  }
```
(ii)
```
# include <iostream..h>
main()
   {
       char ch;
       char *p;
       ch ='A';
       p=&ch;
       cout << "\n " <<  ch << " " << (*p)++);
       }
```
4. What will be the output of the following program:
```
# include <iostream.h>
main()
   {
    int list[5], i;
    *list =5;
    for (i=1; i < 5; i++)
       *(list + i) =*(list + i-1)*i;
    cout << "\n";
    for (i=0; i < 5; i++)
          cout <<" " << *(list + i);
   }
```
5. Find the errors in the following program segment:
```
struct xyz {
     char *A;
     char *B;
     int val;
     };
```

```
xyz s;
A = "First text";
B = "Second text";
```

6. What will be the output of the following program segment?

```
# include <iostream.h>
main()
  {
    struct Myrec {
        char ch;
        Myrec *link;
        };
    Myrec x,y,z, *p;
    x.ch='x';
    y.ch='y';
    z.ch ='z';
    x.link=&z;
    y.link =&x;
    z.link=NULL;
    p=&y;
    while (p!= NULL)
        {
          cout << p->ch;
          p=p->link;
        }
  }
```

7. What will be the output of the following program?

```
# include <iostream.h>
main()
   {
   float cost []={ 35.2, 37.2, 35.42, 36.3 };
   float *ptr[4];
   int i;
   for ( i=0; i < 4; i++)
       *(ptr +i)=cost + i;
   for ( i=0; i < 4; i++)
       cout << " " << *(*(ptr +i));
   }
```

Assume the base address of the array called 'cost' to be 2025.

8. What will be the output of the following program?

```
# include <iostream.h>
main()
   {
```

```
    char item[]="COMPUTER";
    int i;
    for (i=7; i >=0 ; i--)
    cout << " " << *(item + i);
  }
```

9. What would be the output of the following program?

```
# include <iostream.h>
  main()
  { char *ptr = "abcd";
    char ch = ++ *ptr ++;
    cout << "\n ", ch;
  }
```

10. What would be the output of the following program?

```
# include <iostream.h>
  main()
    {
      struct val {
          int Net;
          };
        struct val x;
        struct val *p;

        p = &x;
        p->Net = 50;
        cout << "\n", <<(x.Net)++;
    }
```

11. What would be the output of the following program?

```
# include <iostream.h>
  main()
    {
      struct val {
            int Net;
            };
        struct val x;
        struct val *p;

        p = &x;
        p->Net = 50;
        cout << "\n", (x.Net)++;
     }
```

12. Explain how new and delete operators manage memory allocation and deallocation.

13. Write a program that creates a linked list of dynamic nodes consisteing of N nodes. The structure of an individual node is given below

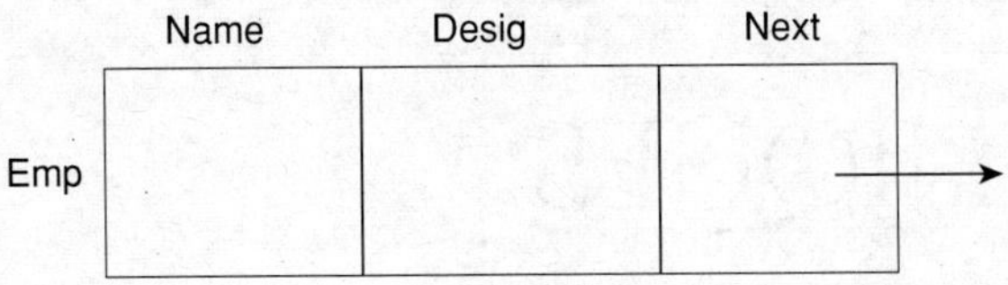

ANSWERS

4. 5 5 10 30 120 **6.** *y x z* **7.** 35.2 37.2 35.42 36.29 **8.** RETUPMOC **9.** b
10. 50 **11.** 51

PROGRAMMING TECHNIQUES: A SURVEY

3

3.1 INTRODUCTION

FORTRAN, a computer language, was developed in mid-1950s. Nowadays, there are hundreds of programming languages available in the market. However, only a small number of them are popular among the programmers. For example, FORTRAN, BASIC, COBOL, Pascal, 'C', 'C++', PROLOG, JAVA, etc. are very popular computer languages.

Since a programming language is responsible for human–system communication, it consists of symbols, characters, and grammar rules which allow programmers to communicate with computers. As discussed earlier in Chapter 1, a programming language can be defined as "a language used for expressing a set of computer instructions" The set of instructions is called a program.

In fact, a computer program is written for the following tasks:

1. **To save time by performing complex calculations** Examples: weather forecasting, design of civil structures, continuous simulation of aircrafts, etc.
2. **To process large amount of data** Examples: transaction processing applications such as banks, nation wide common entrance tests such as AIEEE, GATE, MAT, etc.
3. **To control machinery** Examples: guided missiles, command aircrafts, automated industries, modern cars, etc.
4. **Entertainment.** Examples: multimedia applications, virtual reality, etc.

The programming practice has evolved through the following four major phases:

1. Unstructured programming
2. Procedural programming
3. Modular programming
4. Object-oriented programming

A brief discussion on each of the phases is given in following sections.

3.2 UNSTRUCTURED PROGRAMMING

In the beginning of the programming era, the main emphasis was to write a program that simply produced correct results. The programmers wrote programs consisting of a sequence of statements, operating upon variables which were most of the time global (see Fig. 3.1). The 'goto' statement of FORTRAN was a preferred tool for uncontrolled jumps.

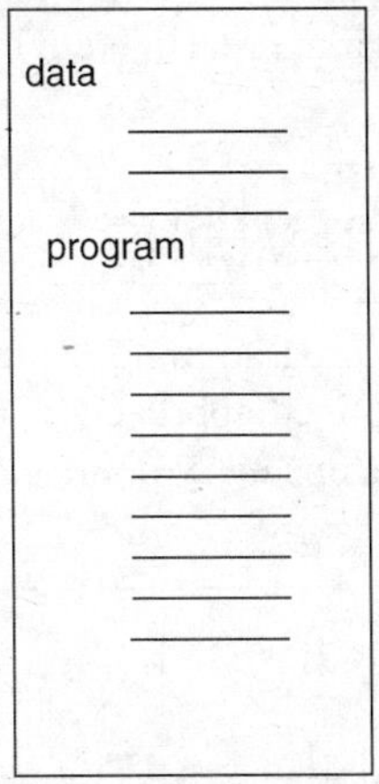

Figure 3.1 *A program with global data*

The global variables coupled with 'goto' statements rendered the program a mess of statements making it very difficult to understand as shown in Fig. 3.2

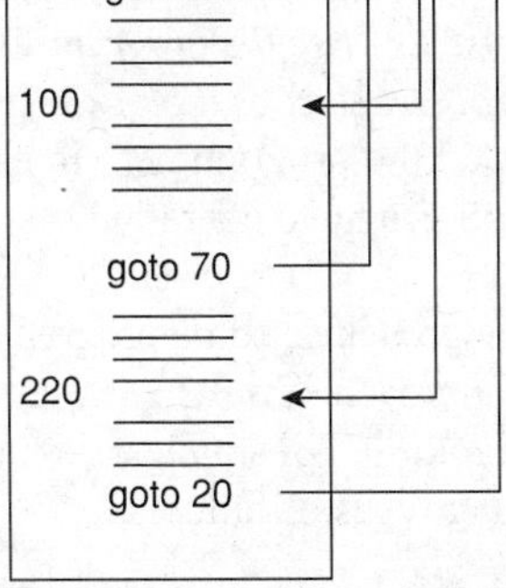

Figure 3.2 *An unstructured program*

It may be noted that the 'goto' statement makes a program unstructured in the sense that program control flows from here to there without making any sense to the reader. Moreover, in case of large programs, it becomes equally difficult to keep track of the history of the global variables. Therefore, it becomes very difficult to understand and maintain the program.

In 1960s, the computing community realized that the cost of maintaining unstructured programs was even more than the cost of rewriting. This realization was the turning point whereby discipline was enforced on the programmers to follow *structured programming* techniques such as block structured approach, modular approach, etc. The use of 'goto' statements in particular was discouraged.

3.3 STRUCTURED PROGRAMMING

With the advent of block structured programming languages such as Pascal and 'C', the programmers started following a disciplined approach of programming. 'C' supports constructs called blocks wherein each block has one entry point and one exit point as shown in Fig. 3.3.

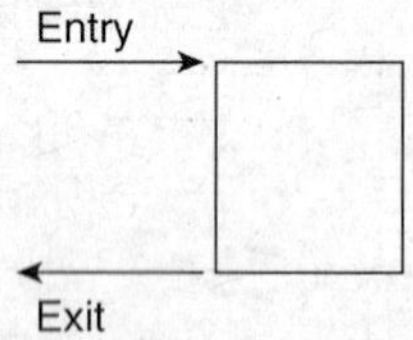

Figure 3.3 *A block*

It may be noted that a code enclosed between a pair of curly braces can be termed as a block. The following constructs of 'C' are examples of blocks.

- Compound statement
- Loop (for, while, do–while)
- Function
- File

Structured programming: *this programming technique allows a limited set of control structures which the programmer can use to write the programs. The control structures are while, for, do–while, if–else, etc. Each control structure is a block.*

The disciplined approach helped the programmers in easily managing large programs. No wonder that the first version of UNIX, a huge operating system, was written using 'C'. Even the compiler of 'C' is written in 'C'

But in-spite of the structured approaches, some programmers try to quickly assemble a program that some how works. The approach of quickly assembling a set of statements to produce a program is generally called as **hacking**. For smaller programs, hacking may work but for large programs, it results in the following types of failures:

1. The program may contain bugs, i.e. do not gives correct results.
2. Abnormal program termination, i.e. the program may crash.

3. The program becomes unstructured, i.e. expensive to maintain.
4. The program may contain time bombs, i.e. hidden errors – which may affect the program in future.

Since hacking is generally practiced by beginners, they can also be taught to follow structured programming rules which would help them to write reliable and robust programs.

Precisely, the *structured programming refers to techniques that produce programs with clean flow, clear design, and hierarchical program structure.* It can be broadly classified into two categories: *procedural* programming and *modular* programming.

3.3.1 Procedural Programming

In procedural programming, importance is given to procedure that can solve a given problem, i.e. "what do we have to do to solve the problem?". The problem at hand is divided into sub-problems. Then each sub-problem is divided into sub-sub-problems and so on till each of them can be solved separately. Each sub-problem is coded as a procedure or function. The arrangement is as shown in Fig. 3.4. The advantage of a procedure is that if it is correct then on every call it produces correct results.

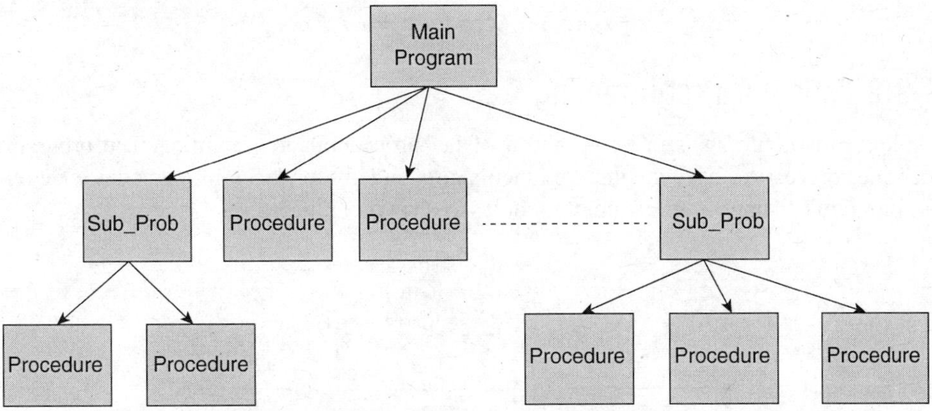

Figure 3.4 *Hierarchy of procedures*

Since a procedure can call another procedure, the program can be provided with a carefully designed structure. In simple words, we can say that "**a structured program is a collection of organized procedures with a clear control flow** as shown in Fig. 3.5.

It may be noted from Fig. 3.4 that the program control flows through a sequence of procedures. The various procedures work under the control of the main program. Each procedure is a block with one entry point and one exit.

Procedural programming: *in this technique of programming the programmer gives more importance to the steps that must be followed to solve a problem. The problem is divided into a collection of small and manageable functions. The emphasis is more on operations than the data on which the operations take place.*

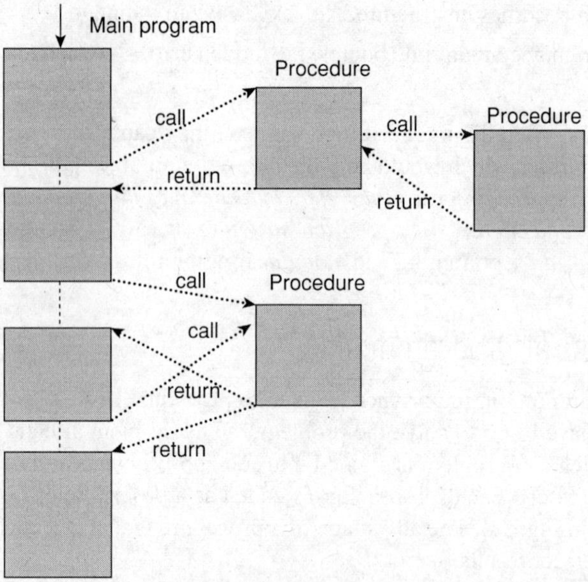

Figure 3.5 *Organized procedures*

3.3.2 Modular Programming

Modular programming is one step ahead of the procedural programming. The programmer identifies procedures having common functionality and groups them into a module. Therefore, the program becomes a collection of modules as shown in Fig. 3.6.

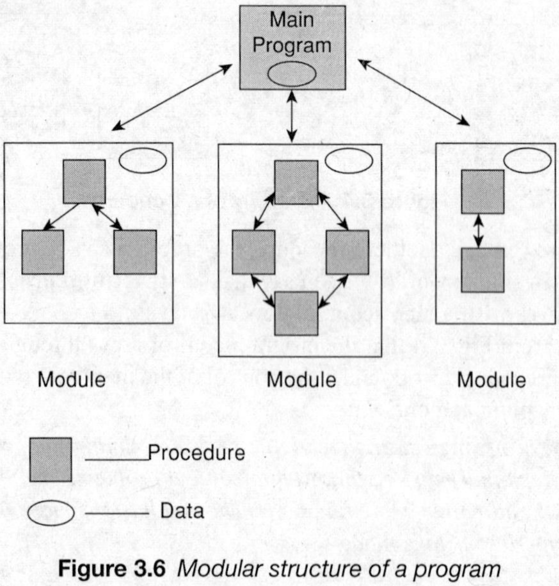

Figure 3.6 *Modular structure of a program*

Each module has its own set of data and procedures. The procedures work on internal data of the module. Every module controls its own procedures.

Modular programming: *in this technique of programming, the program creates a collection of interacting modules as a solution to a given problem.*

3.4 DRAWBACKS OF STRUCTURED PROGRAMMING

In procedural based approach, the main emphasis is on how to solve the problem, i.e. to look for procedure that can give the required results. This approach works well with small and medium sized programs. However, for very large programs such as writing compilers/operating systems/CAD packages/simulators, etc., the complexity increases which only the experienced and matured programmers can handle.

Consider the following 'C' program that implements a Queue. It uses three procedures/functions addQ(), removeQ(), and display() to do the required tasks:

```
/* This program implements a Queue wherein items are
   added to the Queue at rear end and removed from front end
   The add and remove operations are done through respective functions
*/

# include <stdio.h>
# include <conio.h>

        /* prototypes of functions */
void addQ( int queue[], int *rear, int item, int size);
void removeQ( int queue[], int *front, int *rear, int *item);
void displayQ (int queue[], int front, int rear);

void main ()
  {
    int queue[30];
    int front, rear;
    int size; /* size of the queue */
    int item; /* item to be added/removed from the queue */
    int choice;

    printf("\n Enter the size of the queue");
    scanf ("%d", &size);

    front = rear = 0; /* indicates that the queue is initially empty

       show a menu */
    do
      {
   printf ("\n Menu");
   printf ("\n");
   printf ("\n Add -----    1");
   printf ("\n Remove ----- 2");
   printf ("\n Display ---- 3");
   printf ("\n Quit -----   4");
```

```
  printf ("\n");
  printf ("\n Enter your choice");
  scanf ("%d",&choice);
  clrscr();          /* clrear screen */

  switch (choice)
     {
       case 1 :printf ("\n Enter the item to be added");
        scanf("%d", &item);
        addQ(queue,&rear,item,size);
        break;
       case 2 :removeQ(queue, &front, &rear, &item);
        if (item != 9999)
      printf ("\n the removed item = %d",item);
        break;
       case 3 :displayQ(queue, front, rear);
        break;
       }
     }
       while (choice != 4);
       }                        // End of main

/* This function adds an item on the queue */

void addQ( int queue[], int *rear, int item, int size)
  {
    if (*rear < size)
  {
   *rear = *rear + 1;
    queue [*rear] = item;
  }
    else
  printf ("\n the queue is Full");
  }

 /* This function removes an item from the queue */
void removeQ(int queue[], int *front, int *rear, int *item)
 {
   if (*front == *rear)
  {printf ("\n The queue is empty");
    *item = 9999;
  }
   else
      {
       *front = *front + 1;
       *item = queue[*front];
      }
  }

/* This function displays the contents of the queue */
void displayQ (int queue[], int front, int rear)
```

```
{
 int i;
 printf ("\n The items are...");
 if (front < rear)
 for (i = front + 1; i <= rear; i++)
  printf ("%d", queue[i]);
}
```

From the above program, the following **observations** can be made:

1. The queue works only for 20 locations.
2. It only works with integers.
3. The variables front and rear can be corrupted.
4. It is visible to the user that the queue has been implemented using arrays as data structure.
5. Without major modification, it is difficult to reuse any part of the program.

In fact the focus has been to implement the queue that can work on a fixed number of integers. No consideration has been given to produce a reusable code.

In **modular programming**, all the functions related to queue can be grouped together in a module. The common functions work upon the data supplied by the main(). However, the following **observations** can be made:

1. The emphasis is on to group the functions, i.e. operations.
2. As per the requirements of the functions, the data representation is chosen.
3. The functions are then later on made to work on the data.
4. Data and data structures usually remain unprotected.

Therefore, a module suffers from the following drawbacks:

1. The emphasis is on to operations instead of the data.
2. Multiple instances of modules are difficult to create.

3.5 OBJECT-ORIENTED PROGRAMMING

The remedy to the above-mentioned drawbacks is that we put more emphasis on data and try to create reusable software components. The reusable components can further be combined to get bigger and powerful software.

Let us consider the case of assembly of computer systems. In the market, following components are available:

1. Mother board.
2. Microprocessor-based CPU.
3. CPU fan.
4. RAM.
5. HDD.

6. CD-ROM drive.
7. Video card.
8. Sound card.
9. Mouse.
10. Keyboard.
11. LCD monitor.
12. Cabinet with SMPS.
13. Connectors and cables.

Each component given above is an object capable of providing services through an interface. The CPU, RAM, video card, and sound card are plugged into the mother board through their respective interfaces, i.e. the slots. HDD and CD-ROM drives are connected to the mother board through connectors and cables. This assembly of objects is encased in a cabinet. The LCD monitor, keyboard, and mouse are connected externally through ports which extrude from the cabinet. An expert can assemble a system in an hour or so. The process is fast because the components are available and we have to connect them properly.

It may be noted that while assembling the computer system, we did not bother about the internal working of the objects or who made them how. Rather, we emphasized more on their proper interfacing and inter-connection with each other. Moreover, the components like RAM, sound card, mouse, etc. are reusable, i.e. these components can be used with any other computer system.

Similarly, if we have reusable software objects then we can assemble them to quickly produce a software system of interacting components, connected through their interfaces as shown in Fig. 3.7.

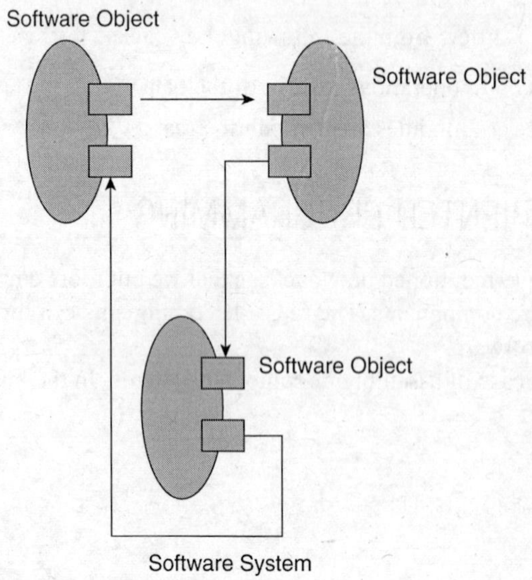

Figure 3.7 *Software objects interacting with each other*

It may be noted that the data and logic are encased in an object and are hidden from other objects. In fact they provide services to each other only through their interfaces. The access to internal components is controlled and limited.

Therefore, the only option to manipulate the objects is through their interfaces. For example, on a mobile phone we press the various buttons or touch on the screen to get services such as: make a call, terminate a call, search a contact name/number, etc. Similarly on an ATM machine, we only work on the 4–6 buttons provided on its interface. What and how it happens inside these machines is none of our business.

From the above discussions, we can say that the object-oriented programming involves programming using objects. An object can be any real time entity which is capable of providing services. The examples of objects are ***you, me, chair, fan, air, bank account, bank clerk***, etc. Object-oriented programming has following three prominent aspects:

1. **Encapsulation:** grouping and hiding data, information and implementation in a unit behind an interface. For instance there are many things in a house but only the doors and windows are provided as interface to the outside world. The inside of the house can be changed or re-configured without changing the doors and windows. Similarly, data and implementation within an object can be changed without changing its interface. This OOP technique is called as '*separateness*', i.e. in an object the interface and implementation are separated from each other.
2. **Inheritance:** this feature of OOP allows code reuse. All the data, data structures, and implementation of an object become the part of a new object through inheritance. For instance, the services of a Queue object can be inherited by a Queue Manager object of operating system for managing the various queues it maintains while allocating the resources. So, the programmer of Queue manager object need not develop the code for Queue object. This is similar to a son inheriting the wealth and property of his father without making any efforts to earn the same.
3. **Polymorphism:** polymorphism allows dynamic binding of functions, i.e. at run time it is decided as to which function to be called for execution. If a new technology has arrived or developed then it is placed in a new function. Through dynamic binding, the new function is bound and executed instead of the old function. This feature makes the software extensible and easily modifiable.

Object-oriented Programming: *this technique of programming provides a collection of reusable objects that interact with each other to offer a solution to a given problem. The main emphasis is on separating 'what from how', i.e. interface from implementation.*

More discussion on object-oriented programming is given in subsequent chapters.

3.6 SUMMARY

Some characteristics of procedure-oriented programming are:

1. Emphasis is on how to solve a problem or to do a job, i.e. develop algorithms.
2. Program is divided into functions.

3. Little attention is given to the data part of the program.
4. The procedures* share global data.
5. The code is generally not reusable.
6. Top-down, stepwise refinement techniques are used.

Some characteristics of object-oriented programming are:

1. More emphasis is given on data and information. These are generally made hidden to make them inaccessible.
2. A program is a collection of objects.
3. Objects are reusable entities.
4. Objects communicate with each other through public interfaces.
5. Only internal members of an object can change the state of an object.
6. Techniques like polymorphism, encapsulation, inheritance, etc. are used.

MULTIPLE CHOICE QUESTIONS

1. A 'goto' statement is
   (a) a conditional jump (b) an uncontrolled jump
   (c) a loop (d) none
2. Global variables and goto statement make a program
   (a) structured (b) modular
   (c) unstructured (d) none
3. Which of the following is not a block
   (a) loop (b) function
   (c) switch (d) simple statement
4. In procedural programming, the emphasis is on
   (a) data (b) procedure
   (c) reusability (d) sharing
5. In object-oriented programming, we have
   (a) interacting objects (b) collection of modules
   (c) collection of functions (d) emphasis on operations
6. Which of the following feature of OOP supports code reuse:
   (a) encapsulation (b) polymorphism
   (c) inheritance (d) object interface
7. Objects interact with each other through
   (a) functions (b) data
   (c) private members (d) interfaces

* A procedure is an impure function in which data exchange takes place through variables passed by reference.

8. A block has
   (a) many entry and many exit points
   (b) one entry and one exit point
   (c) many entry points and one exit point
   (d) one entry and no exit point.

ANSWERS

1. b **2.** c **3.** d **4.** b **5.** a **6.** c **7.** d **8.** b

EXERCISES

1. Why a program is written? Give the major application areas where a computer program becomes necessary.
2. What are the phases through which the programming practice has evolved?
3. Explain unstructured programming in brief.
4. Explain procedural programming in brief.
5. Explain modular programming in brief.
6. List shortcomings of procedure-oriented programming.
7. What is a procedure?
8. What are the drawbacks of structured pro-gramming?
9. Define the terms: encapsulation, inheritance, and polymorphism.
10. List out the characteristics of procedural programming.
11. List out the characteristics of object-oriented programming.

CLASSES AND OBJECTS

4

4.1 INTRODUCTION TO OBJECTS

We perceive the world around us through our senses. The senses recognize objects present around us. For instance, *visible objects* like human beings, buildings, cars, soil, earth, water, cloud, etc. are all perceived by eyes. The *non-visible* objects like air, sound, and smell are perceived through touch, ears, and nose respectively. *Distant or abstract* objects are generally perceived through spoken words of an expert. For instance, the structure of an atom or existence of BOSON, the God particle, can only be perceived through their description by experts. Thus, the world around us is composed of nothing but objects of varying descriptions as shown in Fig. 4.1.

Figure 4.1 *Some of the objects present around us*

An object can be precisely defined as: *an entity around us, perceivable through our senses.* If we look around, we find that we are surrounded by several objects (Fig. 4.1). For example in a University, students, professors, desks, fans, pens, writing pads, computers, etc. are all examples of objects.

Now, a closer look at various objects around us reveals that there are many types of objects as described below:

- *Objects that operate independently*. Examples: toys, photocopying machines, cameras, etc.
- *Objects that work in associations with each other*. Examples: computer–mouse, company–employee, car–driver, etc.
- *Objects that frequently interact with each other*. Example: telephones, fax machines, nodes of computer networks, etc.
- *Objects that are contained in other objects*. Example: ALU contained in a CPU, engine contained in a car, speaker contained in a phone, etc.

An object has following three characteristics:

1. *Identity*: it is the name associated with an object. It helps in identifying the object, i.e. what we call the object as? For example, cup is the name of the object that is used to store, serve and drink hot beverages such as tea or coffee.
2. *States*: an object can be in many states, for example, a cup, can be in the following states:
   a. Full
   b. Empty
   c. Cold/hot
   d. Broken
3. *Behaviours*: what the object does or what is it capable of doing? For example, a cup can be filled, drunk from, washed, broken, etc. Similarly, a person can sit, stand, sleep, walk, talk, etc.

Consider the clay pitcher given in Fig. 4.2.

Figure 4.2 *A clay pitcher*

It has the following characteristics:

1. Identity: pitcher
2. States:
   a. Upright/upside down
   b. Full/empty
   c. Broken

   d. Material – clay
   e. Colour – brown
3. Behaviours:
   a. Can be filled
   b. Can be emptied
   c. Can be transported
   d. Can be broken

In normal programming, when we write a program about (say) pitcher. The states are represented by variables and the behaviours as functions. The main() function sends the variables to various functions to model the overall functionality or behaviour of the pitcher. Thus, by nature, we first break the pitcher into variables and functions (i.e. pieces) then we try to glue the pieces through function calls to model its behaviour as shown in Fig. 4.3.

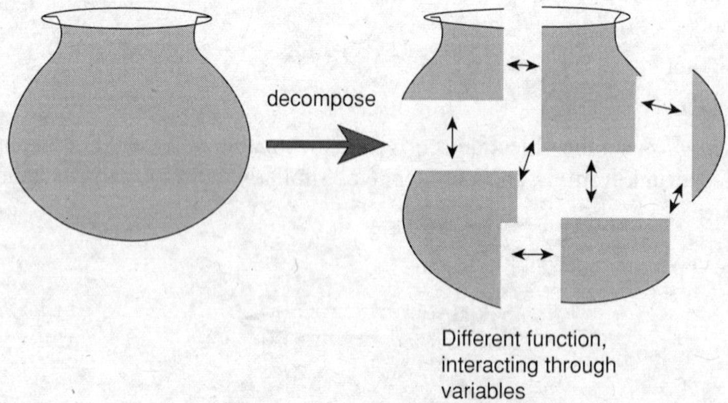

Figure 4.3 *Normal programming*

Now the problem is that in a very large program, when we have large number of broken objects at hand then it becomes difficult for a programmer to keep track of the history of all the variables which are time and again passed to hundreds of functions and the results received from them. As the size and complexity of a program increases, the function and module management becomes equally difficult for the programmer. Therefore, the programming becomes cumbersome and difficult and only few hardcore programmers succeed.

However, *in real life we don't break the pitcher or for that matter we don't break any object at all.* The objects interact with each other without losing their characteristics (see Fig. 3.7). Therefore, their management is quite easy and comfortable in real life.

Now the question is – can we create a software object that doesn't lose its characteristics while being maneuvered in a program. Yes the answer is Object Oriented Programming (OOP) wherein we can define and create software object which behave like real life objects. Before we delve more into OOP, let us first understand another concept called 'class' as discussed in following section.

4.2 CLASSES

Human has a very strong ability to categorize objects. When we see an object we immediately identify it to be belonging to a particular group or category. Consider the objects given in Fig. 4.4.

Figure 4.4 *Collection of objects*

The collection of objects shown in Fig. 4.4 can be easily identified to be belonging to the category called cups. But the question is how we can say that these objects belong to a group or set called cups? The simple answer is that all these objects have common characteristics belonging to the category called cups. In OOP, a category is called a **class**.

In fact, the objects around us can be categorized into classes. For instance, we can easily locate a class of "furniture", representing the objects such as: chairs, tables, desks, etc. In OOP terminology, we can say that a chair is an instance of the class furniture. Similarly, a dining table is also an instance of the class furniture and so on. If we consider book as a class then Ramayana, Gita, Jungle book are also instances of the class book. Thus, it can be said that *an* **object** *is an instance of a class.*

Note: The objects belonging to a class may have different states but their behaviours remain the same. For instances, the cups given in Fig. 4.4 differ from each other in shape but the behaviours such as '*can be filled*' or '*can be carried*' remain the same for all instances of cups.

The precise definition of **class** is: "*A class defines common states and behaviours of a group of objects*". Pictorially a class is represented as shown in Fig. 4.5.

Class name
States
Behaviours

Figure 4.5 *Pictorial representation of a class*

The class that models a pitcher is given in Fig. 4.6.

In fact in OOP, we develop a program using the concept similar to building a system from its basic components. For a given problem, the following steps are followed:

1. Identify the objects that comprise the problem.
2. Categorize the objects into classes.

Pitcher
Upright / Upside down Full / Empty Broken Material – clay Colour – brown
Can be filled Can be emptied Can be transported Can be broken

Figure 4.6 *Pitcher class*

3. Establish the relationship between the classes.
4. Create instances of objects as per the requirement.
5. Manage the objects to solve the problem.

4.3 DECLARATION OF CLASSES IN C++

From the above discussion it is evident that the classes are central to OOP and a class can be used to create objects of its type. In C++, a class can be defined by the keyword "class". The format of class declaration is given below:

```
class  <name  >
   {private :
         variable declarations
         function declarations
   public :
         variable declarations
         function declarations
   };
```

where *class* is a keyword; *<name>* is the user defined name of the class. It is a C++ identifier. *Private* is a keyword; *public* is a keyword.

It may be observed that a class declaration is similar to a structure declaration. Therefore, everything related to structure applies to classes. However, there is a difference in the sense that a structure is open and accessible to all whereas the access to members of the class is rather restricted. The class has clearly two sections: *private* and *public*. There is also a third special section available in a class. This section called *protected* and is discussed later in this book.

Private members: the members declared in private section are not accessible outside the class. Therefore, the most important members that need to be secured are placed in private section. The states (i.e. variables) are always made private. The reason being that the internal *state of an object should only be changed by an internal behaviour or function and not by outside stimuli*. For example, the temperature of human body remains constant irrespective of climatic conditions being summer or winter. However, an infection in the body may give rise to high body temperature. This feature of hiding states and data structures is called *data or information hiding*.

Similarly, the behaviours (i.e. the functions) which implement the business logic are also hidden from outside by making them private members. The *set* functions which can modify a state of the object are also made private. This feature of hiding implementation or set functions is also called as *implementation hiding*.

Public members: the functions that need to interact with outside world are made public. These functions interact with the outside world for the following purposes:

1. *Taking input from users or other objects*. For example, the function that reads data from a user (say read_data()) needs to be made public.
2. *Providing information about states of the object to users*. These functions are also called as *get* functions. For example, the function that informs about the grade of a student (say get_grade()) has to made public.
3. *Providing services offered by the object to users or other objects*. For instance the push() and pop() functions of a stack object are made public.

It may be noted that the public functions act as interface to the outside world. In other words we can say that the important data, information, and implementation are hidden in private section behind a public interface as shown in Fig. 4.7.

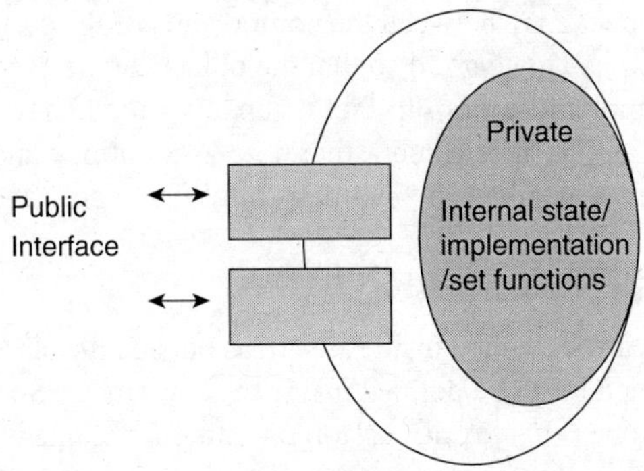

Figure. 4.7 *Data and implementation hiding behind public interface*

4.3.1 Abstraction and Encapsulation

From Figure 4.7, the following points are observed:

1. Only public interface is visible.
2. The data, information, and implementation are hidden.

The visible part which provides only the bare minimum details about the object is called *abstraction*. The data, information and implementation are hidden. In other words, we can say that data, information and implementation have been placed in a capsule and the activity is called as *encapsulation*. An example of abstraction and encapsulation is given in Fig. 4.8.

In a human head, there are many components like arteries, veins, muscles, eyes, ears, nose, mouth, cheek bones, retina, iris, brain, etc. But most of these have been encapsulated. Only the necessary components that are needed to interact with others have been abstracted as interface (see Fig. 4.8).

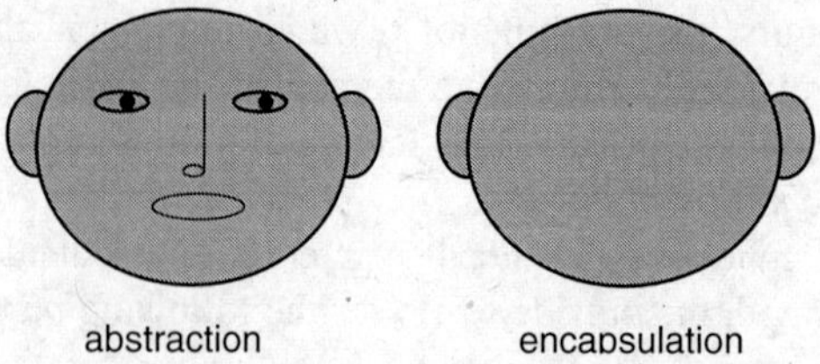

Figure 4.8 *Abstraction and encapsulation*

By default, a class contains private members, i.e. all states and behaviours are private and not accessible to outsiders. Thus, the class encapsulates the data, information, and the implementation. When a user, by design, declares some members as public then those members become the interface or abstraction. Thus, the unnecessary details are ignored. The terms abstraction and encapsulation can be precisely defined as:

Abstraction: the activity of separating essential members of a class in the form of public interface is known as abstraction. It provides a simple view of the object so that the user can easily use the object.

Encapsulation: the activity of hiding data and implementation within a class as a unit is called as encapsulation. It creates a separation between the interface and the implementation thereby reducing the dependency between the components of the system.

In fact the abstraction has to be good so that the object can be used with ease without going into the details of the implementation. In fact it separates the behaviour of the object from its implementation. For example, in a camera there are 2–3 buttons and an eye-piece to interact with. Similarly, a house encapsulates many things but offers doors and windows as abstraction.

4.3.2 Member Function Definition

The member functions can be defined inside as well as outside the class declaration. If a member function is very small then it can be defined inside the class itself. Such function definitions are considered by default to be *inline*. A discussion on inline functions is given later in this book. Let us consider the following class declaration:

```
//Example of member function definition inside class declaration
     class test { private:
     int val;
     public :
       void readvar()
          {
          cin  >>val;
          }
       void dispvar()
          {
          cout  <<val;
          }
     };
```

In this class two public functions readvar ( ) and dispvar ( ) have been defined. It may be noted that the actual code for the function is written inside the class definition itself. On the contrary, if a member function is large then it should be defined outside the class declaration. The prototypes of such functions, however, must be provided in the class definition. For example, the above defined class can be rewritten as given below:

```
//Example of member function definition outside a class declaration
      class test
      {
      private:
             int val;
      public :
             void readvar();
             void dispvar();
      };
      void test :: readvar()
             {
             cin  >>val;
             }
      void test :: dispvar()
             {
             cout  <<val;
             }
```

The operator '::' is known as *scope resolution* operator. This is used to associate member functions to their corresponding class. For example, in the above function declarations, it conveys to the compiler that the functions readvar( ) and dispvar( ) belong to the class called test. The format of a member function declaration is given below:

```
type class_name :: function_name (parameter list)
   {
    function body
   }
```

where type: is the data type of value to be returned;
class_name: the name of the class to which the function belongs;
function_name: the name of the function being declared;
parameter list: list of formal arguments.

From the above discussion, it is clear that a class combines data and functions into a single programming unit.

Example 1. *Define a class called student which models the following states and behaviours of a student:*

States

Name
Roll
Marks
Grade

Behaviours

Read_data()
Display_grade()
Compute_grade()

Compute the grade as per the following rules:

Marks	*Grade*
>=50 < 60	D
>=60 < 70	C
>=70 < 80	B
>=80	A

Solution: We would model the states as variables and place them in private section for the purpose of data hiding. The behaviours read_data() and display_grade() would be modeled as functions and placed in public section as these functions are needed by the user to interact with the student object. Since the compute_grade() is an **implementation function**, it would be placed in private section from implementation hiding point of view. The required class is given below:

```
# include <iostream.h>

class student {

private:
  char name[20];
  int roll;
  int marks;
  char grade;
  void compute_grade(); //implementation function

public:
  void read_data();
  void display_grade();
  };
      // Function to read data of a student
  void student:: read_data()
   {
    cout <<"\n Enter Name:";
    cin >> name;
    cout << "\n Enter Roll:";
    cin >> roll;
    cout << "\n Enter Marks:";
    cin >> marks;
    compute_grade(); // compute the grade
    }
      // Function to display grade
```

```
void student:: display_grade()
     {
       cout<< "\n Name:" << name;
       cout << "\n Roll:" << roll;
       cout << "\n Grade:" <<grade;
     }
   // Function to compute grade
  void student::compute_grade()
      {
        if (marks >= 80) grade = 'A';
        else
       if (marks >=70 ) grade ='B';
       else
         if (marks >=60) grade ='C';
         else
           if (marks >=50) grade ='D';
           else
             grade ='E';
         }
```

4.4 CREATING OBJECTS

An object is an instance of a class and it can be created of its class type. The syntax for defining an object is given below:

```
<class_name>   <object_name>;
```

where <class_name> is the name of the class and <object_name> is the name of the object being defined.

For example, we can create an object **studObj** of class **student** by the following declaration :

```
student   studObj;
```

The above declaration says that *studObj* is an object of class student.

In some situations, especially while sorting of objects, it is required that one object may be copied to another object. C++ allows assignment of objects of same type. It copies the source object bit-wise to the destined object. The concept is illustrated through the statements given below:

```
class xyz {                     // CLASS DECLARATION
      :
      };
      xyz obj1, obj2;          // OBJECT CREATION
      :
      obj2 = obj1;             // OBJECT ASSIGNMENTS
```

4.4.1 Calling Member Functions

Once an object has been created, its member functions (public) can be called in the program with the help of a dot operator, i.e. the object name is connected to the function name with a dot. For example, if we desire to call read_data( ) function of object 'studOb' then the following statement can be used.

```
studOb.read_data();
```

The above statement says that a function read_data() of object studOb is being called / invoked.

Example 2. *Use the class student defined in Example 1. Write a menu driven program that tests the class student for following services:*

1. *Read the data of a student.*
2. *Display the grade of a student.*

Solution: We would use a do–while loop to display a menu for asking the choice from the user. The required program is given below:

```
# include <iostream.h>
# include <conio.h>

class student {
private:
  char name[20];
  int roll;
  int marks;
  char grade;
  void compute_grade();
public:
  void read_data();
  void display_grade();
  };

  // Function to read data of a student
  void student:: read_data()
   {
    cout <<"\n Enter Name:";
    cin >> name;
    cout << "\n Enter Roll:";
    cin >> roll;
    cout << "\n Enter Marks:";
    cin >> marks;
    compute_grade(); // compute the grade
    }
   void student:: display_grade()
```

```
  {
    cout<< "\n Name:" << name;
    cout << "\n Roll:" << roll;
    cout << "\n Grade:" <<grade;
  }
 void student::compute_grade()
   {
     if (marks >= 80) grade = 'A';
     else
    if (marks >=70 ) grade ='B';
    else
    if (marks >=60) grade ='C';
    else
    if (marks >=50) grade ='D';
    else
      grade ='E';
    }
void main()
{
int choice;
student studOb;

do
  {
   clrscr();
   cout << "\n Menu";
   cout <<"\n";
   cout <<"\nRead data\t 1";
   cout <<"\n";
   cout <<"\nDisplay grade \t 2";
   cout <<"\n";
   cout <<"\nQuit\t\t 3";
   cout <<"\n";
   cout <<"\nEnter your choice:";
   cin >> choice;

      switch (choice)
      {
       case 1 : studOb.read_data();
       break;
       case 2 : studOb.display_grade();
  }
       getch();
  }
      while (choice != 3);
  }
```

Example 3. *Define a class called employee with the following specifications:*

States

name
BP: basic pay,
DA: dearness allowance
HRA: house rent allowance
salary

Behaviours

computeSal(): computes the salary
readData (): accepts the data values
dispSal(): prints the data on the screen.
The salary is computed by the following formula:
Salary = BP + DA + HRA
where DA and HRA are 65% and 20% of the BP, respectively.

Write a program that reads the name and BP of the employee and prints the salary.

Solution: We would model the states as variables and place them in private section for the purpose of data hiding. The behaviours readData() and dispSal() would be modeled as functions and placed in public section as these functions are needed by the user to interact with the employee object. Since the computeSal() is an implementation function, it would be placed in private section from implementation hiding point of view.
The required class with a complete program is given below:

```
// This program reads, compute, and displays the data
   // of an employee

   #include   <iostream.h>
   #include   <stdio.h>
   class employee
   {
      private:
      char name[20];
      float BP, DA, HRA, Salary;
      void computeSal();          // hide implementation
      public:
      void readData();
      void dispSal();
    };
      void employee :: computeSal()
        {
           DA = 0.65 * BP;
           HRA = 0.2 * BP;
           Salary = BP + DA + HRA;
        }
```

```
void employee :: readData()
    {
    cout  <<"\n Enter name of the employee:";
    gets(name);
    fflush(stdin);
    cout  <<"\n Enter Basic Pay:";
    cin  >> BP;
    computeSal();
    }
void employee :: dispSal()
  {
    cout  <<"\n Name :"   << name;
    cout  <<"\n Salary= "   << Salary;
  }
void main()
  {
employee empOb;
    empOb.readData();
    empOb.dispSal();
  }
```

4.5 ARRAY OF OBJECTS

C++ allows declaration of arrays of objects like arrays of any other type. An individual object within the array can be accessed by a subscript. The following example illustrates the usage of an array of objects of class student type.

Example 4. *Use the student class of Example 1. Write a program which reads records of N number of students in an array of objects and prints the list of students in the following format:*

List of Students			
S. No.	*Name*	*Roll*	*Grade*
⋮	⋮	⋮	⋮

Solution: The required program, that uses an array of objects of class student type to read and print a list of students, is given below:

```
// This program reads a list of students and prints their grade
```

```
# include <iostream.h>
# include <conio.h>

class student {
private:
char name[20];
int roll;
int marks;
char grade;
void compute_grade();
public:
void read_data();
void display_grade();
};

 // Function to read data of a student
 void student:: read_data()
  {
   cout <<"\n Enter Name:";
   cin >> name;
   cout << "\n Enter Roll:";
   cin >> roll;
   cout << "\n Enter Marks:";
   cin >> marks;

   compute_grade(); // compute the grade
   }
     void student:: display_grade()
   {
      cout<< "\n" << name;
      cout << "\t" << roll;
      cout << "\t" <<grade;
   }
      void student::compute_grade()
   {
      if (marks >= 80) grade = 'A';
      else
       if (marks >= 70 ) grade ='B';
       else
       if (marks >= 60) grade ='C';
       else
      if (marks >= 50) grade ='D';
      else
      grade ='E';
     }
void main()
  {
   int n;
```

```
student stud_list[50];
cout  <<"\nENTER THE NUMBER OF STUDENT";
cin  >>n;
for(int i = 0;i < n;i++)
stud_list[i].read_data();
clrscr();
cout  <<"\n     LIST OF STUDENTS:        \n";
cout  <<"\nNAME\t ROLLNO\t GRADE";
for(i = 0;i < n; i++)
 stud_list[i].display_grade();
}
```

4.6 OBJECTS AS FUNCTION ARGUMENTS

C++ considers objects as built-in data type and therefore, an object can be passed to a function as an argument. An object can be passed in either of the two ways given below. However, each method has its own merits and demerits.

1. Pass by value
2. Pass by reference

1. *Pass by value*: in *pass by value* method of argument passing, the objects are passed to functions by value. A copy of the object is received by the called function, not the actual object. The called function can only use the services of the object because only public members of the object are accessible to the function. For instance, consider the following function (test()) that receives an object of student type through '*pass by value*' and reads its data and displays its grade.

```
void test (student sOb)
    { sOb.read_data();
      cout <<"\n Display in test()";
      sOb.display_grade();
    }
void main()
      {
      student studOb;
      clrscr();
      test (studOb);                  // call test() by pass by value
       cout <<"\n \n Display in main()";
      studOb.display_grade();
      }
```

The output of the program is given below:

```
Enter Name :Atul
Enter Roll :101
Enter Marks :98
```

```
Display in test()
Atul     101     A
Display in main()
Atul     1382    √
```

It may be noted that the function main is also trying to display the grade but only garbage is being shown. The reason being that the object studOb, created in main() is different from the object sOb created in test() as shown in Fig. 4.9. Therefore, the grade computed by sOb is shown by sOb only and not by studOb of main().

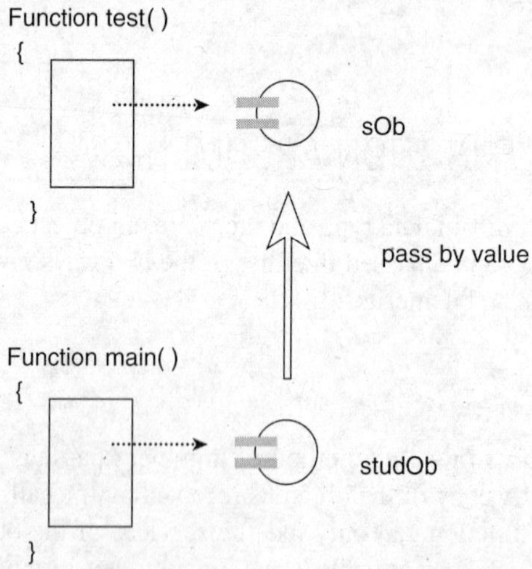

Figure 4.9 *The object being passed by 'pass by value' method*

2. *Pass by reference*: in some situations, it is desired that the changes done to an object in the called function should be reflected back into the calling function. This can be resolved with the help of pass by reference method of argument passing of C++. In this method, the address of an object is passed to the function as an argument. The address of the object is represented by preceding the object name with the character '&'.

   For instance, consider the following modified function (test()) that receives an object of student type by *'pass by reference'* and reads its data and displays its grade.

```
void test (student &sOb)    // pass by reference
   { sOb.read_data();
     cout <<"\n Display in test()";
     sOb.display_grade();
   }
void main()
  {
     student studOb;
     clrscr();
     test (studOb);           // call test() by pass by value
```

```
        cout <<"\n \n Display in main()";
       studOb.display_grade();
    }
```

The output of the program is given below:

```
Enter Name :Atul
Enter Roll :101
Enter Marks :98

Display in test()
Atul      101     A
Display in main()
          101     A
```

It may be noted that the function main is also able to display the grade. The reason being that in pass by reference, only the address of the object has been passed resulting in both test() and main() referring to the same object as sOb and studOb, respectively, as shown in Fig. 4.10.

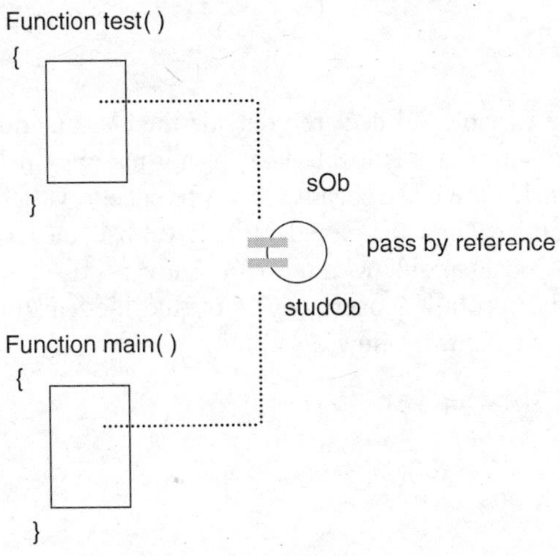

Figure 4.10 *Pass by reference – sOb & studOb refer to the same object*

A function can return an object if it has been declared to return the corresponding class of objects. For example, a function some( ) which returns an object of class (say) student type can be defined as shown below:

```
student some ( )
{ student temp;
.
.
   return (temp);
}
```

4.7 SCOPE RESOLUTION OPERATOR

From our earlier discussion in this chapter we know that, when a member function of a class is large then it is prototyped inside the class and defined outside with the help of a scope resolution operator. The scope resolution operator is a double colon (::) used to connect the definition of functions to their classes. The general form of usage of this operator is shown below:

```
<return type> < class_name > :: < function _name > (parameter list)
```

In addition to above, we can use the scope resolution operator to access hidden global variables inside a class definition. Consider the program segment given below:

```
int val; // global variable
class xyz {
int val // local variable
:
public :
int int_val()
{
return ++ val
}
};
```

We can observe that the variable val declared outside the class is global and the variable val declared separately inside the class is local. Now, in normal circumstances we cannot access such a global variable inside the class because any reference to variable val would be considered as local by the compiler. Thus, the global variable val becomes hidden inside the class on account of presence of a local variable with the same name.

We can use the scope resolution operator (::) on the hidden global variable to make it accessible inside the class as shown below:

```
int val; // global variable
int count;
class xyz {
int val; // local variable
public:
void in_val()
{
        :: val = ++ val;
        cout  <  <"\n THE LOCAL VAL ="   <  <    val;
        cout  <  <}\n THE GLOBAL VAL ="  <  < :: val;
}
}
```

Note: The major difference between scope resolution operator and the dot operator in context of classes and objects is: "The dot operator is used to specify a member of an object whereas the scope resolution operator is used to specify the class name while defining a member function of the class". The scope resolution operator is also used to make hidden global variable visible inside a class or a block.

Example 5. *Give the output of following program:*

```
#include   <iostream.h>
    int a = 10;
    void main()
    {
    void test (int &, int, int &);
    int a = 30, b = 10;
    test (::a, a, b);
    cout   <<::a << " " << a << " " << b << "\n";
    }
    void test (int &x, int y, int &z)
    {
            a += x;
            y *= a;
            z = a + y;
            cout << x << " " << y << " " << z << "\n";
    }
```

Solution: The output would be:

20	600	620
20	30	620

Example 6. *Write a class matAdd that is capable of adding two matrix objects matOb1 and matOb2 of its own type. Also write a main() function to test the working of the class.*

Solution: Let us include the members in the required class called addMat as shown in the class diagram

addMat
i, j mat [][]
readMat() displayMat() addOb()

where readMat() reads a matrix; displayMat() displays a matrix; addOb() adds two objects of type addMat class.

Note: The function addOb() has been included as one of the functions of the class. In the absence of this function it would be impossible to add two matrix objects because the data members have been declared private and hence not accessible out side the class. It is left as an exercise for the readers to declare addOb() as stand alone function (not part of the class) and try to add the matrix objects.

The required program is given below:

```
// This program adds two matrix objects

# include <iostream.h>
# include <conio.h>
  class addMat
     {
       int i,j, m,n;
       int mat[10][10];

       public:

       void readMat();
       void displayMat();
       void addOb(addMat ob1,addMat ob2);
     };

       void addMat:: readMat()
     {
      cout << "\n Enter the order of the matrix : m, n";
      cin >> m >> n;
      cout << "\n Enter the matrix elements one by one\n";
      for (i =0; i < m; i++)
  {
        for (j = 0; j < n; j++)
     {
       cin >> mat[i][j];
     }
  }
     }
  void addMat :: displayMat()
     {
      cout << "\n the matrix :\n";
      for (i =0; i < m; i++)
  {
   for (j = 0; j < n; j++)
     {
       cout << mat[i][j] << " ";
     }
     cout <<"\n";
  }
      }
  void addMat :: addOb(addMat ob1, addMat ob2)
     {
       if (ob1.m == ob2.m && ob1.n == ob2.n)
       {m = ob1.m; //copy order of the matrices
```

```
 n = ob1.n;
for (i =0; i < m; i++)
{
for (j = 0; j < n; j++)
   {
     mat[i][j] = ob1.mat[i][j] + ob2.mat[i][j];
   }
}
}
else
  cout << "\n addition not possible";
   }
   void main()
     {
 clrscr();
addMat matOb1, matOb2, matOb3;
matOb1.readMat();
matOb2.readMat();
matOb3.addOb(matOb1, matOb2);
matOb3.displayMat();
}
```

A sample output of the program is given below:

```
Enter the order of the matrix : m, n 2 3
Enter the matrix elements one by one
2 1 4
4 2 1
Enter the order of the matrix : m, n2 3
Enter the matrix elements one by one
2 0 3
1 1 1
the matrix :
4 1 7
5 3 2
```

Example 7. *A class called clock24 has following members:*

States
hour
minute

Behaviours
readtime();
showtime();

Write a complete program in C++ to input two different objects timeOb1 and timeOb2 of type clock24. Print their sum (assuming 24 hours clock time).

Solution: The required program is given below:

```
#include  <iostream.h>
# include <process.h>
  class clock24
    {
     int hour;
     int minute;
     public:
     void readtime();
     void showtime();
     void addtime(clock24, clock24);
    };
     void clock24::readtime()
   {
     cout <<"\nEnter the time\n" <<"hours:";
     cin >> hour;
     cout << "min:";
     cin >> minute;
     if ((hour > 12)||(minute > 60))
     {cout << "\n wrong time data";
     exit(0);
    }
   }
     void clock24::showtime()
     {
     cout << "\nTime is:" << hour <<":" << minute <<"\n";
     }
           void clock24::addtime(clock24 timeOb1 ,clock24 timeOb2)
     {
           hour = timeOb1.hour+timeOb2.hour;
           minute = timeOb1.minute+timeOb2.minute;
           if(minute > 60)
     {
           minute = minute - 60;
           hour++;
     }
           if(hour > 12)
     hour = hour - 12;
   }
     void main()
   {
     clock24 ob1, ob2,ob3;
     ob1.readtime();
     ob2.readtime();
```

```
        ob3.addtime(ob1,ob2);
        cout << "\n The time of object 1 :";
        ob1.showtime();
        cout << "\n The time of object 2 :";
        ob2.showtime();
        cout << "\n The sum of time of object 1 & 2 :";
        ob3.showtime();
    }
```

The sample output of the program is given below:

```
Enter the time
hours :5
min :34
Enter the time
hours :6
min :56
The time of object 1 :
Time is :5:34
The time of object 2 :
Time is :6:56
The sum of time of object 1 & 2 :
Time is :12:30
```

Example 8. *Compute the size of the object of class matAdd.*

Solution: The member wise size and the total size are given below:

1. $i, j, m, n = 4 * 2$ bytes (each) = 8 bytes
2. mat[10][10] = 100 * 2 bytes = 200 bytes

   Total size = 208 bytes – **Ans.**

4.8 STATIC DATA MEMBERS

When different instances of a class are created then each instantiated object gets its own set of states, i.e. variables. For example, every student object (Examples 1 & 2) gets its own set of variables to store name, roll no., marks, etc.

However, a data member can be declared as **static** within a function of a class so that it becomes common to all instances of the class. In simple words we can say that a static variable is shared among all instantiated objects of the class.

A static variable, declared within a function of a class has following characteristics:

1. The static variable is initialized to zero at the time of creation of first object of the class.

2. It is shared by all instances of the class.
3. The scope of the static variable is within the function of the class.
4. Its lifetime starts with the creation of first object and ends with the destruction of last object of the class.

Example 9. *Write a class called **testStatic** that declares a normal integer variable called individual as its private member. It uses public function called disp() which declares a static variable called common and displays the contents of both individual and common variables for various instances of objects.*

Solution: The required program is given below. It may be noted that in function main(), we are passing the number of the object as an argument to the function disp():

```
// This program illustrates the usage of static variables

# include <iostream.h>
# include <conio.h>

class testStatic
  {
   int individual;
   public:
  void disp(int val)
    {
     static int common;
     individual = val;
     common = common+ val;
     cout <<"\nstatic ="<< common <<"\n";
     cout <<"normal ="<< individual <<"\n";
    }
    };
     void  main()
   {
    testStatic ob1, ob2, ob3;
    clrscr();
    cout << "\n The object1";
    ob1.disp(1);
    cout << "\n The object2";
    ob2.disp(2);
    cout << "\n The object3";
    ob3.disp(3);
    }
```

The output of the program is given below:

```
 The object1
Static =1
```

```
normal =1

 The object2
Static =3
normal =2

 The object3
Static =6
normal =3
```

Kindly note that the static variable is common to all the three objects and its contents are getting accumulated (1–3–6) with each invocation of the disp(). However, the normal variable of each object has independent location and stores only the number of the object. Therefore, the variable (normal) that contains data of an individual object is also called an ***instance variable***. Similarly, the static variable that holds data that is common and relevant to all objects is also called as a ***class variable***. In fact, there is always only one copy of the class variable irrespective of the number of objects instantiated from the class.

In the light of above we can say that the variables individual and common of class testStatic are instance and class variables, respectively.

Example 10. *What is wrong with the following class declaration?*

```
class test {
    int val = 10;
    char ch;
    public
    int setvar ( );
    char read var ( );
    void setvar ( );
     };
```

Solution:

1. The keyword public must be followed by a colon.
2. No variable can be initialized inside a class declaration.

4.9 PROPERTIES OF CLASSES AND OBJECTS

From our discussions on various features of classes, we can observe that the general properties of classes are:

1. Classes consist of both data (variables) and functions.
2. Since a class is only processed at compiler level, no variable can be initialized inside a class declaration.

3. Classes allow private, protected and public members.
4. A member function defined inside the class is by default an inline function.
5. A member of a class is by default a private member unless otherwise specified.
6. A private member is not available outside the class. However, a member function can always access such a member.
7. Objects can be passed as parameters to functions.
8. Objects can be returned from a function.

The general properties of objects are:

1. *Objects are alive* because an object comes into existence. It gets the resources like memory. It has a lifetime.
2. *Objects are active* because an object provides services through its interface.
3. *Objects are intelligent* because every object has the coded logic to provide a service or to solve the problem at hand.

4.10 SUMMARY

Any perceivable entity is an object. Every object can be identified as belonging to a class. The activity that combines data and functions into one unit is known as encapsulation. Data and functions are linked on a fundamental level in the form of encapsulation. It enables data, information, and implementation hiding. An abstraction separates the essential part from the implementation details. A static variable, defined in a member function, is common to all instances of the class.

MULTIPLE CHOICE QUESTIONS

1. The world around us is composed of:
   (a) functions (b) modules
   (c) data (d) objects
2. An object can be perceived through our:
   (a) imagination (b) senses
   (c) intuition (d) emotions
3. Which of the following is not a characteristic of a general object?
   (a) identity (b) structure
   (c) states (d) behaviours
4. A class defines common ____ and ____ of a group of objects.
   (a) identity, states (b) identity, behaviours
   (c) states, behaviours (d) data, data structure
5. Implementation hiding is carried out by:
   (a) encapsulation (b) abstraction
   (c) static functions (d) scope resolution operator

6. An interface is composed of:
   (a) private members
   (b) public members
   (c) stand alone functions
   (d) none of these
7. A private member can be accessed by:
   (a) a stand alone function
   (b) the interface of the object
   (c) only the private members of the class
   (d) by all the members of the class
8. A global variable can be accessed within a class by:
   (a) prefixing it by a scope resolution operator
   (b) by declaring it as static
   (c) by a dot operator
   (d) none of these
9. A member of a class is by default:
   (a) public
   (b) static
   (c) private
   (d) global
10. An object is ____ of a class.
    (a) copy
    (b) part
    (c) property
    (d) instance

ANSWERS

1. d **2.** b **3.** b **4.** c **5.** a **6.** b **7.** d **8.** a **9.** c **10.** d

EXERCISES

1. Describe the basic concepts of object-oriented programming.
2. What do you understand by a class in C++?
3. Write the differences between a structure and a class.
4. Define the terms class and object. What is the relation between the two?
5. How does a class accomplish data hiding?
6. Define the terms: abstraction and encapsulation.
7. Explain how classes are declared in a C++ program.
8. Explain the purpose of access specifiers in a class.
9. Why it is considered a good practice for declaring data members as private?
10. Explain in brief the rules for definition and declaration of functions in a class.
11. Write a class called boxVolume with length, width and height as data members and readData(), dispData() and computeVol() as functions. Also write a main() function to test the boxVolume class.
12. Write a class called *bankACNT* that models a bank account having following members:

    States

    Name of the client
    Account number

Type of account
Balance amount

Behaviours:

initVal() – to initialize the values
depAmount() – to deposit amount
withdrawAmount() – to withdraw some amount
checkBalance() – to check the balance amount
dispInfo() – to display the A/C No. and balance
Write a main() function to test the class bankACNT.

13. Create a class to represent a book. With following members:

States

Book
Title
Author
Acc_No
Code
date_issued
date_received

Behaviours

read_data( )
compute_fine( )
dispFine()

14. Write a program that uses the class book of excercise 13 and manipulates the data of a book through various member functions. Assume rules for the computation of fine for the late return of a book.

15. Write a program that creates a list of *N* number of employee objects having following members.

States

Name
Age
empID
sex
address
H.No.
Street
Dist.
State

Behaviours:

readData()
dispData()

The program prints the list of employees in the format given below:

Name	EMP_ID	Address			
		H. NO	Street	Dist	State

16. Write a C++ program that inputs today's date: mm/dd/yy and determines and prints tomorrow's date correctly. Choose appropriate class declaration and its member data and functions.
17. Differentiate between instance and class variables.
18. Write a program that counts the number of objects in a class.
19. What are the general properties of classes?

MORE ON FUNCTIONS: ADVANCED CONCEPTS 5

5.1 POLYMORPHISM

"The meeting ends with thanks to the Chair", announced the secretary. This message was taken differently by different persons. The Chairman went to his/her office. The accounts clerk distributed the remuneration to the members. The internal members proceeded it to their respective departments. The external experts marched towards the parking place to pick up their vehicles. The secretary took his/her personal assistant along to his/her office for dictation of the minutes of the meeting. And the peon began picking up the papers, littered over the tables. This behaviour is called as *polymorphic* in the sense that the same message was processed in different forms by different group of people.

The word 'polymorphism' has its roots in 'polymorphous', a Greek word meaning: 'poly' (many) and 'morphe' (forms), i.e. many forms. For example, graphite, diamond, coal, etc. are different polymorphic forms of carbon.

In OOP, the programming efforts can be drastically reduced by suitably incorporating polymorphism. In this chapter, we introduce polymorphism in the form of function overloading as discussed in the following section.

5.2 FUNCTION OVERLOADING

A significantly large program contains an equally large number of variables and functions. The programmer has to remember the following:

1. The names of all variables and their types.
2. The names of the functions and their return types.
3. The number of arguments to be sent to the function.
4. The type of each argument.
5. The mechanism of sending the arguments, i.e. pass by copy, pass by ref., etc.

Therefore, the programmer spends more time in keeping track of the history of the variables going to various functions and their returned values. Consequently, the productivity of the programmer reduces because of not giving the desired attention to the logic of the program.

Object-oriented programming (OOP) tackles this problem by providing '***Function polymorphism***'. In C++ this term is better known as '***Function overloading***' wherein the message or data can be processed in more than one form by a group of similar functions.

Let us consider a situation wherein a programmer desires to have following functions in his/her program.

1. A function to compute area of a circle.
2. A function to compute area of a triangle.
3. A function to compute area of a rectangle.

In a non-OOP language like 'C', the programmer will have to declare three functions with unique names (say Area_Cir( ) Area_Tri( ), and Area_Rect( )) in his/her program. After the functions have been declared, he/she has to remember their names and history of related arguments for the computation of area for each trigonometric shape.

C++ allows the programmer to give same name to more than one function having unique parameters. For example, same name (**areaShapes( )**) has been given to following three different functions.

1. float **areaShapes**(int radius);
2. float **areaShapes**(int base, int height);
3. float **areaShapes**(float length, float width);

The name of the function has been overburdened, i.e. it caters to many functions. Therefore, this kind of polymorphism is called 'Function name overloading' or simply '**Function overloading**'.

It may be noted that each function has unique parameter list in terms of number of arguments or types of arguments. For example, the first function has one argument and the second has two arguments. Though both the second and third functions have two arguments each but their arguments differ on types, i.e. the arguments of second are of type int whereas the third function has float type arguments.

Now the programmer has to be careful in providing the right kind of arguments in the function call so that the compiler intelligently maps this call to the desired function. For example, if it is desired to compute the area of a triangle then the programmer should include two arguments of type int in the call to areaShape().

In fact the compiler matches the number and types of the actual arguments with the various **signatures** of the overloaded functions. A *signature* of the function is nothing but the header of the function declaration minus the return type. The signatures of the above overloaded functions are given below:

1. **areaShapes**(int)
2. **areaShapes**(int , int)
3. **areaShapes**(float, float)

Example 1. *Write a program that uses function overloading to compute the area of different shapes like circle, triangle and rectangle.*

Solution: We would use the above given overloaded functions sharing the same name, i.e. areaShapes(). The user would be prompted to choose from a menu item to compute the area of a desired shape. The required program is given below:

```
// This program demonstrates the working of function overloading

# include<iostream.h>
# include<conio.h>

float areaShapes(int); // area of a circle
float areaShapes(int, int); // area of a triangle
float areaShapes(float, float); // area of a rectangle

  void main()
    {
     int radius;
     int base, height, choice;
     float area, length, width;

             // display menu
     do
       { clrscr();
      cout << "\n Menu - Compute area";
      cout << "\n";
      cout << "\n Circle\t\t 1";
      cout << "\n";
      cout << "\n Triangle\t 2";
      cout << "\n";
      cout << "\n rectangle\t 3";
      cout << "\n";
      cout << "\n Quit\t\t 4";
      cout << "\n";
      cout << "\n Enter your choice";
      cin >>choice;
       switch (choice)
          {
           case 1: cout << "\Enter the radius: ";
            cin >> radius;
            area = areaShapes(radius);
            cout << "\n The area of circle is = " << area;
            break;
           case 2: cout << "\Enter the base and height: ";
            cin >> base >> height;
            area = areaShapes(base, height);
            cout << "\n The area of triangle is = " << area;
            break;
           case 3: cout << "\Enter the length, width: ";
            cin >> length>> width;
            area = areaShapes(length, width);
            cout << "\n The area of rectangle is = " << area;
            break;
          }
        getch();
```

```
      }
      while (choice != 4);
      }
float areaShapes(int radius) // area of a circle
 {
   float Area;
   Area = 3.1415 * radius * radius;
   return Area;
 }
float areaShapes(int base, int height) // area of a triangle
 {
   float Area;
   Area = 0.5 * base * height;
   return Area;
 }
float areaShapes(float length, float width) // area of a rectangle
 {
   float Area;
   Area = length * width;
   return Area;
 }
```

A sample output of the program is given below:

```
Menu- Compute area
Circle          1
Triangle        2
rectangle       3
Quit            4

Enter your choice2
Enter the base and height: 4 5
  The area of Triangle is  =  10_
```

Example 2. *Write a program in C++ that uses function overloading to do the following tasks:*

- *Find the maximum of two numbers (integers).*
- *Find the maximum of three numbers (integers).*

Solution: We will use two functions having the name max(). One of the functions will have two arguments of integer type and the other will have three arguments of integer type as shown below:

```
int max(int num1, int num2);
int max(int num1, int num2, int num3 );
```

The required program is given below:

```
// This program uses function overloading to find out
// the maximum of two or three numbers
 int max (int, int); // overloaded functions
 int max (int, int, int);

 #include <iostream.h>
    void main()
   {
    int num1,num2,num3;
    int choice;
    cout << "\n Menu - Options";
    cout << "\n Max of two numbers\t 1";
    cout << "\n";
    cout << "\n Max of three numbers\t 2";
    cout << "\n";
    cout << "\n Enter your choice";
    cin >> choice;
    if (choice == 1)
     {
       cout << "\n Enter two integers";
       cin >> num1 >> num2;
       cout << "\n The Max is = :" << max (num1,num2);
     }
   else
     {
       cout << "\n Enter three integers :";
       cin >> num1 >> num2 >> num3;
       cout << "\n The Max is = :" << max (num1, num2, num3);
     }
   }
   int max (int x, int y)
     {
       if (x > y)
        return x;
       else
        return y;
     }
   int max (int x, int y, int z)
     {
       int lar;
       if (x > y)
         lar = x;
       else
         lar = y;
       if (lar < z)
         lar = z;
       return lar;
     }
```

Example 3. *Write a program that uses function overloading to perform the following:*

1. *Increment the value of a variable of type float.*
2. *Increment the value of a variable of type char.*

Solution: Let us give a common name **inc ()** to both the functions and declare them as follows:

```
float inc (float);
char inc (char);
```

Notice that both the functions carry the same name and same number of arguments but are of different types. During the function call, the C++ compiler would check the arguments and select the corresponding correct function. The required program is given below:

```
/* In this program function overloading with different argument types
is illustrated. We will use two functions with same name: inc with
different arguments */

#include<iostream.h>
#include<conio.h>

float inc(float); // function prototypes
char inc(char);
void main()
  {
    float val;
    char ch;
    clrscr();
    cout << "\n This program increments a float or a character value";
    cout << "\n Enter 'f' for float and 'c' for character : ";
    cin >> ch;
    if ((ch=='f')||(ch=='F'))
    {
       cout << "\n Enter the numerical value : ";
       cin >> val;
       cout << "\n The incremented value is : " << inc(val);
    }
    else
    if ((ch == 'c')||(ch == 'C'))
      {
        cout << "\n Enter the character : ";
        cin >> ch;
        cout << "\n The next character is : " <<  inc(ch);
      }
    }
      // overloaded functions
  float inc(float x)
   {
     return(++x);
   }
```

```
char inc(char y)
 {
   return(++y);
 }
```

Sample outputs for both cases are given below:

```
This program increment,a,float or a character value
Enter 'f' for float and 'c' for character : f

Enter the numerical value : 3.12

The incremented value is : 4.12_
```

```
This program increment,a,float or a character value
Enter 'f' for float and 'c' for character : c

Enter the Charecter : G

The next charecter is : H
```

The *rules* for function overloading can be summarized as:
Each overloaded function must differ either by number of its formal parameters or their data types.

1. The return type of overloaded functions may or may not be same.
2. The default arguments of overloaded functions are not considered by the C++ compiler as part of the parameter list.
3. Do not use the same function name for two unrelated functions. This is against the basic philosophy of OOP and will be rated as a poor design.

The *advantages* of overloaded functions are:

1. The programs become easier to read.
2. The programmer need not waste time in searching for a new name for similar functions.
3. The programmer can devote more time on logic development and need not remember different function names.
4. The program's maintainability increases.

Note:

1. The overloaded functions must be declared in the same scope. For instance, two functions with same name, declared in two different classes cannot be accepted for overloading as they are appearing in different scopes.
2. The pointer variable and array type are identical and cannot be considered as part of separate signatures. For instance, the following overloading is invalid

```
void testFunc(char *);
void testFunc(char []);
```

5.3 INLINE FUNCTIONS

From our previous discussions on functions, we know that a function is a set of instructions that can be called by another function by its name. After the task is over, the control is transferred back to the calling function and the normal program flow continues. In fact the code of a function is stored at one place and not duplicated anywhere. It can be called as many times as needed in a program.

In the parlance of structured programming, there were always two schools of programmers: one which would create a function for every need and occasion, and the other which would restrain from creating functions especially the smaller ones. The difference of opinion was about choosing between *program understandability* and the *program efficiency*.

The *advantages* of creating a function are given below:

1. The problem is divided into sub-programs called functions. Each function handles a smaller portion of the problem.
2. A function can be easily modified as compared to a whole program.
3. If the size of the function is large and it is frequently needed in the calling program then the overall size of the program reduces.
4. Debugging becomes easier.
5. The program becomes more understandable and manageable.

However, a function call is a costly exercise as far as program execution time is concerned. For instance, a function call involves the following activities to be carried out at lower level:

a. Save the return address on the stack.
b. Save the status of the various registers.
c. Transfer the control to the called function.
d. Pass the arguments to the called function.
e. Execute the code of the function body.
f. After the job is over, return the status of the registers.
g. Take care of the value returned from the called function.
h. Pick up the return address from the stack.
i. Transfer control to the return address.

Thus a normal program will become slower in case a function is abstracted out of a program without any reason. In fact, for very small functions, the function call overhead becomes significant and cannot be ignored because it would adversely affect the performance of the program execution.

Hence the controversy: whether to abstract a function from a program or not?

C++ takes care of this tussle by providing inline functions. The compiler substitutes the entire text of the inline function body into the calling program for all instances of an inline function call as shown in Fig. 5.1.

It may be noted that the size of the program has become larger after the compilation. However, the overheads of function calls have been removed and therefore the program has become much faster than before.

Now, this solution satisfies both the parties because at editing and source code level the inline function is available to the programmer as a normal function. At run time, the body of the inline function has been substituted into the body of the calling function resulting in faster execution of the code.

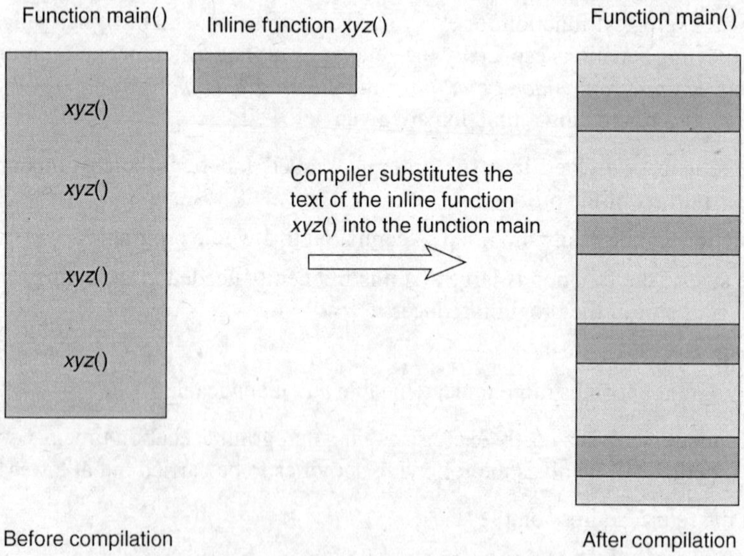

Figure 5.1 *Treatment of an inline function by a compiler*

A keyword *inline* is used to declare an inline function. Let us write an inline function called mult that returns multiplication of two variables.

```
// This program illustrates the use of an inline function

#include <iostream.h>
inline int mult(int a,int b) // Inline function declaration.
  {
    return a*b;
  }

    void main()
    {
     int x = 10, y = 8, z;
     z = mult(x+2, y);
     cout <<  "\n The result is :" << z;
    }
```

After, the above program is executed, the following output is produced:
The result is: 96

Note:

1. The size of an inline function should be kept as very small.
2. The inline function should be defined before it is called in the program. This care should be taken to avoid compilation errors.
3. However, it should be defined in a header file if it is being called within a program made up of several source files.
4. The inline functions can also be overloaded.

The *benefits* of inline functions are:

1. Eliminates function call overheads.
2. Improves program readability.
3. Programs run more efficiently.

Example 4. *Write a function which takes the height of the person in inches and returns the height in feet and inches in two separate variables.*

Solution: Since the task to be performed by the function is simple and its size is likely to be small, we will write an inline function. Let us name the function as convert ().

```
inline int convert (int & inches)
  {
   int feet;
   feet = inches/12;
   inches = inches%12;
   return feet;
  }
```

The function convert () receives the height in inches by reference through the argument called inches. It returns the equivalent height in feet through the return statement and the inches part through the variable called inches.

Example 5. *Use the inline function of Example 4 to write a program that reads the height of a person in inches and prints its equivalent height in feet and inches.*

Solution: The required program is given below:

```
// This program converts height given in inches to feet & inches

# include <iostream.h>
inline int convert (int & inches)
  {
    int feet;
    feet = inches/12;
```

```
    inches = inches % 12;
    return feet;
  }
void main()
  {
    int feet, inches;
    cout << "\n Enter the height in inches";
    cin >> inches;
    feet = convert (inches);
    cout << "\n The height in feet = " << feet;
    cout << "\n Inches = " << inches;
  }
```

The only drawback of inline functions is that they increase the size of the program. It may be noted here that the C++ compiler handles the inline functions as true functions and, therefore, there is no room for macro side effects.

Let us consider the following macro named mult.

```
# define mult (a, b) (a*b);
```

If this macro is called as given below:

```
z = mult (10 + 2, 8);
```

the results are unexpected because the macroprocessor will do the text substitution as shown below:

```
z = (10 + 2 * 8);
```

This will evaluate 26 instead of desired 96. However an inline function is free from such side effects.

It may be noted that a function declared and defined inside a class is by default considered as inline by the compiler of C++.

5.4 FRIEND FUNCTIONS

In Chapter 2, we defined a class called student. It is reproduced below:

```
class student {
private:
    char name[20];
    int roll;
    int marks;
    char grade;
    void compute_grade();
public:
    void read_data();
```

```
    void display_grade();
    };
```

Let us try to use this class in creating a merit list of a batch of (say) 30 students. The student objects can be easily stored in an array of 30 locations of type student as shown below:

```
student studObList [30];
```

Now to create the desired merit list, the student objects will have to be sorted in decreasing order of their marks. Let us define a function called sortList() which takes an array of student type to do the required task. The declaration of the prototype is given below:

```
void sortList ();
```

However, the variable 'marks' is not accessible to function sortList(). The reason being that 'marks' has been defined as a private member in the class and the function sortList() is a stand alone function, i.e. it is not part of the class student. In fact either of the following measures could have solved the problem:

1. Had the programmer of the class included the function sortList() as part of the class student then the function would have automatically got the access to all internal members including the variable 'marks'.
2. The other solution could be that the programmer should have provided a get function (say getMarks()) as a public member to supply the contents of marks to function sortList().

The fact is that none of the arrangement has been made to make the contents of 'marks' available to outsiders like sortList(). Therefore, it is a *design error* as far as the current requirement is concerned.

In the event of a design error, an impurity can be brought to the design of a class by introducing a stand alone outside function as a *friend* of the class. Once a function is declared friend of a class then it gets access to all the members of the class.

A function can be specified as a friend of a class by including its prototype in the class preceded by the keyword friend. For example, a function sortList() can be made friend to a class student as shown below:

```
class student {

private:
    char name[20];
    int roll;
    int marks;
    char grade;
    void compute_grade();
    friend void sortList (); // The friend function

public:
    void read_data();
    void display_grade();
    };
```

Since a friend function violates the encapsulation property of its friend class, the large-scale usage of friend functions will degrade the overall OOP system. In fact, the usage of friend functions in a program indicates a definite design error. *Therefore, "a friend function is not a friend but a **foe**".*

Example 6. *Write a program that uses the above defined student class and the friend function sortList() to display the merit list of N number of students.*

Solution: The required program is given below:

```
// This program illustrates the usage of a friend function

#include <iostream.h>
#include <conio.h>

class student {
  private:
   char name[20];
   int roll;
   int marks;
   char grade;
   void compute_grade();
                                 // The friend function
   friend void sortList(int N);
  public:
   void read_data();

   void display_grade();
   };

  // Function to read data of a student
  void student :: read_data()
   {
     cout << "\n Enter Name:";
     cin >> name;
     cout << "\n Enter Roll:";
     cin >> roll;
     cout << "\n Enter Marks:";
     cin >> marks;

     compute_grade(); // compute the grade
   }
  void student :: display_grade()
     {
       cout << "\n" << name;
       cout << "\t" << roll;
       cout << "\t" << marks;
       cout << "\t"<<grade;
```

```
    }
   void student :: compute_grade()
     {
       if (marks >= 80) grade = 'A';
       else
       if (marks >= 70 ) grade = 'B';
       else
       if (marks >= 60) grade = 'C';
       else
       if (marks >=50) grade = 'D';
       else
       grade = 'E';
     }
   student studOb[30]; // Global list of student objects
   void sortList (int N);
void main()
   {
  int i;

  int N;
  cout << "\n Enter the number of students :";
  cin >> N;
  cout << "\n Enter the data of students one by one";
  for (i = 0; i< N; i++)
  {
    studOb[i].read_data();
  }
  sortList (N);
  cout <<"\n\t\t The merit List ...";
  cout<< "\n Name\t roll\tmarks\tgrade";
  for (i =0; i< N; i++)
   {
    studOb[i].display_grade();
   }

   }
  void sortList (int N)        // The friend function
      {
   int i,j, largest, pos;
   student tempOb;
    for (i = 0; i < N - 1; i++)
      {
        largest = studOb[i].marks;
        pos = i;
         for (j= i + 1; j < N; j++)
      {
       if (largest < studOb[j].marks)
         {
```

```
            largest = studOb[j].marks;
            pos = j;
          }
        }
        tempOb = studOb[i];
        studOb[i] = studOb[pos];
        studOb[pos] = tempOb;
         }
    }
```

It may be noted that the friend function defined in the above program has violated the OOP ideology in the sense that it is an outsider but has the access to all the members of the class called student. Moreover, the student object list has also been declared as global – another drawback of the above program.

However, by introducing a suitable get function in the student class *at design level*, we could have avoided the use of the unwanted friend function. The modified student class that uses a function called getMarks() to provide the contents of the 'marks' variable is given below:

```
class student {

private:
   char name[20];
   int roll;
   int marks;
   char grade;
   void compute_grade();

public:
   void read_data();
   void display_grade();
  int getMarks(); // The get function
  };
```

Note: The above class is a correctly designed class without any unwanted friend function.

Example 7. *Write a program that uses the above-defined student class containing a get function called 'getMarks()' and a stand alone function sortList() to display the merit list of N number of students.*

Solution: The required program is given below:

```
// This program illustrates the usage of a get function as an alterna-
tive to a friend function
```

```
#include <iostream.h>
#include <conio.h>
class student {
  private:
  char name[20];
  int roll;
  int marks;
  char grade;
  void compute_grade();

  public:
  void read_data();
  void display_grade();
  int getMarks(); // The get Function
  };
  // Function to read data of a student
  void student :: read_data()
   {
    cout <<"\n Enter Name:";
    cin >> name;
    cout << "\n Enter Roll:";
    cin >> roll;
    cout << "\n Enter Marks:";
    cin >> marks;

    compute_grade(); // compute the grade
    }
   void student :: display_grade()
     {
       cout<< "\n" << name;
       cout << "\t" << roll;
       cout << "\t" << marks;
       cout << "\t"<<grade;
     }
   int student :: getMarks()
     {
      return marks;
     }
    void student :: compute_grade()
      {
        if (marks >= 80) grade = 'A';
        else
        if (marks >=70 ) grade ='B';
        else
        if (marks >=60) grade ='C';
        else
        if (marks >=50) grade ='D';
        else
```

```
        grade ='E';
     }

   void sortList (student ob[], int N); // stand alone function

  void main()
   {
  int i;
  int N;
  student studOb[30];
  cout << "\n Enter the number of students :";
  cin >> N;
  cout << "\n Enter the data of students one by one";
  for (i = 0; i< N; i++)
  {
   studOb[i].read_data();
  }
  sortList (studOb,N);
  cout <<"\n\t\t The merit List ...";
  cout<< "\n Name\t roll\tmarks\tgrade";
  for (i =0; i< N; i++)
   {
    studOb[i].display_grade();
   }

   }
  void sortList (student studOb[], int N) // stand alone function
    {
  int i,j, largest, pos;
  student tempOb;
   for (i = 0; i < N - 1; i++)
     {

       largest = studOb[i].getMarks();
       pos = i;
        for (j = i + 1; j < N; j++)
   {
    if (largest < studOb[j].getMarks())
      {
       largest = studOb[j].getMarks();
       pos = j;
      }
    }
    tempOb = studOb[i];
    studOb[i] = studOb[pos];
    studOb[pos] = tempOb;
    }
   }
```

It may be noted that the get function is part of the class. It gives only the current contents of the variable called 'marks'. Moreover, no global variable has been used. In fact the student object list is local to the function main() that sends it to function sortList() as an argument. On the contrary, the friend function gets access to all the members of the class and hence a programming disaster. Therefore, the *motto* is as given below:

"If you are requested to let a function be friend of your class, this indicates that the object's interface is poor. Try to change the interface instead of allowing the friendship".

5.4.1 Member Functions of a Class as Friends of Another Class

A member function of a class can also act as a friend of another class. However, in this case the name of the friend function has to be qualified by the name of its corresponding class.

Let us consider the following classes:

```
class xyz
{
  friend void ABC :: myfun()
}
```

```
class ABC
{
    void myfun();
}
```

It may noted that the function myfun() is a member of a class called ABC. In class *xyz* this function has been declared as a friend but its name has been qualified by ABC, i.e. its corresponding class name.

5.4.2 Friend Function as a Bridge Between Two Classes

There is a saying "Use a member function when you can and a friend function when you have to". Let us consider a situation where two classes called person and student were created with members as shown in Fig. 5.2.

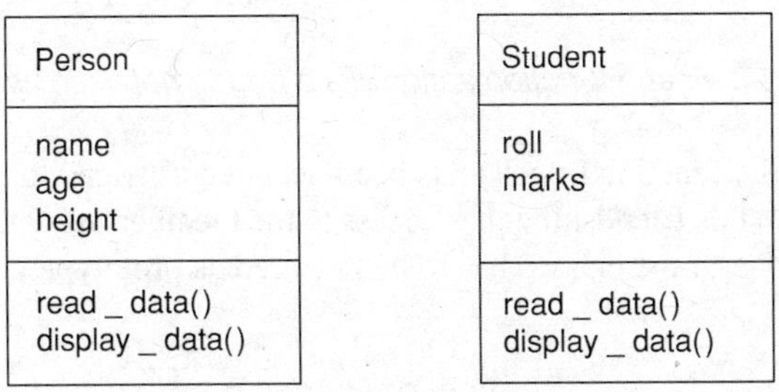

Figure 5.2 *Two independent classes*

The basic idea behind the creation of these classes was that a student, who is basically a person, would be selected for a job depending upon the following criteria:

```
if (marks < 60%) and (height >= 1.7 m)
  then select for "Supervision"
if (marks >= 60% and marks < 70) and (height < 1.7 m)
  then select for "Desk job"
```

```
if (marks >= 60% and marks < 70) and (height >= 1.7 m)
  then select for "Marketing"
if (marks >= 70% and marks < 80) and height >= 1.6 m)
  then select for "Planning"
if (marks >= 80%) then select for "Design".
```

However, there is a design error in the sense that there is no provision of interaction between the two classes: Person and Student. Moreover there is no method or function that can take height from person and marks from student to make the necessary decision for the selection of a student for the job.

In this situation, a friend function (say select()) can be used that acts as a bridge between the two classes as shown in Fig. 5.3.

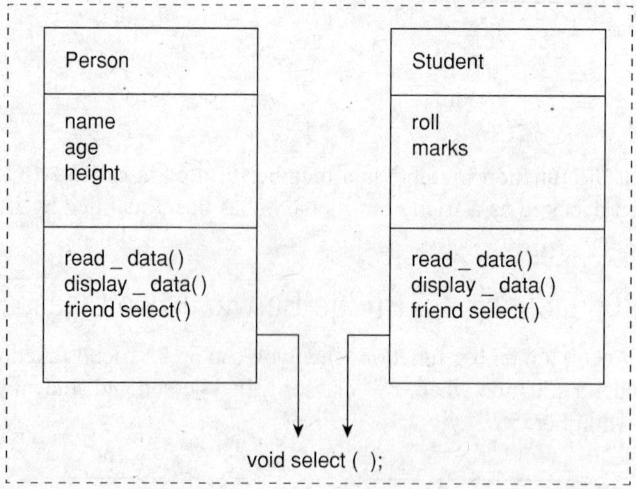

Figure 5.3 *Friend function action like a bridge between two classes*

It may be noted that the function select() has been declared as friend to both the classes person and student and due to this friendship it has access to the members of both the classes. However, in this arrangement one of the classes has to be declared as prototype before the other class as shown below:

```
class student;     // prototype of the class
class person
 { __
   __
 friend void select (person Pob, student Sob);
   __
   __
 };
 class student    // forward class declaration
```

```
{ __
   __
friend void select (person Pob, student Sob);

   __
   __
};
```

This type of class declaration is also known as **forward class declaration**.

Example 8. *Write a program that implements the concept of a bridge function select() which is common friend to two classes person and student. A student or a person is selected for a job depending upon the following criteria:*

```
if (marks < 60%) and (height >= 1.7 m) then select for "Supervision"
if (marks >= 60% and marks < 70) and (height < 1.7 m) then select for
"Desk job"
if (marks >= 60% and marks < 70) and (height >= 1.7 m) then select
for "Marketing"
if (marks >= 70% and marks < 80) and height >= 1.6 m) then select for
"Planning"
if (marks >= 80%) then select for "Design".
```

Solution: A complete program that implements the above concept of a friend function getting as a bridge between two classes is given below:

```
/* This program illustrates the friend function acting as a bridge
between two different classes */

 #include <iostream.h>
 # include <stdio.h>

   class student; // forward class declaration
   class person
     {
       private:
   char name [20];
   int age;
   float height;
       public:
        void read_data();
        void display_data();
        friend void select(person pob, student sob);
      };
   void person::read_data()
    {cout << "\n Enter name of the Person";
      gets(name);
      fflush(stdin);
```

```
      cout << "\n Enter Age";
      cin >> age;
      cout << "\n Enter height";
      cin >> height;
    }
  void person :: display_data()
   {  cout << "\n Name of the Person" << name;
      cout << "\n Age"<< age;
      cout << "\n Enter height" << height;
    }
  class student
  {
    private:
  int roll;
  float marks;
    public :
  void get_data();
  void show_data();
  friend void select(person pob, student sob);
  };
  void student :: get_data()
   {cout << "\n Enter roll";
  cin >> roll;
  cout << "\n Enter marks;";
  cin >> marks;
  }
    void student :: show_data()
    {
      cout << "\n Roll" << roll;
      cout << "\n Marks" << marks;
    }
     void select(person pob, student sob)
    {
     if ((sob.marks < 60) && (pob.height >= 1.7))
      cout << "\n" << pob.name << " is selected Supervisor";
     else
if (((sob.marks >= 60) && (sob.marks < 70)) && (pob.height < 1.7))
cout << "\n" << pob.name << " is selected for Desk Job";
else
if (((sob.marks >= 60) && (sob.marks < 70)) && (pob.height >= 1.7))
cout << "\n" << pob.name << " is selected for "Marketing";
   else
   if (((sob.marks >= 70) && (sob.marks < 80)) && (pob.height >= 1.6))
   cout << "\n" << pob.name << " is selected for Planning";
   else
   if (sob.marks >= 80)
      cout << "\n" << pob.name << " is selected as Designer";
```

```
else
     cout << "\n NOT Selected";
}

void main()
 {
 student sob;
 person pob;
 pob.read_data();
 sob.get_data();
 select (pob,sob);
 }
```

A programmer should follow the following guidelines for the usage of friend function:

1. Do not allow friend functions so easily. Use such a function in extreme conditions.
2. A friend function may be allowed for operations related to public interface of the class.
3. The friend function should not be allowed outside the team working on the project.

5.5 FRIEND CLASSES

Sometimes we are not only interested to hide the implementation but also want to hide the implementation technique. This can be achieved by putting all implementations in a class and the abstraction in another class. Consider the classes shown in Fig. 5.4. The interface class has been made friend of apply class as shown in Fig. 5.4.

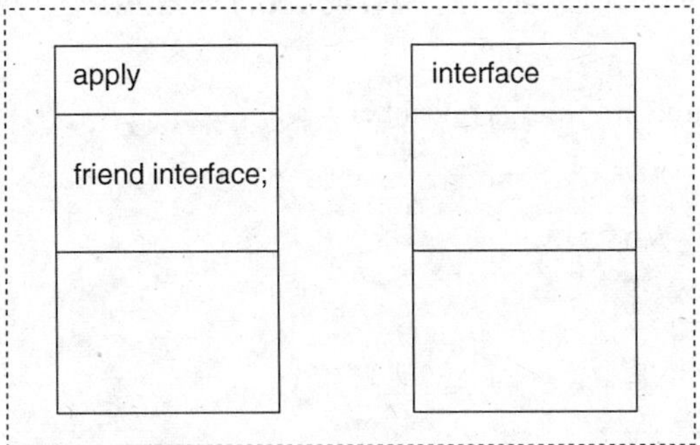

Figure 5.4 *A class declared as friend of another class*

It may be noted that *interface* has access to all the members of *apply.* Now the apply class can be designed to contain all the implementations needed by the interface class. The interface class will only contain interfaces through which the user can obtain services offered by this system of classes.

For example, we can modify the student class to contain only the interfaces and move the implementation functions to another class called *secret* as shown in Fig. 5.5. It may be noted that the secret class contains two implementation functions: compGrade() and chekPass(). The compGrade() computes the grade of a student and the chekPass() verifies the password entered by the user who wants to input data for a student.

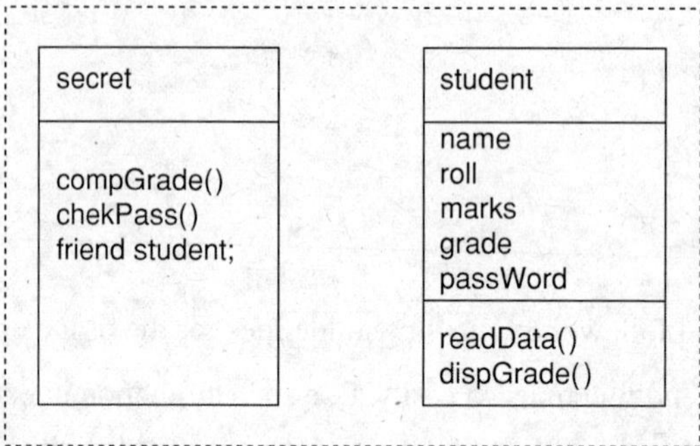

Figure 5.5 *Student class acting as friend of secret class*

It may be noted that we have made the system of classes more secured by pushing the implementation function compGrade() into the secret class. A new function called chekpass() has also been included in the secret class. This will verify the password supplied by the user to the readData() function of the student class.

Example 9. *Write a program that uses the above designed classes called 'secret' and 'student' to manipulate the data of a student. Let the password for the user of readData() be "YMCA" or 'ymca".*

Solution: The required program is given below:

```
// This program illustrates the use of friend class

# include <iostream.h>
# include <conio.h>
# include <string.h>
# include <process.h>

class secret {
  void compGrade(int marks, char & grade);
  int chekPass(char pass[10]);
  friend student;
  };
void secret::compGrade(int marks, char &grade)
  {
   if (marks >= 80) grade = 'A';
```

```
    else
    if (marks >= 70) grade ='B';
    else
    if (marks >=60) grade = 'C';
    else
    if (marks >= 50) grade = 'D';
    else
    grade = 'E';
    }
int secret :: chekPass(char pass[10])
    {
     if (! (strcmp ("YMCA", pass) || strcmp ("ymca", pass)))
       {
   return 1;
       }
   else
   return 0;
       }
class student {
   private:
    char name[20];
    int roll;
    int marks;
    char grade;
    char passWord[10];
    secret secOb;
   public:
    void readData();
    void dispGrade();
    };

   // Function to read data of a student
   void student :: readData()
    {
     cout << "\n Enter Password";
     cin >> passWord;
        if (secOb.chekPass(password))
          {
            cout <<"\n Error";
            exit(0);
          }
     cout <<"\n Enter Name:";
     cin >> name;
     cout << "\n Enter Roll:";
     cin >> roll;
     cout << "\n Enter Marks:";
     cin >> marks;
    secOb.compGrade(marks, grade); // compute the grade
```

```
    }
  void student :: dispGrade()
    {
      cout << "\n Name:" << name;
      cout << "\n Roll:" << roll;
      cout << "\n Grade:" <<grade;
    }

  void main()
    {
  int choice;
  student studOb;

  do
    {
     clrscr();
     cout << "\n Menu";
     cout <<"\n";
     cout <<"\n Read data\t 1";
     cout <<"\n";
     cout <<"\n Display grade \t 2";
     cout <<"\n";
     cout <<"\n Quit\t\t 3";
     cout <<"\n";
     cout <<"\n Enter your choice:";
     cin >> choice;

        switch (choice)
    {
      case 1 : studOb.readData();
         break;
      case 2 : studOb.dispGrade();
    }
     getch();
    }
   while (choice != 3);
  }
```

Note: The friend class helps the programmer in hiding the implementation and the data as well. Therefore, a friend class is closer to OOP ideology. In fact *a friend class is a friend indeed.* On the contrary, *a friend function is a foe.*

5.6 RECURSION

We have already discussed *iteration* through various loop structures discussed in Chapter 1. Iteration can be defined as *the computations that are performed each time by the same method and the result of computation is utilized as the source of data in the next repetition of the loop.* For example the factorial of an integer N can be computed by the following iterative loop:

```
:
fact = 1;
for (i = 1; i <= N; i++)
fact = fact * i;

cout << "The factorial of " << N << "= " << fact;
```

We can also use an alternative approach wherein *we reduce the problem into a smaller instance of the same problem*. For instance, factorial of N can be reduced to a product of N and the factorial of $N - 1$ as given below:

```
Fact (N)= N * Fact (N - 1)
```

In the above statement, a function Fact(N) has been defined in terms of Fact($N - 1$), where Fact($N - 1$) is a smaller problem as compared to Fact(N). This type of definition is known as recursive definition. Recursion can be defined as *the ability of a concept being defined within the definition itself.* In programming terms recursion is defined as *the ability of a function being called from within the function itself.*

Now, by the same definition, the factorial of ($N - 1$) can be defined as given below:

```
Fact(N - 1) = (N - 1) * Fact(N - 2)
```

We can continue this process till we end up with Fact(0) which is equal to 1, which is also the terminating condition for this reduction process. The terminating condition for a recursive function is also called the *basic solution*. For instance, the basic solution for a list of elements is that *if the list contains only one element then this element is the largest as well as the smallest element.* Similarly, if a list contains only one element then it is already sorted.

The process described above can be implemented by using a recursive function fact() which is defined in terms of itself as shown below:

$$\text{Fact}(N) = \begin{cases} 1 \text{ if } N = 0 \text{ or } N = 1 \\ N * \text{Fact}\,(N-1) \text{ otherwise} \end{cases}$$

In C++ such recursive functions can be implemented by making the function call itself. For example, the recursive function Fact(N) can be defined as given below:

```
int fact (int N)
  {
   if (N = = 0)
       return (1);
   else
       return (N * fact (N-1);
  }
```

It may be further noted that the function fact is being called by itself but with parameter N being replaced by $N - 1$. A trace of Fact (N) for $N = 4$ is given in Fig. 5.6.

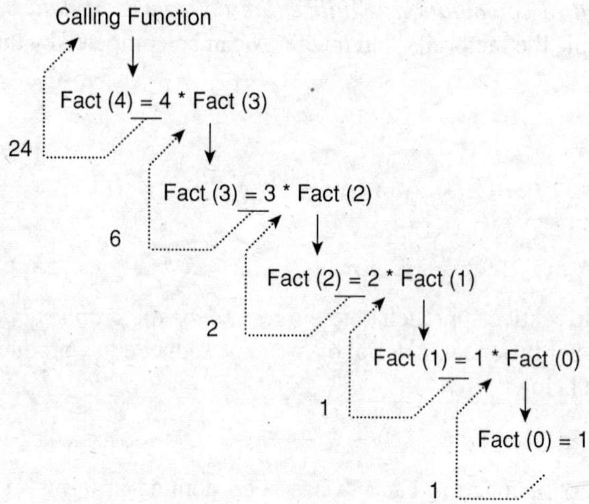

Figure 5.6 *Trace of Fact(4)*

Example 10. *Write a program that uses recursive function* **Fact(*N*)** *to compute the factorial of a given number N.*

Solution: A complete program to compute factorial of a number using recursion is given below.

```
// A program to compute factorial of a number using recursion

   #include<iostream.h>
   #include<conio.h>
   long int fact(int);
   void main()
      {
        int num, factorial;
        clrscr();
        cout <<"\n This program computes the factorial of a number";
        cout<< "\n Enter the number :";
        cin >> num;
        factorial = fact(num);
       cout << "\n The factorial of " << num << " is = " << factorial;
      }
      long int fact(int n)
       {
       if (n == 0)
          return(1);
       else
          return(n*fact(n - 1));
       }
```

Recursion can be used to write simple, short and elegant programs. However, a recursive algorithm requires a basic condition that must end the recursive calls. The absence of this condition would result in an infinite loop. For example, in function fact the condition "$N = = 0$" is the required terminating condition. Since recursion involves overheads such as CPU time and memory storage, it is suggested that recursion should be used with care.

Note: Inline functions cannot use recursion.

Example 11. *Write a function that computes x^y by using recursion.*

Solution: We can use the property that x^y is simply a product of x and x^{y-1}. For example, $6^4 = 6 * 6^3$. The recursive definition of x^y is given below:

$$\text{power(x,y)} = \begin{cases} 1 \text{ if } y = 0 \\ x * \text{power(x,y-1) otherwise} \end{cases}$$

```
// Function to compute x^y
int power(int x, int y)
   {
   if (y == 0)
      return (1);
      else
             return (x * power(x, y - 1));
   }
```

The required function is given below:

Example 12. *Write a program that uses recursive power() function to compute x^y for following types of data:*

1. *x of type int and y of type int*
2. *x of type float and y of type int.*

Solution: We would use overloaded power() functions to do the required task. The complete program is given below:

```
// This program uses function overloading to compute
// power of arguments of different types

   int power (int x, int y); // overloaded functions
      float power (float x, int y);

      #include <iostream.h>
      void main()
        {
```

```
        int a, b;
        float A;
        int choice;
    cout << "\n OPTIONS";
    cout << "\n X ^ Y (X & Y both are integers) .. 1";
    cout << "\n";
    cout << "\n X ^ Y (X is float & Y is integer) .. 2";
    cout << "\n";
    cout << "\n Enter your choice :";
        cin >> choice;
        if (choice == 1)
          {
    cout << "\n Enter two integers :";
          cin >> a >> b;
    cout << "\n" << a <<"^"<< b <<" = :"<< power (a, b);
   }
   else
   {
    cout << "\n Enter a float and an integer :";
    cin >> A >> b;
    cout << "\n" << A << "^" << b << " = :" << power (a, b);
   }
   }
  int power (int x, int y)
   {
    if (y == 0)
      return (1);
    else
      return (x * power (x, y - 1));
   }
  float power (float x, int y)
   {
    if (y == 0)
      return (1);
    else
      return (x * power (x, y - 1));
   }
```

Example 13. *Write a program that computes GCD (greatest common divisor) of given two numbers.*

Solution: The greatest common divisor of two numbers can be computed by the algorithm given below:

Algorithm gcd()

Steps:

1. Find the larger of the two numbers and store larger in *x* and smaller in *y*.
2. Divide the *x* by *y* and store the remainder in rem.
3. If rem is equal to 0 then the smaller number (*y*) is the required GCD and stop. Else store *y* in *x* and rem in *y* and repeat Steps 2 and 3.

The above given algorithm can be used to develop a recursive function called GCD which takes two arguments *x* and *y* and integer type and returns the required GCD.

```
// This function computes GCD
int gcd(int x, int y)
{
int rem;
rem = x%y;
if(rem == 0)
return y;
else
      gcd(y, rem);
  }
```

The required program that uses the function gcd(*y*) is given below:

```
// This program computes GCD of two numbers with the help of a func-
   tion gcd().

#include<iostream.h>
  int gcd(int,int);
    void main()
    {
     int x,y,ans;
     cout << "\n Enter the integers whose gcd is to be found :";
     cin >> x >> y;
     if (x > y)
       ans = gcd(x, y);
     else
       ans = gcd(y, x);
     cout << "\n The GCD is :" << ans;
    }

 // This function computes the GCD
 int gcd(int x, int y)
  {
   int rem;
   rem = x%y;
   if(rem == 0)
     return y;
   else
     gcd(y, rem);
  }
```

Example 14. *Write a program that generates the first n terms of Fibonacci sequence by recursion. The sequence is given below:*

0, 1, 1, 2, 3, 5, 8, ...

Solution: In a Fibonacci series each term (except the first two) can be obtained by the sum of its two immediate predecessors. The recursive definition of this sequence is given below:

$$\text{Fib}(n) = \begin{cases} 0 & \text{if } n = 1 \\ 1 & \text{if } n = 2 \\ \text{Fib}(n-1) + \text{Fib}(n-2) & \text{if } n >= 2 \end{cases}$$

Let us now write a program that uses a function Fib() to compute the first *n* terms of the series.

```
// This program generates Fibonacci series

   #include<iostream.h>
   int fib(int);
   void main()
   {
    int n;
    int i,term;
    cout << "\n Enter the terms to be generated: " ;
    cin >> n;
    for(i = 1;i <= n;i++)
     {
       term = fib(i);
       cout << term << " ";
     }
   }

  // Function to return a Fibonacci term

  int fib(int n)
   {
     if (n == 1)
       return 0;
     else
      if (n == 2)
       return 1;
      else
       return(fib(n - 1)+fib(n - 2));
   }
```

From above, we can summarize the *characteristics of recursion* as given below:

1. There must exist at least a basic solution called terminating condition. This statement is processed without recursion.

2. There must exist a method of reducing a problem into a simpler version of the problem.
3. Throw back the simpler problem back to the recursive function.

5.6.1 Types of Recursion

Depending upon the way the recursive function is called, the recursion process can be divided into two categories: *direct* recursion and *mutual* recursion. In direct recursion the recursive function is called from within itself. In mutual recursion, two recursive functions are involved and they mutually call each other as shown in Fig. 5.7.

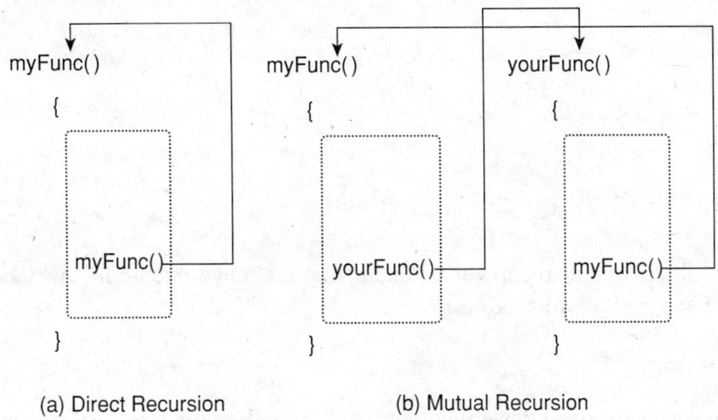

Figure 5.7 *Types of recursion*

The mutual recursion is also called as *indirect recursion*. It may be noted that in direct recursion, the recursive function myFunc() is calling itself whereas in mutual recursion, the two recursive functions myFunc() and yourFunc() are mutually calling each other.

The direct recursion can be further divided into three categories: linear, binary and tail recursions. Though there are many more terms in vogue such as tree recursion, etc., but we will discuss the popular forms of recursion in the following sections.

5.6.1.1 Linear Recursion

When a recursive function has a simple repetitive structure and calls itself once from inside the function then it is called as linear recursion. For example, the recursive function called power(), given below, is a linear recursive function.

```
int power (int x, int y)
   {
    if (y == 0)
      return (1);
    else
      return (x * power (x, y - 1)); //single recursive call
   }
```

It may be noted that it checks the terminating condition and thereafter performs the single recursive call to itself.

5.6.1.2 Binary Recursion

When a recursive function calls itself twice then it is called as binary recursion. For example, the function fib(), given below, calls itself twice, i.e. for fib($n-1$) and fib($n-2$).

```
// Function to return a Fibonacci term

  int fib(int n)
    {
      if (n == 1)
        return 0;
      else
       if (n == 2)
        return 1;
       else
        return(fib(n - 1)+fib(n - 2));
    }
```

Another example of binary recursion is binary tree recursive operations, which are done for both left child and right child subtrees.

5.6.1.3 Tail Recursion

When a recursive call in a recursive function is the last call without any pending operation then the recursion is called tail recursion. Thus, the last result of the recursive call is the final result of the function.

Consider the function fact(), given below:

```
long int fact(int n)
  {
   if (n == 0)
     return(1);
   else
     return(n*fact(n - 1));
  }
```

This function is not tail recursive because the last statement is not recursive call but the multiplication operation:

$$n * \text{fact}\ (n - 1).$$

However, the following modified function fact( ) is tail recursive.

```
long fact(int N, int result)
 {
   if (N == 1)
      return result;
   else
```

```
      return fact(N - 1, N * result); // Tail recursion
  }
```

It may be noted that the last statement in the above function is a recursive call without any pending operation. Hence the function is tail recursive. Since the argument 'result' is acting as an accumulator, its initial value must be set to 1. Therefore, for computing factorial of a given number (say 5), the above function must be called with the following statement:

```
Factorial = fact (5,1);
```

Example 15. *Write a program that computes the factorial of a given number by using the above given tail recursive function fact().*

Solution: The required program is given below:

```
# include <iostream.h>

long fact(int N,int result)
  {
    if (N == 1)
       return result;
    else
       return fact(N - 1, N * result);
  }

 void main()
   {
     long factorial;
     int num;
     cout << "\n Enter the number";
     cin >> num;
     factorial = fact(num, 1);
     cout << "\n factorial =" << factorial;
   }
```

Sample outputs for the program are given below:

```
Enter the number 5
factorial  =120
Enter the number 8
factorial =-25216
```

Example 16. *Write a tail recursive function for computing x^y.*

Solution: The required function power(x, y) is given below:

```
long power(int x, int y, long result)
  {
    if (y == 0)
       return result;
    else
       return power(x, y - 1, x * result); // Tail recursion
   }
```

Example 17. *Write a program that tests the tail recursive function of Example 16 for given values of x and y.*

Solution: The required program is given below:

```
# include <iostream.h>

long power(int x, int y, long result)
  {
    if (y == 0)
       return result;
    else
       return power(x, y - 1, x * result); // Tail recursion
   }

void main()
   {
     long pow;
     int x, y;
     cout << "\n Enter the x,y";
     cin >> x >> y;
     pow = power(x, y, 1);
     cout <<"\n x ^ y =" << pow;
    }
```

Sample output of the above program are given below:

```
Enter the x,y 4 3
x ^ y =64
Enter the x,y 5 3
x ^ y =125
Enter the x,y 27
x ^ y =128
```

Example 18. *Write both normal and tail recursive versions of a function sum(N) that adds the first N integers. For example, sum(6) is computed as following:*

```
Sum(6) = 1 + 2 + 3 + 4 + 5 + 6
```

Solution: The normal recursive function is given below:

```
long sum (int N)
  {
    if (N == 1)
       return 1;
    else
       return N + sum (N - 1);
  }
```

The tail recursive version of function sum() is given below:

```
long sum (int N, int result)
  {
    if (N == 1)
       return result;
    else
       return(sum (N - 1, N + result)); // Tail recursion
  }
```

Example 19. *Write a complete program that takes the tail recursive version of the function sum() to compute the first N integers.*

Solution: The required program is given below:

```
# include <iostream.h>
long sum (int N, int result)
  {
    if (N == 1)
       return result;
    else
       return(sum (N - 1, N + result));
  }
 void main()
   {
     int N;
     long total;
     cout << "\n Enter N";
     cin >> N;
     total = sum(N,1);
     cout <<"\n sum =" << total;
   }
```

Sample output of the program is given below:

```
Enter N 5

sum =15

Enter N 10

sum =55
```

Note: Recursion is a costly option in terms of usage of both memory and CPU time. Therefore, it should be used with care. For instance, the following example is totally unnecessary rather an abuse of this elegant tool.

Example 20. *Write a C++ program that uses a recursive function to compute sum of two non-negative integers X and Y.*

Solution: The required program is given below:

```
# include <iostream.h>
int sum (int X, int Y)
  {
   if (X == 0)
     return Y;
   else
     return(sum(--X, ++Y));
  }
 void main()
  {
    int Val1, Val2, total;
    cout << "\n Enter two values :";
    cin >> Val1 >> Val2;
    total = sum(Val1,Val2);
    cout <<"\n sum =" << total;
    }
```

A sample output is given below:

```
Enter two values :12 8
sum =20
```

This problem could have been very easily solved in one statement as given below:

```
Sum = X + Y;
```

5.7 SUMMARY

Polymorphism means many forms. Overloaded functions are polymorphic in nature. This property helps a programmer to declare a set of different versions of a given function such that all versions carry the same name but different parameters.

When the size of the code of a function is so small that the overhead of the function call becomes prominent then the function should be declared as inline. If the size of the code of a function is very small then an inline function, in fact, reduces the overall size of the program. However, an inline function with larger code explodes a program to a substantial length of code.

During *iterations*, computations are performed each time by the same method and the result of computation is utilized as a source of data in the next repetition of the iteration process. On the other hand, a *recursive* function calls itself with a smaller version of the original problem. By every call it comes nearer to a basic solution.

MULTIPLE CHOICE QUESTIONS

1. The overloaded functions must have a unique:
   (a) names (b) argument list
   (c) return type (d) loop
2. A function call is an overhead on program's:
   (a) computation time (b) size
   (c) logic (d) none
3. Function overloading is a way of implementing:
   (a) recursion (b) iteration
   (c) polymorphism (d) none
4. ________ functions cannot use recursion.
   (a) inline (b) polymorphic
   (c) user defined (d) friend
5. After the compilation of a multiple call inline function, the size of a program becomes/remains:
   (a) small (b) large
   (c) same
6. The ability of a function to call itself is called:
   (a) repetition (b) recursion
   (c) iteration
7. The size of an inline function should be:
   (a) large (b) very large
   (c) small (d) very small
8. A friend function indicates:
   (a) a good design (b) a bad design
   (c) a design error (d) a friendly program

9. In extreme conditions, a friend function can act as a ________ between two classes
   (a) bridge (b) hill
   (c) bond (d) road
10. The terminating condition of a recursive function is called its:
   (a) only solution (b) basic solution
   (c) necessary solution (d) alternate solution

ANSWERS

1. b **2.** a **3.** c **4.** a **5.** b **6.** b **7.** d **8.** b **9.** a **10.** b

EXERCISES

1. What is meant by polymorphism?
2. What is meant by function overloading? Use this concept to create three functions with name 'abs' each of which returns the absolute value of its arguments. The arguments can have any of the three types: int, double, and long.
3. What is the need for overloading functions?
4. What is an inline function?
5. Define recursion. Write a program that reads a line of text and prints it out backward.
6. What are the activities carried out at the system level during a function call?
7. What are the benefits of an inline function?
8. Differentiate between iteration and recursion.
9. Suppose you have two function definitions with the following prototypes.

```
double xyz (double temp, double length);
int xyz (double set);
```

   which function definition would be used in the following function call and why?

```
result = xyz (s);
```

   (assume *s* is of type double).
10. Write a program that uses a recursive function to compute an integer power of a floating point number.
11. Use the concept of function overloading to compute area of rectangle (given length of two sides, area of a triangle (given length of the three sides – use Hero's formula) and area of a circle (given length of a radius).

   Given three sides of a triangle: *a*, *b*, *c*. Its area can be computed by Hero's formula as given below:

$$S = (a+b+c)/2)$$

$$\text{Area} = \sqrt{S*(S-a)*(S-b)*(S-c)}$$

12. Give the output of the following program

```
#include <iostream.h>
        int area (int s)
        {
                return (s * s);
        }
        float area (int b, int h)
        {
                return(0.5*b*h);
        }
        void main()
        {
                cout << area(5) << "\n";
                cout << area(4,3) << "\n";
                cout << area(6,(area(3)));
        }
```

13. Write an inline function that converts a temperature given in centigrades to degree Fahrenheit.

14. Indicate the error(s) in the following function.

```
void show_data (float x = 5.27, int y, int z)
                {
                        cout << "x = " << x;
                        cout << "y = " << y;
                        if (x != 5.27) z = z + x;
                        cout << "z = " << z;
        }
```

15. Write an interactive C++ program to accept two positive integer numbers *n* and *r* and computes ^nC_r and ^nP_r where:

$$nC_r = \frac{n!}{r!(n-r)!}$$

$$nP_r = \frac{n!}{(n-r)!}$$

16. Write a program that uses function overloading to add the elements of a matrix of type int or float.

17. Write a program that finds the sum of the following series for a given *N* terms.

$$\text{Sum} = 1 + \frac{1}{2!} + \frac{1}{3!} + --- \frac{1}{N!}$$

18. Define the term mutual recursion. How it is different from linear recursion?

19. Define the term tail recursion. Explain it with the help of an example.

20. What is a friend class? Give an example where use of a friend class becomes necessary.

21. Give your view on the comment: “Friend class is a friend indeed – Friend function is a foe”.

ANSWERS

12. 25
6
27

14. The function show_data() is employing a default value for the dummy or formal parameter x; since x is not the last parameter of the parameter list, it is an error. The second error is that the expression $z = z + x$ has a type conflict, i.e. z is of type int and x is of type float.

CONSTRUCTORS AND DESTRUCTORS

6

6.1 CONSTRUCTORS

We know that a class is more important than the objects it represents. The reason being that once a class is defined, any number of objects of the class type can be churned out at the run time of the program. We also know that the class is a set of specifications that are used by the compiler for the purpose of construction of objects.

In fact for the creation of an object, the compiler creates a function having the same name as the class itself as shown in Fig. 6.1. It may be noted that the name of the class is *myClass* and the name of the function created by the compiler is also *myClass*. This function is called as a **constructor** function. As the name suggests, the constructor function creates an object of its corresponding class type on demand in a program.

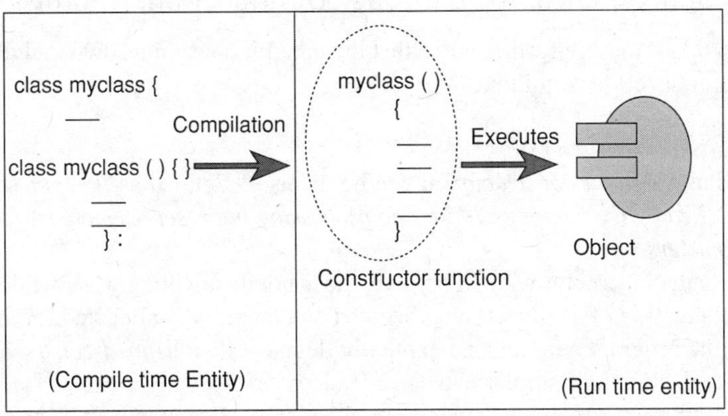

Figure 6.1 *The constructor function and its operation*

Thus, the constructor function 'myClass()' would create an object 'myOb' of myClass type as and when the following object creation statement is executed:

```
myClass myOb;
```

It may be further noted that the class is a compile time entity whereas the object is a run time entity. Therefore, the object will get the memory and the resources and not the class.

For that reason, the constructor function allocates the memory space for the data items or state variables of each object. However, the member functions are allocated space only once for all instances of objects. But the inline functions are duplicated for every created object.

Now the most important question is that, who calls the constructor function especially when it is a run time entity? The answer is that the compiler inserts the following line in the class (say myClass) at compile time and binds it with its constructor function (see Fig. 6.1).

```
myClass ( ) { };
```

It is important to know that the syntax of the constructor is special in the sense that not only its name is same as the name of the class but also it has no return type (not even void).

Since the constructor is the first function to be called before the construction of an object, the programmer can use constructors for variety of purposes as discussed in the following sections.

6.2 TYPES OF CONSTRUCTORS

In C++, there are four types of constructors:

1. The default constructor.
2. User defined constructor.
3. Parameterized constructors.
4. The copy constructor.

6.2.1 Default Constructor and User Defined Constructor

Consider Fig. 6.1. It may be further noted that the compiler has on its own included the following statement in the class definition:

```
myClass() { }
```

This is called as a *default constructor*. It can be precisely defined as *the constructor which is defined and called by the compiler. It does no processing but reserves memory for the object. It takes no parameters.*

Thus, a default constructor with empty body does not do anything worthwhile but it is legal. At the time of creation of an object, it is executed and memory is allocated for the object.

However, the programmer can also explicitly define *a user defined constructor* for his/her own advantage in situations similar to as given below.

Many programming situations demand initialization of data members of an object before it is used in a program. For example, in a stack object, the top of the stack must be initialized to −1 to indicate that the stack is initially empty. Let us initialize the top to −1 in the class called stack, given below, and see what happens.

```
class stack {
int stak [20]; // the stack of 20 locations
int top = -1; // initialize the top to a location out side stack, i.e. -1
```

```
public:
  void push (int item);
  int pop ();
};
```

When the class is compiled, the compiler gives an error on the following statement because we know very well that the class is a compile time entity and will not get the memory and therefore no variables can be initialized within the class.

```
int top = -1;
```

In fact, in almost every useful program, some data elements are needed to be initialized before they are used. We can use a default constructor in these situations by putting the initialization statements inside the body of the constructor as shown below:

```
stack () {int  top = -1;}
```

Now the above arrangement is valid and at the time of creation of object it will work as follows:

1. The constructor function called *stack()* would be called.
2. The constructor will provide the memory to the various elements of the class, i.e. the array called *stak[]* and the *top*.
3. At the time of providing space to the variable top, it will load the desired value −1 into it.

The modified class called *stack* is given below:

```
class stack {

    int stak [20]; // the stack of 20 locations
    int top;

    public:
    stack ()// the user defined constructor
    {top = -1; }// initialize the top

    void push (int item);
    int pop ();
};
```

Example 1. *Write a program that demonstrates the working of a constructor by using the class called stack to simulate its operations: push and pop, for integer values. Modify the push and pop functions so that the following messages are displayed in the calling function main().*

"Stack is full", "Stack is empty"

Solution: We would modify the push() and pop() functions to return following values as per the remarks given against them and accordingly the messages would be displayed in function main().

```
int push (int item); // returns 0 when stack - full and 1 otherwise
```

int pop ( ) // returns –9999 when stack – empty and a valid item otherwise

The complete menu driven program is given below:

```
// This program demonstrates the working of a default constructor
// by simulating the stack operations

# include <iostream.h>

class stack {

    int stak [20]; // the stack of 20 locations
    int top;

public:
  stack ()// the user defined constructor
   {top = -1;}// initialize the top
  int push (int item);
  int pop ();
};

int stack :: push (int item)
  {
    if (top < 19)
      {
        top++;
        stak [top] = item;
        return 1; // operation successful
       }
         else
         return 0;
      }

  int stack ::  pop ()
   {
     int val;
     if (top < 0)
     return -9999; // stack is empty
     else
        {
    val = stak[top];
    top--;
    return val; // valid item
        }
   }
void main()
  {
    int item;
    int choice, result;
```

```
stack sOb;

do
  {
 cout << "\n Menu";
 cout << "\n";
 cout << "\ Push 1";
 cout << "\n";
 cout << "\ Pop 2";
 cout << "\n";
 cout << "\ Quit 3";
 cout << "\n";
 cout << "\n Enter your choice :";
 cin >> choice;

 switch (choice)
   {
     case 1: cout <<"\n Enter the number to be pushed";
             cin >> item;
             result = sOb.push(item);
             if (result == 0)
             cout << "\n Stak full";
             break;
     case 2: result = sOb.pop();
             if (result == -9999)
             cout <<"\n Stack empty";
             else
             cout <<"\n The popped item =" << result;
             break;
          }
     }
     while (choice != 3);
 }
```

It may be noted that the stack class is inflexible in terms of size of the stack, i.e. it will always create a stack of 20 locations. This problem can be solved by parameterized constructors.

6.2.2 Parameterized Constructors

We can also include arguments in the constructor function definition. *The constructors with arguments are also known as parameterized constructors*. This is helpful in a situation where the programmer wants to provide explicit initial values at the time of creation of an object.

Consider the stack class defined in above sections. As explained above that it will always create a stack of 20 locations. If the user desires to create a stack of a particular size then he can do so by sending the size (say Sz) as an argument at the time of creation of the object. The parameterized stack constructor is given below:

```
stack (int Sz) // parameterized constructor
{top = -1;
size = Sz;
}
```

The modified class is given below:

```
class stack {
int stak [20]; // the stack of 20 locations
    int top;
    int size;

public:
  stack (int Sz)// the parameterized constructor
   {top = -1;
                 size = Sz;// size of stack specified
            }

  void push (int item);
  int pop ();
};

int stack :: push (int item)
  {
    if (top < size - 1) // stack size as per the user specification
      {
        top++;
        stak [top] = item;
        return 1; // operation successful
      }
     else
   return 0;
   }

  int stack ::  pop ()
   {
     int val;
     if (top < 0)
     return -9999; // stack is empty
     else
       {
   val = stak[top];
   top--;
   return val; // valid item
       }
   }
```

The programmer would now create the stack object by the following statements:

```
stack sOb (Sz);
```

where Sz is the size of the stack as specified by the user.

Example 2. *Design a class called Queue that simulates the queue data structure for N locations, where N is user defined. The class must initialize the Front and Rear location indicators to suitable values through a constructor function. The elements are added and removed from the locations pointed by Rear and Front respectively.*

Solution: We would use a parameterized constructor that takes the user specified number of locations (say *N*) for the proposed Queue class and will also initialize Front and Rear to location 0 to mark that the queue is empty.

The required class is given below:

```
class Queue {
    int Q[20]; // the Queue of 20 locations
    int Front, Rear;
    int size;

public:
  Queue (int N)                         // the parameterized constructor
    {Front = Rear = 0;
    size = N;
    }

  int add (int item);
  int  remove ();
};

int Queue :: add (int item)
  {
    if (Rear < size)
    {
        Rear++;
        Q [Rear] = item;
        return 1; // operation successful
        }
     else
     return 0;
    }

  int Queue ::  remove ()
    {
     int val;
     if (Front == Rear)
     return -9999; // Queue empty
     else
        {
    Front++;
    val = Q[Front];
    return val; // valid item
        }
    }
```

Example 3. *Write a program that tests the Queue class for a given size of a queue.*

Solution: The required program is given below

```
void main()
  {
    int item;
    int choice, result;
    int Sz;
    cout << "\n Enter the size of the queue";
    cin >> Sz;
    Queue qOb (Sz);

    do
      {
     cout << "\n Menu";
     cout << "\n";
     cout << "\Add 1";
     cout << "\n";
     cout << "\Remove 2";
     cout << "\n";
     cout << "\ Quit 3";
     cout << "\n";
     cout << "\n Enter your choice :";
     cin >> choice;

        switch (choice)
      {
       case 1: cout << "\n Enter the number to be added";
               cin >> item;
               result = qOb.add(item);
               if (result == 0)
               cout << "\n Queue full";
               break;
       case 2: result = qOb.remove();
             if (result == -9999)
               cout << "\n Queue empty";
             else
               cout << "\n The removed item =" << result;
             break;
       }
    }
    while (choice != 3);
  }
```

It may be noted in the above program that the argument for the constructor has been provided during the creation of the object by the following statement:

```
Queue qOb (Sz);
```

The format of passing arguments to constructor function is:

```
<class name> <object name> (argument-list);
```

This method of passing argument to constructor function is called as **implicit** call. It is a widely used way of providing arguments for the constructor function. However, there is also another way of providing arguments to constructors as shown below:

```
Queue qOb = Queue (Sz);
```

This method of passing argument to constructor function is called as **explicit** call. Since implicit call method of providing arguments is shorter, most of the programmers prefer this method more often.

6.2.3 Copy Constructor

An object can be copied to another with the help of an assignment statement. Consider a simple class called 'test' given below:

```
class test {
    int val;
    public :
    test () { }; // default constructor
    test (int item) {val = item; } // parameterized constructor
    void showData() {
    cout << "\n\t Val =" << val; }
};
```

Kindly note that the class 'test' has two constructors: default constructor and a parameterized constructor, i.e. the constructors have been overloaded. Let us construct two objects Ob1 and Ob2 of class test type in such a way that Ob1 is constructed by the default constructor and Ob2 by the parameterized constructor initializing variable val to 50 through the argument item. The main() function, given below, does this task and prints the contents of val of both the objects. Thereafter, it copies the contents of Ob2 to Ob1 by an assignment statement and again prints the contents of val of both the objects.

```
void main()
  {
   test Ob1;
   test Ob2 (35);
   cout << "\n Object Data";
   Ob1.showData();
   Ob2.showData();
     // copy object Ob2 to Ob1
   Ob1 = Ob2;

   cout << "\n Object data after copy operation";
```

```
    Ob1.showData();
    Ob2.showData();
}
```

The output of the above code is given below:

```
object Data
        Val =4129
        Val =35
object Data after copy operation
        Val =35
        Val =35
```

As predicted, the contents of un-initialized val of object Ob1 are random and garbage whereas the val of object Ob2 has been properly initialized to 50. The point worth noting is that after the assignment of Ob2 to Ob1, the val of both the objects have the same contents.

In fact the following statement has copied the object Ob2 to Ob1 bit by bit.

```
Ob1 = Ob2;
```

The above method of copying one object to another of same class type is perfectly alright. However, this method fails in certain situations. For instance, consider an object (say Obptr2) having a pointer (p), pointing to a location containing some information (say 'My Data'). When this object is copied to another object (say Obptr1) by assignment operator then the pointers of both the objects would point to the same location as shown in Fig. 6.2. The reason being that the assignment operator copies the contents of one object to another bit by bit and therefore both the pointers get the same address.

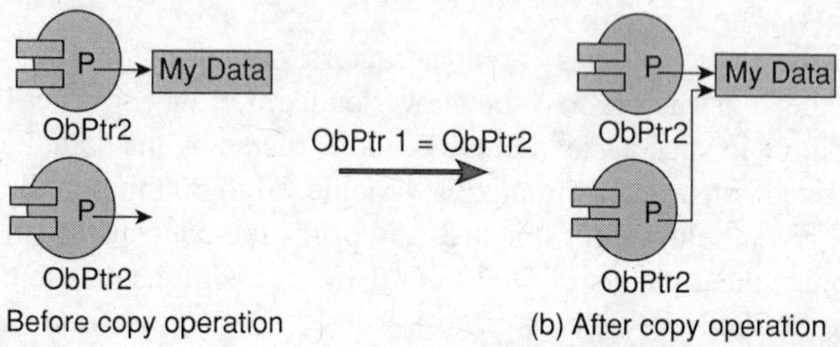

Figure 6.2 *Object copy operation through assignment operator*

Now, this abnormal situation would cause many types of problems such as both the objects work on the same location, the changes done by one object to the common location may not be acceptable to another object, etc.

Thus, for copying objects with pointers, we need a mechanism that allows member-wise copy of the objects so that separate space may be allocated to the pointer of the target object.

C++ provides a special constructor called copy constructor that allows the programmer to member-wise copy of one object to another. However, the programmer must write the code for member-wise copy of various members of the source object to the corresponding members of the target object. The copy constructor is, however, defined in the class as a parameterized constructor receiving an object of its own type as argument passed by reference. Consider the class given below:

```
class myClass {
  public:
     myClass (myClass & ob) { // The copy constructor
     }
  };
```

It may be noted that the above class 'myClass' has a special parameterized constructor that receives an object by reference of its own class type. Now, if we have an obj1 of myClass type and we desire to create a new object obj2 of myClass type, initialized with the contents of obj1 then the following declaration can be used:

```
myClass Obj1;          (i)
:
:
myClass  Obj2 (Obj1); (ii)
```

The declaration (i) declares an object obj1 of class myClass type whereas (ii) it declares another object obj2 of class myClass as well as passes the object Obj1 to the copy constructor for member-wise copy as per the programmer's desire.

Example 4. *Modify the class test, defined above, such that it has a copy constructor that copies an object of test type to another object of test type but while copying the member val of source object, it multiplies it with a number (say 5) and then stores it into the member val of target object.*

Solution: The required modified class 'test' is given below:

```
// This class demonstrates the working of a copy constructor

class test {
  int val;
  public :
  test () { }; // default constructor
  test (int item) {val = item;} // parameterized constructor
  test (test & ob) // Copy constructor
          {
          val = ob.val * 5; // multiply the val of source object by 5
          }
  void showData() {
   cout << "\t Val =" << val;
     }
};
```

Example 5. *Write a function main() that creates an object Ob1 of test type with initial value (say 15) and then copies it to an object Ob2 of test type with the help of the copy constructor. Thereafter, it prints the contents of both the objects.*

Solution: The required function main() is given below:

```
void main()
  {
    test Ob1(15);

    cout << "\n The contents of Val of source object Ob1: ";
    Ob1.showData();

       test Ob2(Ob1); // Copy the object

    cout << "\n The contents of Val of Target object Ob2: ";
    Ob2.showData();
  }
```

The output of the above is given below:

```
The contents of Val of source object ob1:    Val =15
The contents of Val of Target object ob2:    Val =75
```

It may be noted that the copy constructor has not only copied the object but as desired, it has also multiplied the contents of the source object's member val (i.e. 15) by 5 before copying it into the corresponding member of the target code. It may be further noted that this would not have been possible by an ordinary assignment operation that uses a default copy constructor.

Let us now take an example of the following class called 'studData' that uses a pointer to store personal data of a student who studies in a University.

```
struct personal{
   char name[20];
   int idNum;
   char pass[10];
    };

class studData
   {
     char nameUniv[20];
     char secId[5];

     personal * ptr; // pointer to student data
     public:
     void setPass(); // to change the personal data
     void readData(); // to read both common and personal data
     void showData(); // to show complete data
   };
```

It may be noted that the above class has two types of information: common data to all the students such as name of the University and name of the section. For each student there is a personal data accessible through a pointer.

Let us now write a complete program that creates an object ob1 of studData type, reads its data, copies the object to another object Ob2 and prints the data of both the objects. Thereafter, it modifies the personal data of Ob2 and prints the data of both the objects.

```
# include <iostream.h>
#include <conio.h>
#include <stdio.h>

struct personal{
   char name[20];
   int idNum;
   char pass[10];
    };
class studData
   {
     char nameUniv[20];
     char secId[5];

     personal *ptr;
     public:
     void setPass();
     void readData();
     void showData();
   };
   void studData :: readData()
     {
      cout <<"\n Enter Name of the University";
      gets(nameUniv); fflush(stdin);
      cout <<"\n Enter Id of the Section";
      gets(secId);  fflush(stdin);
      ptr = new personal;
      cout << "\n EnterName:";
      gets(ptr->name); fflush(stdin);
      cout << "\n Id:";
      cin >> ptr->idNum;
      cout << "\n password";
      gets( ptr->pass); fflush(stdin);
     }
   void studData :: showData()
     {
     cout <<"\n University Name :" << nameUniv <<"\t Section: "<<secId;
      cout <<"\n Name: "<< ptr->name;
      cout << "\t Id:"<< ptr->idNum<< "\t password: " << ptr->pass;
     }
   void studData :: setPass()
     {
```

```
        cout << "\n Enter new Name:";
        gets(ptr->name); fflush(stdin);
        cout << "\n new Id:";
        cin >> ptr->idNum;
        cout << "\n entr new password";
        gets(ptr->pass); fflush(stdin);
      }
  void main()
    {
     studData Ob1, Ob2;
     Ob1.readData();
     clrscr();
     cout << "\n Object 1"; Ob1.showData();
     Ob2 = Ob1; // Copy the object
     cout << "\n Object 2 after copy ";Ob2.showData();

     Ob2.setPass();
     cout << "\n After Changing the password of Object2";
     cout << "\n Object 1";Ob1.showData();
     cout << "\n Object 2";Ob2.showData();
     }
```

A sample output is given below:

```
    Enter University Name : YMCA University
Section Id : CE302

    EnterName : Ram
Id : 12101
PassWord : ram1234

Object 1
University Name : YMCA  University       Section : CE302
Name : Ram       Id : 12101       Password : ram1234
Object 2 after copy
University Name :  YMCA University       Section : CE302
Name : Ram       Id : 12101       Password : ram1234
Enter new name : Sham
new Id : 12102
new Password : sha2314

After Changing the password of object 2
Object 1
University Name : YMCA University       Section : CE302
Name : Sham       Id : 12102       Password : sha2314
Object 2
University Name : YMCA University       Section : CE302
Name : Sham       Id : 12102       PassWord : sha2314
```

It may be noted that as predicted, both the objects contain same data after the following copy operation.

```
Ob2 = Ob1; // Copy the object
```

However, the strange part is that even after giving new personal data to object Ob2, both the objects show the same data. The only difference is that now the personal data pertains to a student called 'Sham' whereas prior to changes, both the objects had the personal data of a student called 'Ram'. However, the intention was to assign Ob1 to Ram and Ob2 to Sham. The anomaly has occurred because the pointers (ptr) of both the objects are pointing to the same location as was earlier shown in Fig. 6.2.

The solution to above problem is to use a copy constructor to copy the objects member wise as per our requirement. The modified class studData is given below:

```
struct personal{
   char name[20];
   int idNum;
   char pass[10];
    };

class studData
   {
     char nameUniv[20];
     char secId[5];

     personal * ptr;
     public:
     studData(){} // default constructor
     studData(studData &Ob){// copy constructor
     strcpy (nameUniv, Ob.nameUniv);
     strcpy (secId, Ob.secId);
     ptr = new personal;
      cout << "\n EnterName:";
      gets(ptr->name); fflush(stdin);
      cout << "Id:";
      cin >> ptr->idNum;
      cout << "password:";
      gets( ptr->pass); fflush(stdin);
     }
     void readData();
     void showData();
   };
```

It may be noted that we have not only included the copy constructor but have also removed the setPass() function because it had become unnecessary. Let us now write a main() function to test it. We will not repeat the code for readData() and showData() as it remains the same. The required main() function is given below:

```
void main()
   {
```

```
    studData Ob1;

    clrscr();
    Ob1.readData();

    cout << "\n Object 1"; Ob1.showData();
    studData Ob2(Ob1);
    cout << "\n Object 2 after copy ";Ob2.showData();

    }
```

The sample output is given below:

```
    Enter University Name : YMCA University
Section   Id : CE302

EnterName : Ram
Id : 12101
PassWord : ram1234

Object  1
University Name : YMCA  University        Section : CE302
Name : Ram         Id : 12101        Password : ram1234
Enter  name : Sham
new Id : 12102
new Password : sha2314

Object  2  after copy
University Name : YMCA University        Section : CE302
Name : Sham         Id : 12102        Password : sh2314
```

Kindly note that the copy constructor has done the required task, i.e. the pointers (ptr) of both the objects are pointing to two different locations (see Fig. 6.3). Therefore, each object is having its own separate personal data.

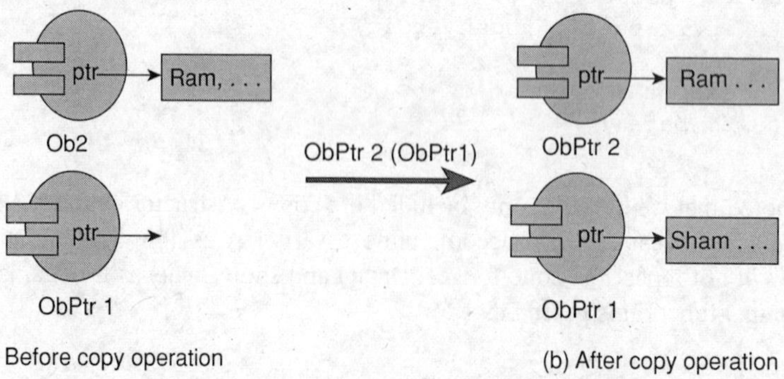

Figure 6.3 *The copy operation through copy constructor*

6.2.4 Constructors with Default Arguments

Similar to a normal function, a constructor can also have default values. For example, we can rewrite the class called stack as shown below:

```
class stack {
    int stak [20]; // the stack of 20 locations
    int top;
    int size;
public:
  stack (int Sz =20) // the parameterized constructor
   {top = -1;
                size = Sz; // size of stack specified
        }
void push (int item);
  int pop ();
};
```

Note: A default argument "int Sz = 20" has been specified in the constructor defined in the above given class. Now, an object of class address can be created without specifying the argument. The compiler will always take the default argument "Sz = 20" for the initialization purpose whenever the argument state is missing. However, care must be taken that the default arguments must be the trailing arguments.

6.2.5 Rules for Constructor Definition and Usage

The rules for constructor definition in C++ and its usages are:

1. The name of the constructor must be same as that of the class.
2. A constructor can have a parameter list.
3. The constructor functions can be overloaded.
4. A constructor with no arguments is the default constructor.
6. If there is no constructor in a class, a default constructor is generated by the compiler.
7. The constructor is executed automatically.
8. The popular abbreviation for constructor is **ctor**.

It may be noted here that an object can be defined at a local level inside a function (say myFun()) or at a global level. When the object is local then it is created as many times as the myFun() is called. Therefore, its constructor is also called every time myFun() is called. When the object is global in nature then its constructor is called at the start of the program.

6.3 DESTRUCTORS

A destructor is an inverse of a constructor in the sense that it removes the memory of an object which was allocated by the constructor during the creation of the object. It carries the same name as the class, but with a tilde (~) as prefix as shown below:

```
class xyz
{
   :
public :
    xyz();    // Constructor
    ~xyz(); // Destructor
};
```

The rules for destructor definition and usage are

1. The destructor has the same name as that of the class prefixed by the tilde character '~'.
2. The destructor cannot have arguments.
3. It has no return type, not even void type.
4. Destructors cannot be overloaded, i.e. there can be only one destructor in a class.
5. If there is no destructor in a class, a default destructor is generated by the compiler.
6. The destructor is executed automatically when the control reaches at the end of class scope.
7. The popular abbreviation for destructor is **dtor**.

Now the most important question is as to of what use is the destructor function to a programmer? Since the destructor function is the last function to be executed, no fruitful use of this function can be made by the programmer. *However, if we have to find its use then it can be best used for debugging purpose.* In fact, some appropriate message can be included in the destructor function to inform that the object in question is being destroyed. If the message is not displayed by an object then the programmer may infer that the object in question is misbehaving and the program control is struck somewhere within the object itself.

Example 6. *Write a class called testDest that illustrates the working of a destructor. It displays the following message as soon as its object is destroyed.*

"I am being destroyed"

Write a smallest possible main() function for testing the working of the destructor.

Solution: The required class with destructor and the minimal main() function is given below:

```
//This program demonstrates the working of a destructor

      # include <iostream.h>
      class testDest {
       public:

       testDest () { cout << "\n I am being created";} // constructor
       ~testDest() { cout << "\n I am being destroyed";} // destructor
   };
```

```
void main()
{
    testDest ob; // object is created
} // object is destroyed
```

The output of above program is given below:

```
I am being created
I am being destroyed
```

It may be noted that the constructor and the destructor are called automatically by the system as and when the object is created or destroyed – as the case may be.

6.4 SUMMARY

Constructor is a function that creates an object. It is a special function that returns no value not even the void. It helps the programmer to automatically initialize certain data members of an object at the time of its creation. The name of the constructor is same as the class. A copy constructor initializes one object with values from another object of the same class type. The destructor function destroys the object. It removes the memory held by an object. It is the last member function to be called. It also carries the same name of the class with a tilde (~) as prefix. The destructor function can be used for debugging purposes.

MULTIPLE CHOICE QUESTIONS

1. A constructor function returns:
   (a) an integer
   (b) a float
   (c) no value
   (d) void
2. A constructor function automatically initializes the data members of an object at the time of its:
   (a) declaration
   (b) creation
   (c) destruction
   (d) compilation
3. The name of the constructor function is:
   (a) same as class name
   (b) same as program name
   (c) user defined name
   (d) none of these
4. Is constructor function a friend of the class?
   (a) yes
   (b) no
5. What happens if an object is passed by value to a copy constructor?
   (a) the size of the object increases
   (b) the size of the object decreases
   (c) system may run out of memory
   (d) compiler runs out of memory

6. A constructor with no arguments is called:
   (a) copy constructor (b) default constructor
   (c) parameterized constructor (d) none of these
7. When an object consists of pointer variables, it must be copied through:
   (a) assignment operator (b) a user defined function
   (c) copy constructor
8. What is the popular abbreviation for constructor?
   (a) conc (b) tor
   (c) cons (d) ctor
9. What is the popular abbreviation for destructor?
   (a) dtor (b) tor
   (c) dest (d) ~des
10. What happens if there is no constructor defined in a class?
    (a) the object is not created (b) the program terminates
    (c) the objects gets created (d) none of these

ANSWERS

1. c **2.** b **3.** a **4.** b **5.** c **6.** b **7.** c **8.** d **9.** a **10.** c

EXERCISES

1. What is a constructor? Explain its utility.
2. Define the terms: default constructor and parameterized constructor.
3. Modify Example 1 of Chapter 4 such that the class contains a constructor function.
4. Design a constructor with default values for Example 4 of Chapter 4.
5. Design a suitable constructor function for Example 9 of Chapter 4.
6. Explain copy constructor in detail.
7. Define the term destructor.
8. Describe the importance of destructor function.
9. Write a program that illustrates the working of a destructor function.
10. Given the following C++ code, answer the questions (a) and (b).

```
# include <<iostream.h>>
class Readbook
  {
    public:
    Readbook() // Function1
    {
    cout << "Open the book" << endl;}
```

```
    void Readchapter() // Function2
  {
    cout << "Read Chapter 1" << endl;}
    ~Readbook()
  {
    cout << "Close the Book" << endl;}
};
```

a. In object-oriented programming, what is Function1 referred to as and when does it get invoked/called?

b. In object-oriented programming, what is Function2 referred to as and when does it get involved/called?

11. Write a program in C++ that creates a class called 'time' with data members: hour, minutes, and seconds of type integer, integer, and float, respectively. The class uses two constructors. One constructor is used to initialize the time data elements to zero. The second constructor is used to set the time components to a predetermined time, passed by the user as arguments. The class also has two member functions: dispTime() and addTime(). The dispTime() displays the time in: hh:mm::ss.ss format. The other function addTime() adds two objects T1 and T2 of time type such that T3 = T1 & T2, where T3 is also of type 'time'.

INHERITANCE: EXTENDING CLASSES

7

7.1 INTRODUCTION TO CODE REUSE

Almost all programming languages support functions that allow a piece of code to be reused again and again in a calling program. However, functions provide rather limited support for code reuse. In object-oriented programming (OOP), code reuse is a central feature. In fact, we can reuse the code written in a class in another class by either of the two mechanisms given below:

1. Containership
2. Inheritance

7.2 CONTAINERSHIP

In day-to-day life, we come across objects which are composed of other objects. For instance, a computer is composed of objects like motherboard, hard disk, CD-ROM drive, monitor, etc. The motherboard contains a CPU and other components. The CPU contains ALU, CU and registers. Similarly, a car is composed of an engine, a steering wheel, a radiator, fan, and so many other objects.

In other words we can say that the CPU object uses the services of its contained objects. It acts as a container for other objects as shown in Fig. 7.1.

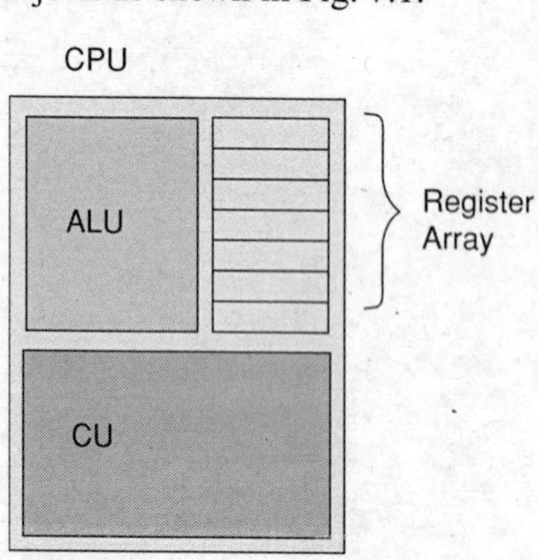

Figure 7.1 *CPU, a container of objects*

It may be noted that the CPU is a more powerful and useful device as compared to its contained objects: ALU, CU and register array. Moreover, we see only the container and the contained objects remain hidden and secured inside the container. The relationship between container and contained objects is called as a 'has-a' relationship. The CPU 'has-a' CU, 'has-a' ALU and, 'has-a' register array. Taking the cue from this, we can also create powerful objects by containing object components in a container object.

C++ allows a class to contain the objects of some other class. This activity establishes 'has-a' relationship among objects. The 'has-a' relationship is also known as **containership** and comes into picture when an object of a class is contained in another class. Consider the following declaration:

```
class address {
    int houseno;
    char colony[15];
    char distt[15];
    char state[20];
    int pincode;
    public:
    void get_data();
    void show_data();
    };
 class person {      // container
    char name [20];
    int age;
    address resAdd; // contained object

    public:
    void read_data();
    void display_data();
    };
```

The above declaration establishes the relationship: a person has an address. Now, an object of class person will always contain an object of class address type. Thus, the person object would become more powerful by using (or reusing) the services offered by the address object. This composition feature of OOP is also known as *aggregation*.

The *containership* can be precisely defined as *a composition of objects in which a contained object is hidden. The access to the contained object is only through the container object.*

Example 1. *Write a program that reads the data of a person and prints it. Use the classes person and address to illustrate the concept of containership.*

Solution: We will use the class declaration of has a relationship between the class person and class address as described above. The required program is given below:

```
// Example Containership

   # include <iostream.h >
```

```
# include <stdio.h >
# include <conio.h >

class address {
    int houseno;
    char colony[15];
    char distt[15];
    char state[20];
    long pincode;
    public:
    void get_data();
    void show_data();
    };
class person {
    char name [20];
    int age;
    address resAdd; // containership :resAdd is an object
                    // of class address
    public:
    void read_data();
    void display_data();
    };
void address :: get_data()
    {
    cout << "\nHouse No:";
    cin >> houseno;
    cout << "\n Colony:";
    gets(colony); fflush(stdin);
    cout << "\n Distt:" ;
    gets(distt); fflush(stdin);
    cout << "\n state:" ;
    gets(state); fflush(stdin);
    cout << "\n PinCode:";
    cin >> pincode;
    }
void address :: show_data()
    {
    cout << "\n Address : ";
    cout << houseno << " ," << colony;
    cout << "\n " << distt << " ," << state;
    cout << "," << pincode;
    }
void person :: read_data()
    {
    cout << "\nEnter the data ..";
    cout   <<  "\n";
    cout << "Name:";
```

```
    gets(name); fflush(stdin);
    cout << "\nAge:";
    cin >> age;
    resAdd.get_data(); // Invoke the function of contained object
    }
void person :: display_data()
    {
    cout << "\n The person data is.. \n" ;
    cout << "\n Name:" << name;
    cout << "\n Age:" << age;
    resAdd.show_data(); // Invoke the function of contained object
    }
main()
    {
    clrscr();
    person obj; // Create an Object of class person type
    obj.read_data(); // Read the data of a person
    obj.display_data();
    return 0;
    }
```

A sample output is given below:

```
Enter the data..
Name:Ram

Age:17

House No:108

  Colony :saket

  Distt:South Dist.

  State:Delhi

  Pincode:110017
```

```
The person data is ..

Name:Ram
Age:17
Address : 108 ,saket
South Dist. ,Delhi,110017
```

It may be appreciated that *most of the programming situations can be easily handled by containership*. Let us consider the following situation:

Assume that an object called '*point*' is available that can display a point (say '*') at coordinates (x, y). We can define a class called line that displays a line on the screen by using the services of the point object. Similarly we may define class called rectangle that displays a rectangle on the screen by using the services of the line object.

Thus, the rectangle class contains a line object which in turn contains an object of point type and the arrangement is given in Fig. 7.2.

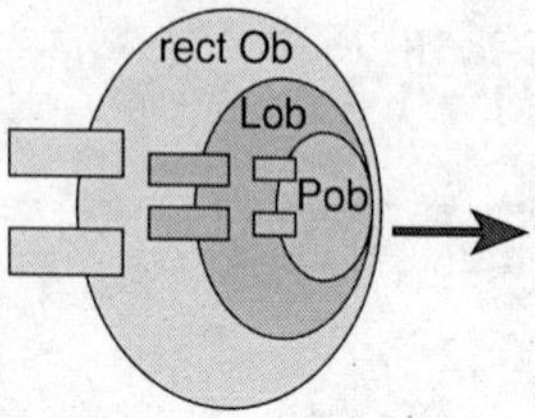


```
Class point
—
—
};
Class line {
—
Point Pob ; // Point object
—
};
Class rectangle {
—
—
line Lob; // line object
};
```

Figure 7.2 *Container and the contained objects*

Example 2. *Write a program that uses the above given container class 'rectangle' to display a user specified rectangle on the screen.*

Solution: We would use the goto*xy*() function of Turbo C++ to display a point ('*') on the screen in text mode. The line class would print contiguous points to display a line. The rectangle class would appropriately draw the lines of the rectangle.

A point worth noting is that Turbo C++ takes top left corner as (0,0) coordinates of the screen.

The required classes and the complete program is given below:

```
// This program displays a rectangle on the screen

# include <iostream.h>
# include <conio.h>

class point {
    int x, y;
    void disp()
      {
      gotoxy(x,y);
      cout << '*';
      }
    public:
    void dispPoint(int Xcord, int Ycord)
      {
```

```
  x = Xcord; y = Ycord;
  disp ();
    }
   };
class line {
  int x1,y1,x2,y2;
  int x,y;
  point Pob; // Object of point type
  void disp();
  public:
  void dispLine(int X1, int Y1, int X2, int Y2)
    {
  x1 = X1; y1 = Y1; x2 = X2; y2 = Y2;
  disp();
    }
    };
 void line :: disp()
  {   if (y1 == y2) // draw horizontal line
      {if (x1 < x2)
       for (x = x1; x <= x2; x++)
       Pob.dispPoint (x, y1);
  else
       for (x = x2; x <= x1; x++)
       Pob.dispPoint (x, y1);
   }
  else
     if (x1 == x2) // draw vertical line
       {if (y1 < y2)
     for (y = y1; y <= y2; y++)
       Pob.dispPoint(x1,y);
     else
       for (y = y2; y <= y1; y++)
         Pob.dispPoint(x1,y);
         }
     }
  class rectangle {
  int x1,y1, x2,y2;
    line lob; // object of line type
    void disp ()
      {
  lob.dispLine (x1,y1, x2,y1);
  lob.dispLine (x1,y1, x1,y2);
  lob.dispLine(x2,y1, x2,y2);
  lob.dispLine(x1,y2, x2,y2);
      }
    public:
    void dispRect(int CorX1,int CorY1,int CorX2,int CorY2)
```

```
        {
         x1 = CorX1; y1 = CorY1; x2 = CorX2; y2 = CorY2;
         disp();
        }
    };
    void main()
    {rectangle RecOb;
     clrscr();
     RecOb.dispRect(12,5,40,10);
        }
```

The output of the program is given below:

```
*****************************
*                           *
*                           *
*                           *
*                           *
*****************************
```

Note: The main advantage of the containership is that it excellently implements the encapsulation feature of OOP. The reason being, that the contained objects are only accessible through their container object and that too only through their interfaces. Therefore, it achieves complete implementation hiding. This arrangement of containership can be pictorially represented in Fig. 7.3.

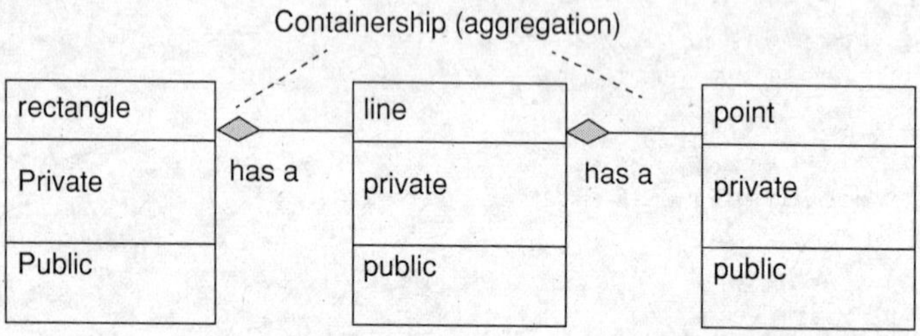

Figure 7.3 *Representation for aggregation*

The diamond indicates the 'has-a' relationship.

7.3 INHERITANCE

The containership works well when a class has two clearly defined sections: private and public. This indicates that the designer of the class is offering public interfaces for interaction and hiding the important information and implementation components of the object inside the private section as shown in Fig. 7.4. However, the usage of such object is rather limited because the user can only use the public services offered by the object.

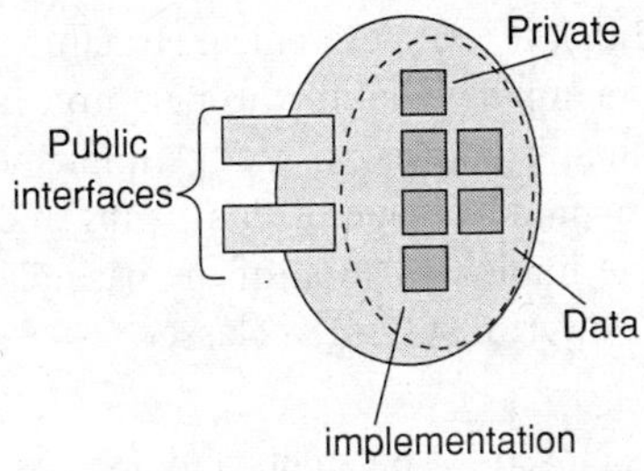

Figure 7.4 *An object suitable for containership*

Consider a situation, where some important implementation of the object (Fig. 7.4) is needed to a programmer who is a member of the same project, i.e. the programmer wants to reuse the implementation in his/her class. The other requirement could be that the programmer may like to add some more features to the implementation to create a more powerful class. With the existing design, it is not possible because the desired implementation is inaccessible, as it has been placed in the private section of the object by its designer. *Thus, the class is closed for modification of any kind*. It can only be used.

The above anomalous situation can be solved by *inheritance*. It is the most central feature of the object oriented design. A class provides a special visibility mode called '*protected*' in addition to the private and public visibility modes.

The protected mode is as good as private as far as its usage by outsiders is concerned. Now the designer of a class can, without fear, place an implementation into the protected section instead of the private. The programmer, who is part of the project and requires the implementation, can use the implementation with the help of inheritance. The inheritance makes the implementation available to the programmer, which was otherwise inaccessible. The arrangement is shown in Fig. 7.5.

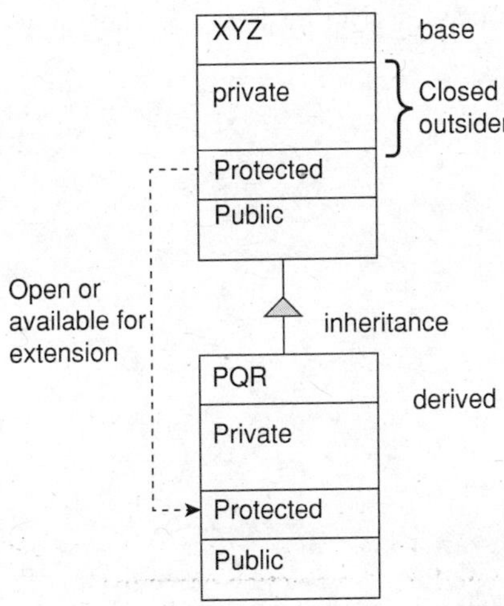

Figure 7.5 *Protected member available through inheritance*

It may be noted from Fig. 7.5 that it is a hierarchical structure of classes XYZ and PQR. The class XYZ which has offered an implementation through protected mode is called a *base* class. The beneficiary class PQR which is allowed to use the implementation through inheritance is called the *derived* class. The main advantage of this arrangement is that not only the derived class is able to access a private implementation of the base class but it can also add its own strength to it to create a more powerful system of classes.

Note: The base class is closed for outsiders and open for extension to the derived class or classes through inheritance. This principle is called **'open close principle'**

1. The relationship between the base and derived class is called ' a kind of' (*AKO*) relationship. For instance PQR is a kind of XYZ. We also describe that PQR is derived from XYZ. In real world, a mango is a kind of fruit and a mammal is a kind of animal.
2. The derived class cannot access the private members of base class.

It may be observed from Fig. 7.5 that inheritance is represented by connecting a base class to its derived classes with the help of a triangle. The apex of the triangle is connected to the base class and its derived classes are connected to the base of the triangle. The derived class inherits the members of its base class without the need to redefine them. The format for defining a derived class is given below:

```
class <derived class> : <visibility mode> <base class> {
:
 };
```

where class is the reserved word; "**:**" is the colon operator indicating inheritance; <derived class> is the name of the subclass or new class being derived; <visibility mode> is the mode of access to items from the base class. The access mode can be either of the following type: *private, public, or protected.*

Consider the hierarchy of classes given in Fig. 7.5. The equivalent skeleton code for this inheritance is given below:

```
class XYZ {
   private
   :
   protected:
   :
   public:
};
class PQR : public XYZ {
   :

   :
};
```

It is reiterated here that most of the code reuse situations can be easily handled by containership. There are fewer situations where inheritance can be used. One of the examples is given below:

Consider a class called University having the following members

```
class University {
  private: //private members closed for modification
   int rollNo [100], i, flag;

   int interMarks [100]; // internal marks of students
      // number of students
   int theoryMarks [100]; // theory marks of students
   void setTheorMarks (); // sets theory marks protected:
   int numStud; // protected members open for extension
   void setInterMarks();
   void issueRollNo();
  public:
   void prepResults();
   void showResults(char ColgName[]);
};
```

Kindly note that the designer of the class has included some very important members in the protected section. Now, consider a class called College having the following members. It inherits the University class for using the protected members of the University class. Now this is a situation suitable for inheritance because containership would have definitely failed in this situation.

```
class College : public University {

  private:
   char collegName [50];
  public:
   College (int N) {
   numStud = N;
   issueRollNo();}
   void inputInterMarks(); // teacher inputs students' internal marks
   void dispResult ();
      };
```

Example 3. *Write a complete program that uses the classes University and College to input and display data of N number of students.*

Solution: The complete program is given below:

```
// This program illustrates inheritance

# include <iostream.h>
# include <conio.h>
# include <stdio.h>

class University {
  private:
```

```
   int rollNo [100], i, flag;

   int interMarks [100]; // internal marks of students
   // number of students
   int theoryMarks [100]; // theory marks of students
   void setTheorMarks (); // sets the theory marks of students pro-
tected:
   int numStud;
   void setInterMarks();
   void issueRollNo();
  public:
   void prepResults();
   void showResults(char ColgName[]);
};
class College : public University {

  private:
   char collegName [50];
  public:
   College (int N) { // Constructor to set No. of students and
      // issue Roll No.
      numStud = N; // number of students
      issueRollNo();
      }
   void inputInterMarks(); // teacher inputs students' internal marks
   void dispResult ();
 };
void University ::  issueRollNo()
  { for (i = 0; i < numStud; i++)
     {
     rollNo[i] = 100 + i; // issue roll nos. starting from 100 onwards
     }
  }
void University :: setTheorMarks ()
  {
   cout << "\n Enter theory marks for the roll number mentioned";
   for (i = 0; i < numStud; i++)
     {cout << "\n Roll" << rollNo[i] << " : ";
       cin >> theoryMarks[i];
     }
   }
void University :: setInterMarks()
   {
    cout << "\n Enter internal marks for the roll number mentioned";
   for (i = 0; i < numStud; i++)
     {cout <<"\n Roll" << rollNo[i] << " : ";
       cin >> interMarks[i];
     }
```

```
    flag = 1;
  }
  void University :: prepResults()
    {if (flag == 1)
      setTheorMarks();
      else
     cout << "\n input internal marks";
    }
void University :: showResults(char colgName[])
  {
   clrscr();
    cout << "\n College :" << colgName;
    cout << "\n The result...";
    cout << "\nRoll\tinternal\tTheory";
    for (i =0; i < numStud; i++)
      {cout <<"\n" <<rollNo[i] << "\t" << interMarks[i] <<"\t  \t" <<
      theoryMarks[i];
      }
   }
void College :: inputInterMarks()
   {
    cout << "\n Enter the college name";
    gets(collegName);
    setInterMarks();
    prepResults();
   }

void College :: dispResult ()
  {
   showResults (collegName);
  }

void main()
  {int N;
   cout << "\n Enter the number of students";
   cin >> N;
   College Cob (N);
   Cob.inputInterMarks();
   Cob.dispResult();
  }
```

A sample output is given below:

```
 Enter the number of students3
 Enter the college nameYMCA University of Sc. & Tech.

 Enter internal marks for the roll number menioned
 Roll-100 : 65
 Roll-101 : 76
```

```
Roll-102 : 71

Enter theory markes for the roll number mentioned
Roll100 : 87

Roll101 : 78

Roll102 : 79

College : YMCA University of Sc. & Tech.
The result...
Roll      internal      Theory
100          65         87
101          76         78
102          71         79
```

It may be noted that the College class is able to use the protected members of University class after inheritance. It may be further noted that the members are being used as if they are part of the derived class, i.e. the College class. This is perhaps the one of the most brilliant way of 'code reuse' of the implementation which otherwise was worthy of being placed in private section.

7.3.1 Visibility Modes

In the examples given above, we have used the access specifier '*public*' while specifying inheritance. This means that all the public and protected members of the base class will also be accessible as public and protected members to the derived class. For example, in the following declaration, all the public and protected members of class XYZ will be accessible as public and protected members to class PQR.

```
class PQR : public XYZ {
    :
     };
```

Precisely, we can say that in *public inheritance*:

1. The public members of base class remain public in the derived class.
2. The protected members of base class remain protected in the derived class.

One can also use the keyword private in place of keyword public as shown below:

```
class PQR: private XYZ{
    :
          };
```

In this type of situation, all public and protected members of the base class XYZ will become private members of the derived class PQR.

Precisely, we can say that in *private inheritance*:

1. The public members of base class become private in the derived class.
2. The protected members of base class also become private in the derived class.

Similarly, we can use the keyword protected while specifying inheritance as shown below:

```
class PQR : protected XYZ {
    :
            } ;
```

In this type of situation, the protected members of the base class XYZ become the protected members of the derived class PQR.

Precisely, we can say that in *protected inheritance*:

1. The public members of base class become protected members in the derived class.
2. The protected members of base class also remain protected members in the derived class.

The access control to various members of a derived class can be summarized in the form of a diagram as shown in Fig. 7.6.

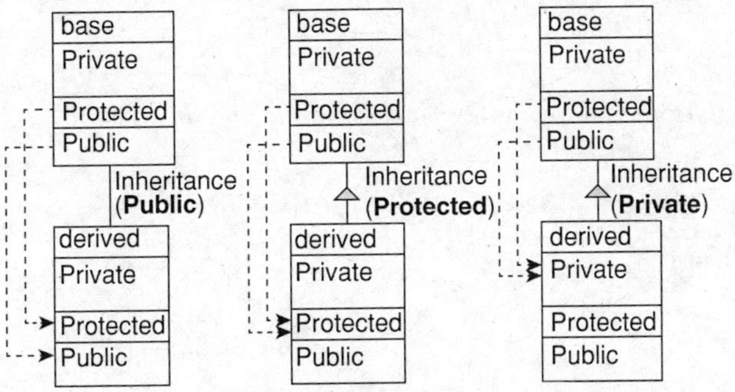

Figure 7.6 *Access control mechanism in class inheritance*

Having tasted the benefits of inheritance, let us now precisely define it. The definition is given below:

Inheritance: it is a mechanism of providing code reuse in a hierarchy of classes. A class called derived is able to inherit (i.e. reuse) the protected code of another class called base without having to redefine the code.

In the following section a discussion on types of inheritance is given.

7.4 TYPES OF INHERITANCE

There are three types of inheritance as given below:

- Multilevel inheritance
- Multiple inheritance
- Graph inheritance

7.4.1 Multilevel Inheritance

We know that a derived class with a single base class is said to form single inheritance. The derived class can also become a base class for some other derived class (see Fig. 7.7). This type of chain of deriving classes can go on to as many levels as needed. The inheritance of this type is known as multilevel inheritance. For example, the class son inherits from class father. The class father in turn inherits from class grandfather.

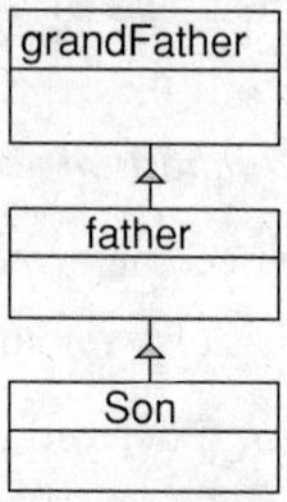

Figure 7.7 *Multilevel inheritance*

Example 4. *Consider the following C++ declarations and answer the questions given below:*

```
class grandFather
  {
   void secVal();
   protected:
    int x,y;
    void protVal();
   public:
    void getvalGf();
    void putvalGf();
  };
class father: protected grandFather
  {
   int a, b;
   protected:
     int c,d;
     void getvalF();

    public:
    void putvalF();
   };
 class son:private father
   {
    int p;
    protected :
```

```
    int q;
    void getvalS();
  public:
    void showvalS();
};
```

Questions:

1. Name all the member functions which are accessible to the user of the objects of class son.
2. Name all the accessible protected members of class father.
3. Name the base and derived classes of class father.
4. Name the data members, which are accessible from the member functions of class son.

Solution:

1. The only member function accessible to the users of objects of class 'son' is showvalS(). The reason being showvalS() is the only public function of the class 'son' and the other function getvalS() is a protected member and therefore not available to the object.
2. The protected members of class 'father' are:

   data items: *c*, *d*, *x*, *y*

   member functions: getvalF(), getvalGf(), putvalGf().
3. The base class of 'father' is class 'grandFather' and derived class of 'father' is class 'son'.
4. The data members available to member function of 'son' are:

   p, *q*: internal members of class son

   c, *d*: by virtue of inheritance

   x, *y*: by virtue of inheritance

7.4.2 Multiple Inheritance

A class can inherit properties from more than one base class as shown in Fig. 7.8. This type of inheritance is called as multiple inheritance. Please note that this inheritance is different from multilevel inheritance wherein a subclass is derived from a class which itself is derived from another class and so on.

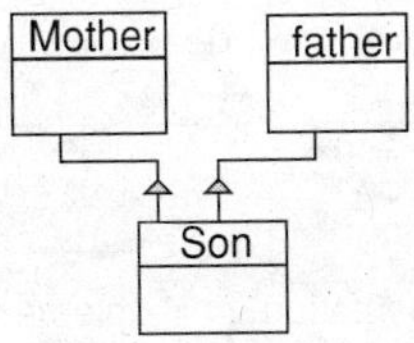

Figure 7.8 *Multiple inheritance*

It can be observed from Fig. 7.8 that the class 'son' inherits properties from both the base classes 'mother' and 'father'.

The format of multiple inheritance is given below:

```
class mother {

};

class father {

};

// multiple inheritance from two classes 'mother' and 'father'
class son : public mother, public father  {

};
```

Discussion on **Graph inheritance** is given in section 7.4.

7.5 FUNCTION OVERRIDING

One of the major advantages of abstraction and encapsulation is that a class separates "what from how". In simple words, we can say that the interface is separated from implementation as shown in Fig. 7.9.

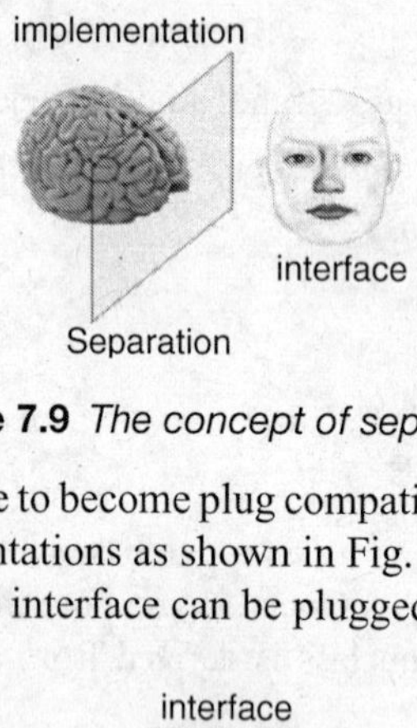

Figure 7.9 *The concept of separation*

The separation enables the interface to become plug compatible, i.e. the interface can be plugged with any of the available implementations as shown in Fig. 7.10. It may be noted that there are two implementations A and B. The interface can be plugged with any of them.

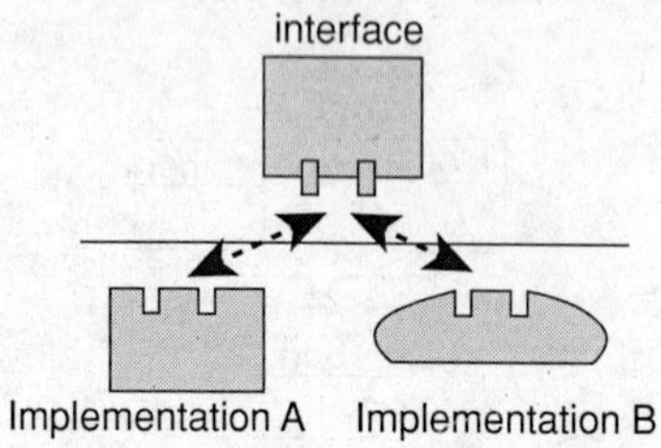

Figure 7.10 *Plug compatibility*

Consider a situation where A and B are versions 1 and 2, respectively, of a software implementation. Now, we can easily unplug implementation A and plug the implementation B without having to change the interface. This will not only save lot of coding effort but also offer the same interface to the user who is already trained to use it. In fact, the user-retraining cost is also saved.

The above *polymorphic* behaviour can be easily achieved through *function overriding* wherein a function of a derived class can run in place of a function of its base class. Let us reconsider the following class called 'student' of Chapter 4:

```
class student {

private:

   char name[20];
   int roll;
   int marks;
   char grade;
   void compute_grade();

public:

   void read_data();
   void display_grade();
   };
```

The implementation function 'compute_grade()' computes the grade of a student as per the following rules:

Marks	Grade
>= 50 < 60	D
>= 60 < 70	C
>= 70 < 80	B
>= 80	A

If it is predicted that in future the above mentioned rules may change then either of the following steps would be needed to handle the situation:

a. Change the class as per new rules. It is a difficult and cumbersome option because an attempt to change the class may lead to a chain of modifications in classes which depend upon the 'student' class. Moreover, where is the guarantee that still further changes to the rules will not take place?

b. The programmer should make a provision in the class such that the changes may be incorporated without changing the existing (i.e. student) class. This can be achieved by declaring the required function as *virtual*.

A brief discussion on virtual functions is given in the next section.

7.5.1 Virtual Functions

Consider the function declaration given below:

```
void read_data();
```

The above function 'read_data()' is compiled by the compiler such that at run time whenever a call to read_data(); is made, a correct correspondence is established between the function call and the function. This kind of binding of function call to the corresponding function is said to be **static binding**. In fact, the address of the function is permanently bound at the compile time.

However, *a programmer would not like to statically bind a function defined in base class especially when he/she predicts the function to be redefined in derived class.* Rather he/she would like to defer the binding to run time so that the correct function out of the two may be called. This type of **run time binding** is supported by C++ through *virtual* keyword.

In a class, a programmer can declare a function as *virtual*. It is a keyword of C++ that precedes a function declaration as shown below:

```
virtual void read_data();
```

The keyword virtual is a directive to the compiler indicating to defer the binding of the function 'read_data()' till run time. If this function, defined in base class, is redefined in derived class then at run time the address of whichever function through its object is made available that function would be bound and executed.

Consider the following arrangement of classes:

```
class student {
  protected:
  char name[20];
  int roll;
  int marks;
  char grade;
  void compute_grade();
public:
  virtual void read_data();
  void display_grade();
};

class changes : public student {

   private:
      void compute_grade();
   public:
      void read_data();
   };
```

It may be noted that the function read_data() of class student has been declared as virtual. A function with same name has been defined in class changes that inherit from class student. The read_data() of class changes calls its own implementation function compute_grade() that uses the following rules to compute grades:

Marks	Grade
>= 45 < 55	D
>= 55 < 65	C
>= 65 < 75	B
>= 75	A

The above rules are different than what are being used by the base class, i.e. the student class. For instance, a student who secures 56 marks will get 'D' grade by old rules and 'C' by new rules.

Example 5. *Write a program that uses the above given 'student–changes' class inheritance and tests the working of virtual functions.*

Solution: We would use a pointer to base class. The pointer would be assigned the address of an object of type changes. The program would be tested for input (marks = 56) to display grade.

The complete program is given below:

```
# include <iostream.h>
class student {

protected:
   char name[20];
   int roll;
   int marks;
   char grade;
   void compute_grade();

public:
   virtual void read_data();        // dynamic binding
   void display_grade();            // static binding
   };

class changes : public student {

    private:
       void compute_grade();
    public:
       void read_data(); // overriding function
    };
// Function to read data of a student
   void student :: read_data()
    {
     cout << "\n Enter Name:";
     cin >> name;
     cout << "\n Enter Roll:";
```

```
    cin >> roll;
    cout << "\n Enter Marks:";
    cin >> marks;

    compute_grade(); // compute the grade
    }
   void student :: display_grade()
     {
       cout << "\n The data:" << name;
       cout << "\t" << roll;
       cout << "\t" <<grade;
     }
    void student :: compute_grade()
      {
      if (marks >= 80) grade = 'A';
        else
        if (marks >= 70) grade = 'B';
        else
        if (marks >= 60) grade = 'C';
        else
        if (marks >= 50) grade ='D';
        else
        grade = 'E';
       }
void changes :: read_data()
   {
    cout << "\n Enter Name:";
    cin >> name;
    cout << "\n Enter Roll:";
    cin >> roll;
    cout << "\n Enter Marks:";
    cin >> marks;

    compute_grade(); // compute the grade
    }
void changes :: compute_grade()
      {
        if (marks >= 75) grade = 'A';
        else
        if (marks >= 65) grade = 'B';
        else
        if (marks >= 55) grade = 'C';
       else
        if (marks >= 45) grade = 'D';
       else
        grade = 'E';
      }
```

```
void main()
  {
   student *ptr;

   changes dob; // create an object of changes type
   ptr = &dob; // assign its address to ptr of type student
   ptr->read_data();
   ptr->display_grade();
   }
```

A sample (for marks = 56) output is given below:

```
Enter Name :Ashok
Enter Roll:101
Enter Marks:56
The data:Ashok 101     C_
```

Note:

1. As per new rules the student gets 'C' grade. Thus, the function 'read_data() of class 'changes' has overridden the function read_data() of class 'student'.
2. The most important point to be noted is that the address of an object of class 'changes' (derived class) has been assigned to a pointer of type class 'student' (base class). The surprise is that the compiler accepted it and has not complained it to be a mismatch. This has become possible because of the '*virtual*' keyword.
3. The non-virtual function 'display_grade()' of class 'student' has been statically bound.

From above we can conclude that a function declared as virtual is bound at run time. The object of a derived class can substitute for object of a base class. This principle is called as **"Liskov's Substitution Principle (LSP)"**.

The type of inheritance that allows a derived class function to override a base class function is also called as **proper inheritance**. However, the condition is that both the functions carry the same name and the base class function is declared as virtual. The proper inheritance allows both *substitutability* and *extensibility*.

Example 6. *Write a program that illustrates the working of 'Liskov's Substitution Principle'.*

Solution: We create two classes called 'parent' and 'child' wherein child inherits from parent. Both contain a function named display() that displays a message. The function of base class would be declared as virtual. Objects of both parent and child classes would be sent to a stand alone function called test() which calls the display function of the object to display the message.

The complete program is given below:

```
#include <iostream.h>
#include <string.h>

class parent {
  char Id[10];
   public:
     parent () { strcpy(Id, "parent");}
     virtual void show () {
     cout <<"\n I am " << Id;
     }
  };

class child : public parent
   {
  char Id[10];
   public:
     child () { strcpy(Id, "child");}
     void show () {
     cout <<"\n I am " << Id;
     }
  };
void test ( parent & ob) // stand alone function designed
 {// to get object of type parent
     ob.show();
  }
void main()
  {
    parent Pob;
    test (Pob); // call test() with an object of type parent
    child Cob;
    test (Cob); // call test() with an object of type child
   }
```

The output of the program is given below:

```
I am parent
I am child
```

It may be noted that the function test() has been defined to receive an object of type parent but it also accepts an object of type child, i.e. the derived class. This is possible because the function show() in class 'parent' has been declared as virtual. The 'child' class is a derived class of parent. Thus, the working of *LSP* has been established because *the object of derived class has been able to substitute the object of base class.*

7.5.1.1 Pure Virtual Functions

We know that the main purpose of an object is to provide services to other objects or users. For instance, the student object computes grade and displays it. Similarly, a stack object offers two services: push and pop. We also know that for each service offered by the interface of an object, there has to be an implementation that provides the service.

Sometimes a situation arises when, out of many implementations, the designer of a class does not have an implementation for a service committed by the interface. If he/she predicts that in future the implementation would become available then he/she can remind the programmer of a derived class to write the implementation. He/she does so by including a pure virtual function for the non-available implementation. A simple format for a pure virtual function is given below:

```
virtual <returnType> <funcName> ( ) = 0;
```

where virtual is a keyword; <returnType> is a type of value supposed to be returned by the function; <funcName> is the user defined name of the function.

Consider the following declaration of a function whose body has been set equal to 0:

```
virtual void compute_grade() = 0;
```

The above statement says that implementation for the function compute_grade() is not available. Now if the above statement is included in a class then its object cannot be created because this function of the class has no body, i.e. no implementation. Such a class is called as an **abstract class**. The abstract class can be precisely defined as *a class which has at least one pure virtual function.* A normal class that does not have a pure virtual function is called as a **concrete class**. An abstract class has the following characteristics:

1. Its object cannot be created.
2. It cannot be inherited by a derived class unless the programmer of the derived class provides an implementation for each pure virtual function declared in the abstract class.

Thus, the programmer of abstract class forces the derived class programmer to provide implementations for all the unimplemented functions (i.e. pure virtual) present in the base class.

Consider the class hierarchy given in Fig. 7.11.

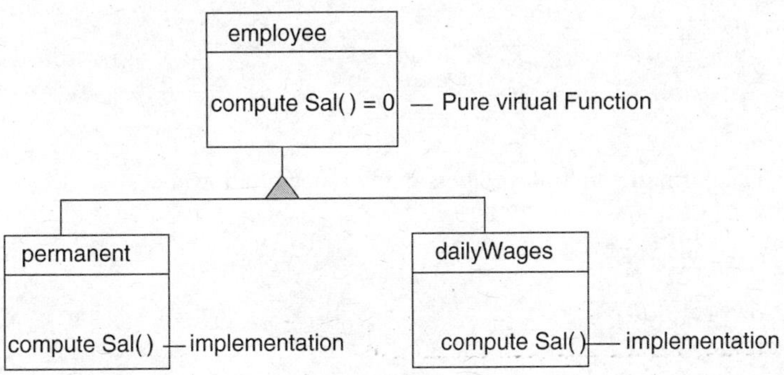

Figure 7.11 *Class hierarchy*

It may be noted that the base class (employee) has a pure virtual function named computeSal(). Since its implementation has not been provided by the base class, the derived classes (permanent and dailyWages) have been forced to provide their version of implementation. Thus, 'employee' is an abstract class and the 'permanent' and 'dailyWages' classes are concrete classes.

Example 7. *Give the class definitions for the class hierarchy given in Fig. 7.11.*

Solution: The classes: employee, permanent, and dailyWages are given below:

```
class employee {
  char name[20];
  char desig [15];

  protected:
  int empType; // 1 for permanent and 0 for daily wages
  void getData();
  virtual void computeSal() = 0; // pure virtual function
     public:
  void showData();
   };
```

It may be noted that the employee class records only the general data of an employee.

```
class permanent :public employee{
  private:
  float basicPay;
  float DA; // dearness allowance
  float HR; // house rent
  int med; // medical allownace
  float salary;
  void computeSal();
     public:
  permanent () {med =500; // consolidated amount
          empType = 1;}
  void readData();
  void dispData();
   };
```

Note: The permanent employee gets many types of allowances.

```
class dailyWages : public employee {
  private:
    float dailyWage;
    int numDays;
    float salary;
    void computeSal();
```

```
  public:
    dailyWages() { empType =0;}
    void readData();
    void dispData();
  };
```

Note: The temporary employee gets only limited salary based on the number of working days.

Example 8. *Give the definitions of various functions of the classes defined in Example 7. Write a main() function that test the classes for permanent as well as daily wages employee.*

Solution: The definitions of functions of various classes are given below:

```
// Functions of employee class
void employee :: getData()
 {
   cout << "\n Enter name :";
   gets (name); fflush(stdin);
   cout << "\n Enter designation :";
   gets(desig);
  };
void employee :: showData()
  {
   cout << "\n Name:" << name << "\t Desig :" << desig;
   if (empType == 1)
       cout << "\n Permanent";
       else
       cout << "\n Temporary";
  }
// Functions of permanent class
void permanent :: readData()
    { getData();
      cout << "\n Enter Basic Pay :";
      cin >> basicPay;
      computeSal();
     }
  void permanent :: computeSal()
     {
      DA = basicPay * 0.76;
      HR = basicPay * 0.2;
      salary = basicPay + DA + HR + med;
     }
  void permanent :: dispData()
     {
      showData();
```

```
    cout << "\n BP =" << basicPay << " DA = " << DA  << " HR = " << HR;
     cout << " med =" << med;
     cout << "\n Salary =" << salary;
    }
// Functions of dailyWages class
void dailyWages:: readData()
   {
     getData();
     cout << "\n Enter Daily wage :";
     cin >> dailyWage;
     cout <<"\n Enter number of days :";
     cin >> numDays;
     computeSal();
    }
  void dailyWages :: dispData ()
      {
       showData();
       cout << "\n Daily Wage = " << dailyWage;
       cout << "\n Number of days = " << numDays;
       cout << "\n Salary = Rs. " << salary;
      }
 void dailyWages :: computeSal()
   {
    salary = dailyWage * numDays;
   }
// The main() function
 void main()
  {
    permanent Pob;
    Pob.readData();
    Pob.dispData(); // Test the object of permanent type
    dailyWages Dob;
    Dob.readData();
    Dob.dispData(); // Test the object of  daily wages type
}
```

A sample output for the above program is given below:

```
Enter name : A. K. Sharma
Enter designation : Manager
Enter Basic pay :30000
Name: A. K. Sharma   Desig : manager
Permanent
BP =30000 DA = 22800 HR = 6000 med =500
Salary =59300
```

```
Enter name : S. K. Verma

Enter designation : Prob. officer

Enter Daily wage :2000

Enter number of days :25

Name: S. K. Verma    Desig : Prob.officer

Temporary
Dialy Wage =2000
Number of days =25
Salary = Rs.50000
```

It may be noted that the base class has provided the basic data and some services and not the implementation. The derived classes have provided individual implementations but have used the basic data and services of the base class. Without inheritance and the virtual keyword, this kind of arrangement would not have been possible.

Another point to be noted is that from ‘employee’ class we have carved out two roles in the form of ‘permanent’ and ‘daily wages’ employees. In fact, *inheritance can be very usefully employed to carve out roles* from an existing class as shown in Fig. 7.12. The base class is a general computer mouse. By adding specific individual features, we can carve out many types of mouse, i.e. mechanical, optical, optomechanical and wireless mouse. Similarly a person can play the roles of Peon, Professor, Vice-Chancellor, Registrar, Clerk, etc.

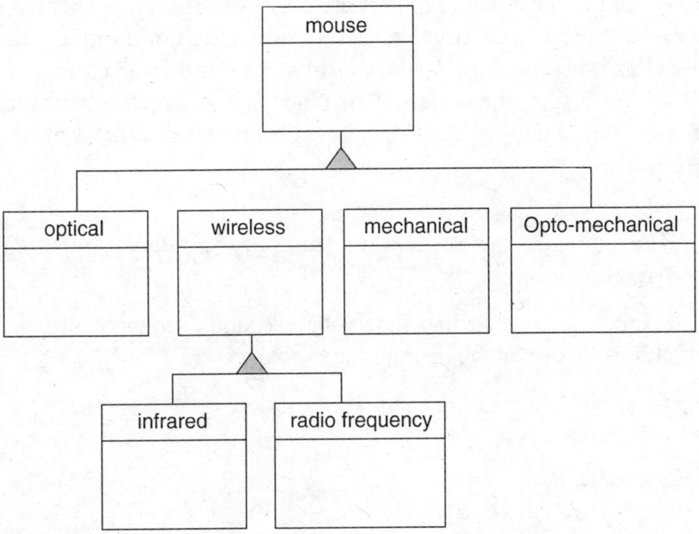

Figure 7.12 *Roles of computer mouse*

It may be further noted that Inheritance can also be used to represent *knowledge*. For example, Fig. 7.12 reveals the knowledge that ‘infrared mouse’ is a kind of wireless mouse. When we go from top to bottom, the classes become specialized. For instance, infrared is a special wireless mouse. Therefore, the **top down approach provides the extensibility** wherein an existing class can be extended to create a more powerful class.

However, when we go from *bottom-up*, the classes become generalized. The bottom-up design allows combination of existing components. If the components are reusable, then this technique provides the much-required *reusability* of the objects.

Function overriding is an entirely different concept than function overloading though both of them depict polymorphic behavior. Overloaded functions have the same scope, i.e. they appear in same class or file. Whereas overriding functions have different scope, i.e. they appear in different classes. A feature-wise difference between the two is given in Table 7.1.

Table 7.1 Difference Between Function Overloading and Overriding

Concept\Feature	Scope	Name	Signature	Virtual Keyword
Functoin overloding	same	same	different	Not required
Function overriding	different	same	same	Required

7.6 ROLE OF CONSTRUCTORS AND DESTRUCTORS IN INHERITANCE

When a class is derived from a base class, there are two types of constructors: constructors of the derived class and the constructors of the base class. At the time of creation of an object of derived type, the execution of constructors starts from top to down in the sense that the constructor of base class is executed before the constructor of its derived class.

At the time of destruction of a derived class object, the destructors are executed in reverse order, i.e. the destructor of derived class is executed before the destructor of its base class.

Example 9. *Write a program in C++ that illustrates the execution process of constructors of base and derived classes.*

Solution: The program given below shows the execution sequence of constructors in the hierarchy of classes by displaying appropriate messages.

```
// This program illustrates the execution of constructors
// of base and derived classes

  #include <iostream.h>
    class xyz { // Base class
     public :
        xyz () // Constructor of Base class
  {
   cout << "\n Constructor of Base class executes";
  }
```

```
        };
    class ABC : public xyz { // Derived class
        public :
    ABC () // Constructor of derived class
    {
     cout << "\n Constructor Of Derived class executes";
    }
};
      void main()
       {
         ABC obj; // object of derived class is created
   }
```

The output of the above program is given below:

```
Constructor of Base class executes
Constructor of Derived class executes_
```

The sequence of messages shows that whenever an object is created, the constructor of base class is executed before the constructor of the derived class.

Example 10. *Write a program in C++ that illustrates the execution process of constructors of base and derived classes.*

Solution: The program given below shows the execution sequence of constructors in the hierarchy of classes by displaying appropriate messages.

```
// This program illustrates the execution of constructors
// of base and derived classes

  #include <iostream.h>
   class xyz { // Base class
    public :
       xyz () // Constructor of Base class
  {
   cout << "\n Constructor of Base class executes";
  }
        };
    class ABC : public xyz { // Derived class
       public :
  ABC () // Constructor of derived class
    {
     cout << "\n Constructor Of Derived class executes" ;
    }
```

```
};
      void main()
       {
         ABC obj; // object of derived class is created
  }
```

The output of the above program is given below:

```
Constructor of Base class executes
Constructor of Derived class executes_
```

The sequence of messages shows that whenever an object is created, the constructor of base class is executed before the constructor of the derived class.

Example 11. *Write a program in C++ that illustrates the execution process of destructors of base and derived classes.*

Solution: The program given below shows the execution sequence of destructors in the hierarchy of classes by displaying appropriate messages.

```
// This program illustrates the execution of destructors
// of Base and derived classes

  #include <iostream.h>
    class xyz { // Base class
     public :
       ~xyz () // Destructor of Base class
  {
   cout << "\n Destructor of Base class executes" ;
  }
       };
     class ABC : public xyz { // Derived class
        public :
   ~ABC () // Destructor of derived class
     {
      cout << "\n Destructor Of Derived class executes" ;
     }
  };
      void main()
       {
         ABC obj;
   } // The object of derived class going out of scope
```

The output of the above program is given below:

```
Destructor of Deriveed class executes
Destructor of Base class executes
```

The sequence of messages shows that whenever an object goes out of scope, the destructor of the derived class is automatically executed before the destructor of the base class is executed by the system.

Example 12. *Consider the following and answer the questions given below:*

```
# include  <iostream.h >
class University
   {
    int NOC; // Number of Colleges
    protected:
       char Uname[25]; // University Name
    public:
       University(){} ;
       char State [25];
       void EnterData();
       void DisplayData();
   };

 class college: public University
   {
     int NOD; // Number of Departments
     char Cname [25]; // College name
     protected:
  void Affliation();
        public:
  college(){};
  void Enrol (int,int);
  void Show();
      };
   class Department: public college
      {
        char Dname[25]; // Department
        int Nof; // No. of faculty members
        public:
        Department(){};
        void Display();
        void Input();
      };
```

Questions:

1. The constructor of which class will be called first at the time of creation of an object of class Department?
2. How many bytes does an object belonging to class Department require?
3. Name member functions which are accessed from the object(s) of class Department.
4. Name the data member() which are accessible from the object(s) of class College.

Solution:

1. The constructor of class University will be called first.
2. 106 Bytes, the reason being that the objects of college and University will also be created along with the object of Department. Therefore, the total size of memory occupied would be:
   Object of University = 52 bytes
   College = 27 bytes
   Department = 27 bytes
   Total = 106 bytes
3. (a) All the public functions of classes – Department, College, and University: EnterData() DisplayData(), Enroll() Show(), Department(), Display(), Input().
   (b) The protected function of class College, i.e. Affiliation().
4. (a) The protected data member of University, i.e. UName
   (b) The private members of self, i.e. DName and NOf.

7.7 VIRTUAL BASE CLASS

Multiple inheritance has its own disadvantages. When a class inherits from two different classes and if both the base classes have a same named member then the problem of name clashing comes as shown in Fig. 7.13.

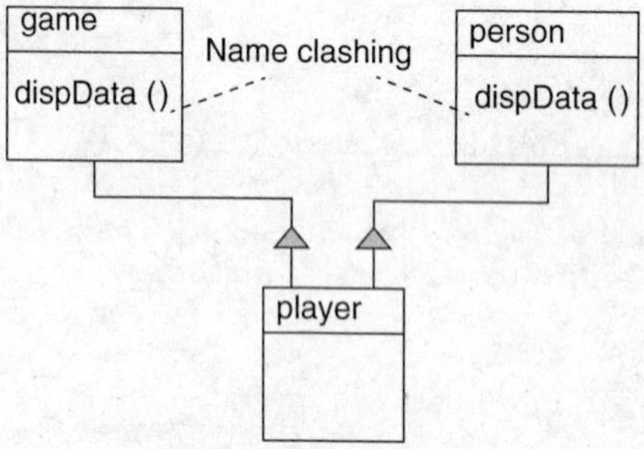

Figure 7.13 *Problem of name clashing in multiple inheritance*

In this situation, the programmer of the derived class player has to necessarily use a scope resolution operator to resolve the problem of name clashing as shown in the following program:

```
// multiple inheritance

# include <iostream.h>
class person {

  protected:
    void dispData() { cout << "\n I am person"; }
      };
class game {

  protected :
    void dispData() { cout << "\n I play a game"; }
     };

class player : public person, public game {
  public:
    void test() {
      person::dispData(); // use of scope resolution operator
                          // to resolve name clashing

      game :: dispData();
      }
  };

void main()
  {
   player pOb;
   pOb.test();
}
```

The output is given below:

```
I am person
I play a game
```

It may be noted that each instance of dispData() has been called in the 'player' class by qualifying it by the name of the class through scope resolution operator.

However, multiple inheritance can also lead to a *graph inheritance* as shown in Fig. 7.14.

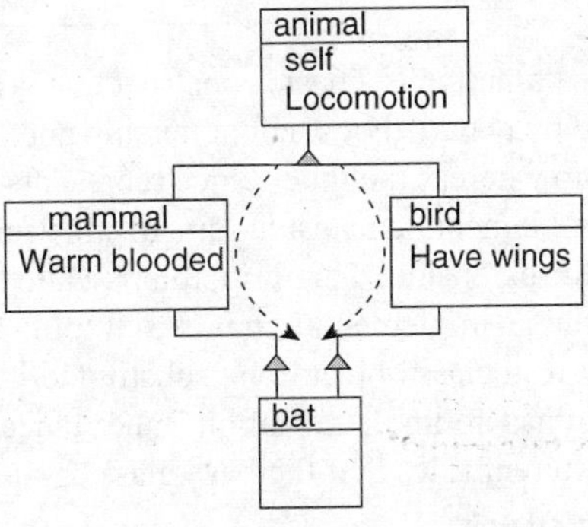

Figure 7.14 *Graph inheritance*

It may be noted that the capability of self locomotion is being inherited by the class 'bat' through two paths: animal–mammal–bat and animal–bird–bat. Thus 'locomotion' property is being inherited twice by the class 'bat'. Moreover, execution of constructor functions can also cause problem. Since, there are two paths, at the time of creation of 'bat' object the 'animal' object would be created twice. This above anomalous situation can be handled by declaring the 'animal' class as virtual by the derived classes as shown below:

```
class animal {


};
class mammal  : public virtual animal {




};
class bird   : public virtual animal {



};
class bat  : public mammal, pubic bird {



};
```

Kindly note that the 'animal' class has been declared as *a virtual base class*, during inheritance declaration. This kind of inheritance makes available only one copy of the inheritable members of the 'animal' class to the derived class 'bat'.

7.8 SUMMARY

In a programming language, a function is a basic construct that is used for 'code reuse'. In OOP, 'code reuse' is accomplished by two methods: containership and inheritance. The containership represents 'has-a' relationship whereas the inheritance represents 'a kind of' (ako) relationship. Containership excellently implements encapsulation. In inheritance, the base class is closed for modification and open for extension. This principle is called 'Open Close Principle'. The separation of an interface from its implementation makes it 'plug compatible'. 'Liskov's Substitution Principle' allows a derived class object to be substituted in place of an object of its base class. A pure virtual function has no implementation. Inheritance can also be used to represent knowledge and carve out different roles that the base class can play. Multiple inheritances can lead to creation of graph inheritance.

MULTIPLE CHOICE QUESTIONS

1. The 'has-a' relationship is depicted by:
   (a) inheritance (b) function
   (c) containership (d) encapsulation
2. A class is called ______ when it has an object of another class.
   (a) base class (b) container class
   (c) derived class (d) virtual class
3. In a composition, the contained object remains:
   (a) hidden (b) visible
4. A containership implements:
   (a) abstraction (b) aggregation
   (c) inheritance (d) polymorphism
5. A protected mode is as good as:
   (a) public (b) private
   (c) global
6. A protected mode allows the base class to be:
   (a) virtual (b) instantiated
   (c) extended
7. In private inheritance, the public members of base class become _______ in the derived class:
   (a) private (b) public
   (c) protected (d) free
8. When a class inherits its properties from more than one base class, it is called as:
   (a) multilevel (b) graph inheritance
   (c) multiple inheritance (d) single inheritance
9. The binding of a virtual function is done at:
   (a) compile time (b) run time
   (c) preprocessing time
10. A class having a pure virtual function is called as:
    (a) concrete class (b) friend class
    (c) base class (d) abstract class

ANSWERS

1. c **2.** b **3.** a **4.** b **5.** b **6.** c **7.** a **8.** c **9.** b **10.** d

EXERCISES

1. What is containership? What is its advantage?
2. In the context of containership, a class is closed for modification. Give your comments.

3. What is inheritance? Explain the different kinds of inheritances with examples.
4. Discuss the use of inheritance in the development of object-oriented programs.
5. In inheritance, discuss the order of invocation of constructors and destructors.
6. Explain virtual function and differentiate it from a pure virtual function.
7. What is the difference between function overloading and overriding.
8. Differentiate between early binding and late binding.
9. What is an abstract class? Differentiate between multiple and multilevel inheritance.
10. What happens when a derived class inherits from a base class using public, private and protected keywords.
11. In this chapter, two classes: university and college have been used. Create a base class, using generalization, so that both these classes inherit from this common base class.
12. From the student class, using specialization, create a 'player' class that has additional members: game, level, giveExtraMarks().
13. Write a main() function that tests the player class developed in Question 12.
14. In the college, it was decided to modify the rules of computation of grades for players. Accordingly modify the classes student and player such that the player class also has a function 'compute_grade'. Use the concept of function overriding such that at run time, for player object, the computation of grade is done using the compute_grade() function of player class. Choose appropriate rules for the computation of grades for the player object.
15. Use a constructor function to instantiate the player object with following default values:

    Game: cricket

    Level: novice
16. Write short notes on the following:
    a. Open close principle
    b. Liskov's substitution principle
17. What is meant by proper inheritance?
18. Define the terms extensibility and reusability.
19. What is a virtual base class? Why it is needed?
20. Explain in brief graph inheritance.

TEMPLATES: CODE SHARING (GENERICITY)

8

8.1 INTRODUCTION TO CODE SHARING

There are many programming situations where same set of operations is applied on different data types. For example, the following function exchanges the contents of two variables of type int.

```
void exchange (int & oldVal, int & newVal)
  {
  int temp;

  temp = oldVal;
  oldVal = newVal;
  newVal = temp;
  }
```

Now, consider a situation where we also need to exchange the contents of variables of type: float and char. Accordingly, we will have to define the following two functions:

Function for float type variables:

```
void exchange (float & oldVal, float & newVal)
  {
  float temp;

  temp     =  oldVal;
  oldVal   =  newVal;
  newVal = temp;
  }
```

Function for char type variables:

```
void exchange (char & oldVal, char & newVal)
  {
  char temp;

  temp = oldVal;
  oldVal = newVal;
  newVal = temp;
  }
```

It may be noted that 99% of the code in the above three functions is same except the type declaration: int, float and char. Now the pertinent question arises that “Can’t we write a *generic* function that can accept all types of parameters?”. If yes, then a tremendous amount of typing effort can be saved. This will not only increase the productivity of the programmer but also reduce the size of the program. However, the programmer must demarcate the program code into two categories: type dependent and type independent codes.

In fact, there are plenty of applications of such generalized (generic) codes. For instance, a compiler needs to maintain variety of tables: symbol table, literal table, opcode table, compiler directive table, function name table, etc. All tables are operated in search–insert fashion and the code for these operations is almost same. Similarly the compiler maintains as many stacks as types of data it works upon.

Code sharing is implemented in C++ through **templates**. A detailed discussion on this feature is given in the following sections.

8.2 TEMPLATES

A template in C++ is used to create generic functions and classes. The format of template declaration is given below:

```
template <class ugType>
```

where template is a keyword; “<” is the standard left angled bracket or sign for less than operator; class is a keyword; ugType, user defined generic type; “>” is the standard right angled bracket or sign for greater than operator.

The user-defined type (ugType) becomes the generic type. Let us now rewrite the function exchange() of Section 8.1 as a generic function.

```
template <class myType> // declare a function template

void exchange (myType & oldVal, myType & newVal)
  {
  myType temp;

  temp = oldVal;
  oldVal = newVal;
  newVal = temp;
  }
```

It may be noted that we have used a generic type called ‘myType’ to declare the variables in the generic function ‘exchange’. This generic type (myType) would get substituted at run time by whichever type of data is sent by the programmer. Thus, templates use run time polymorphism to bind the data with their types.

Example 1. *Write a program that uses the generic function exchange() and tests it for variety of types of data.*

Solution: The required program is given below:

```
// This program creates a function template

# include <iostream.h>

template <class myType> // declare a function template

void exchange (myType & oldVal, myType & newVal)
   {
      myType temp;

      temp = oldVal;
      oldVal = newVal;
      newVal = temp;
   }
void main()
   {
    int val1 = 20, val2 = 30;
    exchange (val1, val2);
    cout << "\n The exchanged integer values  are:" << val1 << " and
    " << val2;

    float fval1 = 15.5, fval2 = 11.7;
    exchange (fval1, fval2);
    cout << "\n The exchanged float values are:" << fval1 << " and "
    << fval2;

   char cval1 = 'A', cval2 = 'C';
   exchange (cval1, cval2);
   cout << "\n The exchanged  character values  are:" << cval1 << "
   and " << cval2;

    }
```

The output of the program is given below:

```
The exchanged integer values are: 30 and 20
The exchanged float values are: 11.7 and 15.5
The exchanged character values are: C and A
```

It may be noted that the generic function exchange() has been able to work with various types of data.

Example 2. *Write a function template called search( ) that searches an element (generic type) from a given list of N elements. It returns 1 when the element is found 0 otherwise. Also write a generic function called readList( ) that reads a list of N elements.*

Solution: We will use an array of *N* locations of generic type. However, the size of array *N* and the index *i* will be declared as integers because these variables are type dependent.

The required functions are given below:

```
// This generic function searches an element in a list of elements of
generic type.

template <class myType>
 int search (myType list[], myType element, int N)
    {
      int i, flag;
      flag =0;
      for (i =0; i < N; i++)
      {
   if (element == list[i])
         {
    flag = 1;
    break;
    }
   }
    return flag;
     }

// This generic function reads a list of N elements
    template <class myType>
    void readList(myType list[], int N)
      {
       int i;
       cout << "\n Enter the elements of the list one by one";
       for (i = 0; i < N; i++)
      {
       cin >> list[i];
      }
       }
```

Example 3. *Write a menu driven function main( ) that tests the working of the generic functions developed in Example 2 for integer and float values.*

Solution: The required function main( ) is given below:

```
void main()
      {
    int intList[20], intVal;
    float realList[20], realVal;
    int size, choice, result;
      cout << "\n Menu";
      cout << "\n";
      cout << "\n Integer list 1";
```

```
    cout << "\n float list 2";
    cout << "\n Quit 3";
    cout << "\n";
    cout << "\n Enter your choice :";
    cin >> choice;
      switch (choice)
      {
       case 1: cout << "\n Enter the size of the integer list";
             cin >> size;
             readList(intList, size);
             cout << "\n Enter the element to be searched";
             cin >> intVal;
             result = search (intList, intVal, size);
             if (result == 1)
               cout << "\n Element found";
             else
               cout << "\n Not Found";
             break;
       case 2: cout << "\n Enter the size of the float list";
             cin >> size;
             readList(realList, size);
             cout << "\n Enter the element to be searched";
             cin >> realVal;
             result = search (realList, realVal, size);
             if (result == 1)
               cout << "\n Element found";
             else
               cout << "\n Not Found";
             break;
       case 3: break;
      }
   }
```

A sample output is given below:

```
Menu

Integer list  1
float   list  2
Quit          3
```

```
Enter your choice :1
Enter the size of the integer list5
Enter the elements of the list one by one23 45 56 67 78
Enter the element to be searched 67
Element found
```

```
Enter your choice :2
Enter the size of the float list 5
Enter the size of the list one by one 4.2 65.4 7.23 5.1 9.2
Enter the element to be searched65.4
Element found_
```

8.3 GENERIC CLASSES

Similar to functions, we can also create generic classes in the form of class templates. The format of a *class template* is given below:

```
template<class ugType>   ⎫
class<name>              ⎪
{                        ⎬ classtemplate
                         ⎪
};                       ⎭
```

where template is a keyword; "< " is the standard left angled bracket or sign for less than operator; class is a keyword; ugType, user defined generic type; ">" is the standard right angled bracket or sign for greater than operator.

Note: The template declaration followed by class declaration is jointly called as a *class template*.

Example 4. *Write a class template called stack that offers the following services for generic type of data.*

1. *Push an element on a stack.*
2. *Pop an element from a stack.*

Solution: The required class is given below:

```
// A class template

# include <iostream.h>
template <class myType>
 class stack {
      myType stak[20];
      int top,N;
   public:
      stack(int size = 20) {top = -1; N = size;};
      int push (myType item); // return 1 if operation successful
                              // 0 otherwise
```

```
    int  pop (myType &item);
  };

template <class myType>
int stack <myType> :: push (myType item)
   {
    if (top < N)
      {
  top++;
  stak[top] = item;
  return 1;
 }
   else
   return 0;
    }
template <class myType>
int stack <myType> :: pop (myType &item)
   {
    if (top > -1)
      {
      item = stak[top];
      top--;
      return 1;
       }
      else
      return 0;
 }
```

It may be noted that when a member function of a generic class is declared outside the class then it has to be separately defined as a template. The format of defining a member function is given below:

```
template <class ugType>
<return type> <class name> <<ugType>> :: <function name> (arguments)
```

Note: <ugType> has to be written within a pair of angled brackets (< and >).

For example, the push() function of generic class called 'stack' has been declared as given below:

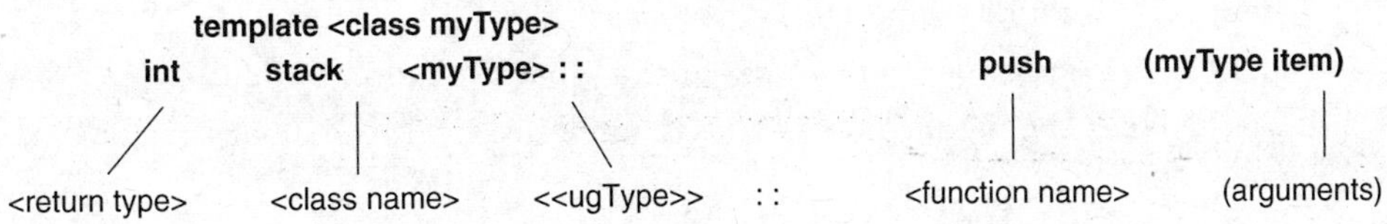

Note: An object of generic type class can be created by qualifying (or type casting) the statement by the type for which the object is desired. The format of object creation for a generic class is given below:

```
<class name> <<typeOb>> <object name>
```

where class name is the name of the class; “<” is the standard left angled bracket or sign for less than operator; typeOb is the type of data for which the object is required; “>” is the standard right angled bracket or sign for greater than operator; object name, name of the object to be created.

For example, an object named ‘chOb’ of type stack that works on char type of data can be created by the following statement:

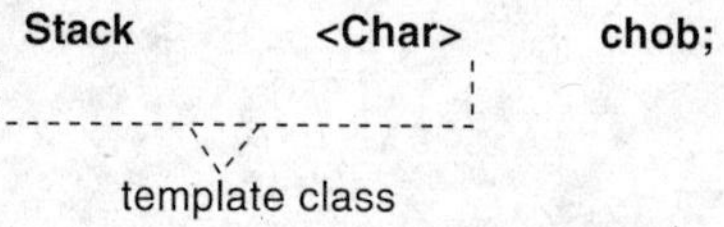

Kindly note that angled brackets are necessary for type casting the required object. The name of the class juxt aposed with the type in angled brackets (i.e. stack <char>) is called a *template class*.

Example 5. *Write the function main to test both the stacks for values 70 and 23.54 to be pushed and popped from the integer and float stacks, respectively.*

Solution: The required function main() is given below:

```
void main()
     {int size = 5;
  int intVal;
  float realVal;
  int result;
  stack <int> intOb(size); // create a stack of int type
  result = intOb.push(70); // push 70 on the integer stack
  if (result == 1)
     cout << "\n item pushed successfully";
  else
     cout << "\n stack full";
  result =intOb.pop (intVal);
  if (result == 1)
    cout << "\n The item popped = " << intVal;
  else
    cout << "\n stack empty";
  stack <float> realOb(5); // create a stack of float type
  result = realOb.push(23.54); // push 23.54 on the float stack
  if (result == 1)
```

```
      cout << "\n item pushed successfully";
   else
      cout << "\n stack full";

   result = realOb.pop (realVal);
   if (result == 1)
     cout << "\n The item popped = " << realVal;
   else
     cout << "\n stack empty";
    }
```

The output of the above program is given below:

```
item pushed successfully
The item popped = 70
item pushed successfully
The item popped = 23.540001
```

It may be noted that same class has been used to instantiate two different objects capable of working on integer and float type data, respectively. Therefore, a generic class is also known as a **parameterized class**.

There is only one piece of generic code which is being shared by different objects working on different types of data. Thus, we can say that *templates help us in* **sharing the code** *among structurally similar family of objects or functions*.

8.4 TEMPLATES WITH MORE THAN ONE GENERIC PARAMETER

A template can have more than one generic parameter as shown by the following declaration:

```
template <class genType1, class genType2>
```

The above template declaration is using two generic types: genType1 and genType2. The advantage of this feature of C++ is that a function template or class template can be called for more number of generic parameters.

Consider the following function template:

```
template <class T, class U>

void test (T x, U y)
  {
    U result;
    result = x + y;
    cout << "\n result = "<< result;
  }
```

It may be noted that it is using two generic types: *T* and *U*. It adds two formal parameters *x* and *y* of type *T* and *U*, respectively. The sum is stored in a variable called 'result' of type U. Thereafter the contents of 'results' are printed.

Example 6. *Write a complete program that uses the generic function test(), developed above and tests it for various combination of parameters of different types.*

Solution: We would test the generic function for various combinations of values of types int, float and char. The complete program is given below:

```
# include <iostream.h>

template <class T, class U>

void test (T x, U y)
  {
    U result;
    result = x + y;
    cout << "\n result = "<< result;
  }

 void main()
   {
   cout << "\n sending int, float, the result would be of float type";
   test (25, 65.34);
   cout << "\n sending char, int, the result would be of int type";
   test ('A', 10);
   cout << "\n sending int, char, the result would be of char type";
   test (5, 'B');
   cout << "\n sending float, int, the result would be of int type";
   test (10.23, 10);
   }
```

The output of this program is given below:

```
sending int, float, the result would be of float type
result = 90.34
sending char, int, the result would be of int type
result = 75
sending int, char, the result would be of char type
result = G
sending float, int, the result would be of int type
result = 20_
```

It may be noted that the generic function is able to work with two generic parameters. It is giving correct results for various combinations of different types of data.

8.5 SUMMARY

A generic function and class can accept parameters of different types. It allows code sharing with a view to reduce typing effort, increase productivity and reduce the size of the program. The code of a program can be comfortably divided into two parts: type dependent and type independent. The 'generic type' gets substituted at runtime by the type of data supplied to the generic function or class. A template declaration followed by a class declaration is jointly called a '**class template**'. The name of class juxt aposed with a type in angled brackets is called a '**template class**'. A template can have more than one generic parameter.

MULTIPLE CHOICE QUESTIONS

1. A generic function increases:
   (a) productivity (b) program length
   (c) typing effort
2. A template in C++ is used to create _______ functions
   (a) virtual (b) generic
   (c) recursive (d) friend
3. The templates use_____ polymorphism to bind the data with their types
   (a) compile time (b) runtime
4. A generic class is called as:
   (a) base class (b) derived class
   (c) parameterized class (d) friend class
5. Templates help us in sharing the code among structurally ______ family of objects or functions
   (a) dissimilar (b) superior
   (c) conflicting (d) similar

ANSWERS

1. a **2.** b **3.** b **4.** c **5.** d

EXERCISES

1. What is a generic function?
2. How 'code sharing' is implemented in C++?
3. What is a template and how it is defined?
4. Write a template called areaSq() that computes and returns the area of a square. It takes an argument called 'side' of generic type. Test this function for a given side of type: int, float, double.
5. Write a generic function called 'sort()' that sorts a list of given N data items of generic type into ascending order.

6. Write a function main() that tests the above function 'sort()' through a menu driven interface.
7. Differentiate between 'class template' and 'template class'.
8. Write a 'class template' called 'queue' that offers the following services for generic type of data.
   a. add an element on a queue
   b. remove an element from a queue
9. Write a template function called 'searchTab()'. It maintains a symbol table having following format:

Symbol	Value

   The symbol is an array of character types whereas the value can be of any one of the available type for a particular table, i.e. int, float, char, etc.
10. Write a function main() that tests the above function 'searchTab()' for a symbol of type int.
11. Write a function main() that tests the above function 'searchTab()' for a symbol of type float.

9 OPERATOR OVERLOADING

9.1 INTRODUCTION

Let us consider a situation where we have a class called 'length' which represents the length of an item (say cloth) in feet and inches. Its class diagram is shown in Fig. 9.1.

length
feet inches
readData() ShowData()

Figure 9.1 *A class called 'length'*

Now if we desire to add two objects of this class type, one of the options is to use a friend function (say **add()**) as shown below:

```
class length {
private:
   int feet;
   int inches;
public:
   void readData();
   void showData();
friend length add(length Ob1, length Ob2); // friend function
};

void length :: readData()
   {
    cout << "\n Enter the length";
    cout << "\n Feet :";
    cin >> feet;
    cout << "\n inches:";
    cin >> inches;
    }
```

```
void length :: showData()
 {
   cout << "\n Feet :" << feet;
   cout << "\n inches:" << inches;
 }

length add(length Ob1, length Ob2) // stand alone friend function
  {
    length tempOb; // create a temporary object
    tempOb.feet = Ob1.feet + Ob2.feet;
    tempOb.inches = Ob1.inches +Ob2.inches;
    if (tempOb.inches > 12)
      {
       tempOb.inches = tempOb.inches - 12;
       tempOb.feet++;
       }
   return tempOb;
  }
```

The following main() function tests the above given class.

```
 void main()
   {
    length Ob1,Ob2,Ob3;
    cout << "\n The first object";
    Ob1.readData();
     cout << "\n The second object";
    Ob2.readData();

    Ob3 = add (Ob1,Ob2);
     cout << "\n The third object";
    Ob3.showData();
   }
```

A sample output is given below:

```
The first object
Enter the length
Feet :5

inches:10

The second object
Enter the length
Feet :7

inches:8

The third object
Feet :13
inches:6
```

The results are correct. However, there are following drawbacks in this program.

1. *We have used a friend function which has violated the very basic principles of object-oriented programming (OOP), i.e. data and information hiding.* The remedy for this drawback is to make the function add() as member of the class and not a friend.
2. We have used the following functional notation to add the two objects Ob1 and Ob2:

    ```
    Ob3 = add (Ob1 + Ob2);
    ```

    However, it would have been better if we could write and use the following natural looking expression:

    ```
    Ob3 = Ob1 + Ob2;
    ```

This can be achieved by overloading the '+' operator.

A detailed discussion on operator overloading is given in the following section.

9.2 OPERATOR OVERLOADING

The term 'operator overloading' seems to be new but the concept is quite old or perhaps as old as programming languages. In fact in almost every programming language, the operators are already overloaded to work on various data types. For example, the '+' operator is used to add two integers, floats, and characters as shown below:

```
intVal = 20 + 30;
realVal = 23.54 + 67.31;
alphaVal = 'A' + 'S';
```

where intVal, realVal, and alphaVal are of int, float and char type, respectively.

It may be noted that the compiler automatically recognizes the data types of the participating variables in arithmetic expressions given above. Similarly, the operators: '–', '*', '/', etc are also overloaded to work on different types of data. In C++, the capacity of these operators can be further enhanced to work on objects of user defined classes. The precise definition of this concept is given below:

Operator overloading: the enhanced capacity of C++ operators to work on objects of user defined classes is called as operator overloading. *An overloaded operator is a user defined function that implements the desired operation on the objects.*

Operator overloading is yet another form of polymorphism supported by C++. Similar to functions, the C++ operators can also be overloaded to perform operations on user defined objects. For example the normal '+' operator can be taught to add two objects (say cup objects) as shown in Fig. 9.2.

Figure 9.2 *Addition of objects*

Let us now understand as to how to overload various types of operators supported by C++. A category wise discussion on overloading of operators is given in the following sections.

9.3 BINARY OPERATORS

The syntax of overloading of an operator in C++ is given below:

```
<return type> operator <op> (argument list)
```

where return type is the type of object or value to be returned by the overloaded operator; operator is a keyword of C++; <op>, the operator which is to be overloaded; <argument list>, the list of formal parameters.

Let us now modify the class 'length' to include an overloaded operator function for operator '+'. The modified class is given below:

```
class length {
  private:
   int feet;
   int inches;
  public:
   length operator + ( length Ob); // overloaded operator function.
   void readData();
   void showData();
};
void length :: readData()
  {
   cout << "\n Enter the length";
   cout << "\n Feet :";
   cin >> feet;
   cout << "\n inches:";
   cin >> inches;
   }
void length :: showData()
 {
   cout << "\n Feet :" << feet;
   cout << "\n inches:" << inches;
 }
length length :: operator + (length Ob) // overloaded operator function
  {
    length tempOb; // create a temporary object
    tempOb.feet = feet + Ob.feet;
    tempOb.inches = inches +Ob.inches;
    if (tempOb.inches > 12)
      {
       tempOb.inches = tempOb.inches -12;
       tempOb.feet++;
       }
   return tempOb;
  }
```

It may be noted that the overloaded operator function is part of an object (say Ob1). The function is designed to receive an object as argument (say Ob2). It returns an object (say Ob3) to the calling function or object. Thus, there are following three objects involved in the above given overloaded operator function for the arithmetic operator '+'.

a. The function itself belongs to an object of type length (say Ob1).
b. The function is receiving a second object of type length (say Ob2).
c. The function is returning back the third object tempOb to a calling object (say Ob3).

The main function that tests the length class is given below:

```
void main()
  {
   length Ob1,Ob2,Ob3;
   cout << "\n The first object";
   Ob1.readData();
    cout << "\n The second object";
   Ob2.readData();
   Ob3 = Ob1 + Ob2; // call the overloaded operator function for '+'
    cout << "\n The third object";
   Ob3.showData();
  }
```

A sample output of the above program is given below:

```
The first object
Enter the length
Feet :5

inches:10

The second object
Enter the length
Feet :7

inches:8

The third object
Feet :13
inches:6
```

It may noted that for same input both the versions of the functions (normal and overloaded) have given the same result. However, the overloaded operator function has allowed us to use the arithmetic operator '+' as an infix binary operator with objects as shown below:

```
Ob3 = Ob1 + Ob2; // Ob1, Ob2, Ob3 are instances of class 'length'
```

From above, it can be summarized that:

1. An overloaded operator '+' is a function which is written little differently than the normal add() function. There is only a notational difference as explained in next two points. It provides a cleaner code that is easier to read.

2. The normal function add() takes two arguments: Ob1 and Ob2. It is called by the following conventional statement for addition of objects:

```
Ob3 = add (Ob1 + Ob2); // conventional function notation
```

3. The overloaded operator '+' function takes only one argument. It is called by the following elegant statement as if the participating objects are as good as data types such as 'int' and 'float' are.

```
Ob3 = Ob1 + Ob2; // The elegant infix notation of adding the objects.
```

4. The logic for the operation has to be provided by the programmer.

Example 1. *Write an overloaded operator function for operator '<' (less than) that compares two 'length' objects and returns 1 if the answer is yes and 0 otherwise.*

Solution: The required overloaded operator '<' is given below:

```
int length :: operator < (length Ob) // overloaded operator function
  {if (feet < Ob.feet)
      return 1;
       else
      if (feet == Ob.feet)
         {
           if (inches < Ob.inches)
           return 1;
           else return 0;
         }
      return 0;
   }
```

Example 2. *Test the overloaded operator '<' of Example 1 to compare two objects Ob1 and Ob2 of class 'length' type.*

Solution: The required main() function that tests the overloaded operator is given below:

```
void main()
    {
     length Ob1,Ob2;
    int result;
     cout << "\n The first object";
     Ob1.readData();
      cout << "\n The second object";
     Ob2.readData();
     result = Ob1 < Ob2; // call to overloaded operator
    if (result == 1) cout << "\n The object 1 is less than object 2";
```

```
    else
       cout << "\n The object 2 is less than object 1";
  }
```

A sample output is given below:

```
The first object
Enter the length
Feet :7

inches:10

The second object
Enter the length
Feet :5

inches:11

The object 2 is less than object 1
```

Similar to the '+' and '<' operators, most of the binary operators can be overloaded as illustrated in example 3.

Example 3. *Write a complete program that uses an operator overloaded function for the equality operator '= =' for comparing the operators of class 'length'.*

Solution: The required complete program is given below:

```
# include <iostream.h>

class length {
private:
int feet;
int inches;
public:
int operator = = (length Ob);
void readData();
void showData();
};
void length :: readData()
  {
    cout << "\n Enter the length";
    cout << "\n Feet :";
    cin >> feet;
    cout << "\n inches:";
    cin >> inches;
    }
```

```
void length :: showData()
 {
   cout << "\n Feet :" << feet;
   cout << "\n inches:" << inches;
 }
int length :: operator == (length Ob) // overloaded operator
                                           function
  {if ((feet == Ob.feet) && (inches == Ob.inches))
       return 1;
       else
       return 0;
    }

  void main()
    {
     length Ob1,Ob2;
     int result;
     cout << "\n The first object";
     Ob1.readData();
      cout << "\n The second object";
     Ob2.readData();
    if (Ob1 == Ob2)
       cout << "\n The objects are equal";
       else
       cout << "\n The objects are not equal";
   }
```

A sample output is given below:

```
The first object
Enter the length
Feet :5

inches:7

The second object
Enter the length
Feet :6

inches:2

The object are not equal
```

It may be noted that, in the above examples, we have overloaded the '+', '<', and '= =' binary operators to work upon objects of 'length' type. Similarly other binary operators can be overloaded to work upon objects of user class type. The only important point to note is that the programmer has to provide the logic for the operations corresponding to the operator being overloaded.

9.3.1 Arithmetic Assignment Operators

C++ supports arithmetic assignment operators such as +=, – =, *= etc. These operators combine two operations: an arithmetic operation and an assignment operation. For example the '*=' operator combines the multiplication ('*') and the assignment ('=') operations as shown below:

```
term *= 5; is equivalent to : term = term * 5;
```

Arithmatic assignment operators can also be overloaded as illustrated by example 4.

Example 4. *Write a complete program that uses an overloaded operator function for the arithmetic assignment operator '*=' to multiply a length object with a given integer number.*

Solution: We would convert the length comprising of feet and inches to inches. The length in inches would be multiplied by the given number (say Num). The resultant length would again be converted back to the format: feet and inches. The required program is given below:

```
# include <iostream.h>

class length {
private:
int feet;
int inches;
public:
void operator *= (int Num);
void readData();
void showData();
};
void length :: readData()
  {
   cout << "\n Enter the length";
   cout << "\n Feet :";
   cin >> feet;
   cout << "\n inches:";
   cin >> inches;
   }

void length :: showData()
 {
   cout << "\n Feet :" << feet;
   cout << "\n inches:" << inches;
 }

void length :: operator *= (int Num) // overloaded operator function
  {
  int temp;
  temp = feet * 12 + inches; // convert the length into inches
  temp = temp * Num; // multiply by Num
```

```
  inches = temp % 12; // convert back the length to feet and inches
  feet = temp/12;
  }
  void main()
    {int Num;
     length Ob;
     cout << "\n The Object";
     Ob.readData();
       cout << "\n Enter the number which is to be multiplied with
object";
     cin >> Num;
     Ob *= Num; // call the overloaded operator function
      cout << "\n The multiplied object :";
     Ob.showData();
    }
```

A sample output of the program is given below:

```
The object
Enter the length
Feet :5

inches:10

Enter the number which is to be multiplied with object: 2

The multiplied object
Feet :11
inches:8
```

9.4 UNARY OPERATORS

A unary operator can also be overloaded. Since a unary operator acts upon only one operand, an overloaded unary operator would obviously take one argument less than the overloaded binary operator. Thus, an overloaded unary operator would take zero arguments, i.e. no formal arguments.

For instance, the following overloaded unary operator '++' increments the contents of the 'inches' component of the length object by one inch.

```
void length :: operator ++ () // overloaded operator function
  {
     inches = inches + 1;
     if ( inches >= 12 )
      {
         inches = inches - 12;
         feet = feet + 1;
      }
  }
```

Example 5. *Write a program that uses the overloaded operator '++' to increment an object of type 'length' class.*

Solution: The required program is given below:

```
# include <iostream.h>

class length {
private:
int feet;
int inches;
public:
void operator ++ ();
void readData();
void showData();
};void length :: readData()
  {
   cout << "\n Enter the length";
   cout << "\n Feet :";
   cin >> feet;
   cout << "\n inches:";
   cin >> inches;
   }

void length :: showData()
 {
   cout << "\n Feet :" << feet;
   cout << "\n inches:" << inches;
 }

void length :: operator ++ () // overloaded operator function
  {
     inches = inches + 1;
     if (inches >= 12 )
     {
       inches = inches - 12;
       feet = feet + 1;
     }
    }
  void main()
    {
     length Ob;
     Ob.readData();
     ++Ob;
     cout << "\n after ++Ob";
     Ob.showData();
     Ob++;
     cout << "\n after Ob++";
     Ob.showData();
    }
```

A sample output is given below:

```
Enter the length
Feet :5

inches:11

after ++Ob
Feet :6

inches:0

after Ob++
Feet :6

inches:1
```

It may be noted that the overloaded operator '++' is working with both the forms, i.e. prefix and postfix forms. However, both the forms increment the object of class 'length' in the prefix mode of the increment operator '++'.

It may be further noted that the overloaded '++' operator does not work in an arithmetic/assignment expression such as given below:

```
Ob2 = ++ Ob1;
```

The compiler gives the error "Not an allowed type".

Similarly, the decrement operator '– –' can also be overloaded.

9.5 INPUT/OUTPUT OPERATORS

The insertion operator '>>' and the extraction operator '<<' can be overloaded to work with user defined types. The main advantage of these overloaded operators is that the input and output operations related to objects become quite elegant and easy to read. Since the input and output operations on objects need to access its private data members, the overloaded operator functions are declared as friends of the class.

The operators '>>' and '<<' use istream and ostream classes, respectively. Therefore, the overloaded operator functions have two operands: *first operand of type stream* and *the second operand is an object*. Both operands are passed by reference. The return type of these functions is the corresponding stream type.

For instance, the prototype of overloaded operator function for '>>' intended for the class length is given below:

```
istream &operator >> (istream &stream, length &lenOb);
```

Similarly, the prototype of overloaded operator function for '<<' intended for the class length is given below:

```
ostream &operator << (ostream &str, length &lenOb);
```

Example 6. *Modify the class called 'length' such that it has the overloaded operator functions for '<<' and '>>', capable of input and output of data for an object of type 'length'.*

Solution: The required class is given below:

```
class length {
private:
int feet;
int inches;
public:
friend ostream &operator << (ostream&, length &); // overloaded
operator '<<'
friend istream &operator >> (istream&,length &); // overloaded operator
'>>'
};
istream &operator >> (istream &stream, length &lenOb)
  {
   cout << "\n Enter Feet :";
  stream >> lenOb.feet;
   cout << "\n Enter inches: ";
   stream >> lenOb.inches;
   return stream;
   }
   ostream &operator << (ostream &str, length &lenOb)
  {
   str << "\n Feet = "<< lenOb.feet << "\n Inches =" << lenOb.inches;
   return str;
   }
```

Example 7. *Write a function main() that tests the class 'length' for input and output through 'cout' and 'cin' statement, respectively.*

Solution: The required function main() is given below:

```
void main()
    {int Num;
     length Ob;
     cout << "\n Read the Object";
     cin >> Ob;
     cout << "\n Show the Object";
     cout << Ob;
    }
```

A sample output of this function main() is given below:

```
Read the object
Enter Feet :9

Read the object
Enter Feet :9

Enter inches: 11

Show the object
Feet = 9
Inches = 11
```

9.6 RULES FOR OPERATOR OVERLOADING

The rules for operator overloading are given below:

1. No new operators can be invented. For instance, we cannot create a power operator such as '**' or '^'.
2. The overloaded operator functions cannot have default arguments.
3. The following operators cannot be overloaded
   a. The dot: '.'
   b. The arithmetic if: '? :'
   c. Size: 'sizeof()'
   d. Scope resolution: '::'
   e. Preprocessing symbol: '#'
4. The assignment operator has a default behaviour for user defined types, i.e. objects. This operator may only be overloaded when the object contains pointers.
5. Operators are inherited by the derived classes except the overloaded assignment operators.

9.7 SUMMARY

Operator overloading is an old concept of exhibiting polymorphism for operators. It is not akin to OOP. In OOP, this concept has been only extended to apply on objects. An overloaded operator is a user defined function that cannot take any default arguments. It is written little differently than a normal function. It provides an elegant infix notation of binary operations on objects. No new operator can be created. An overloaded I/O operator has two arguments: stream and object and both are passed by reference. All operators cannot be overloaded. For instance, the operators like: '::', '#', sizeof(), etc. cannot be overloaded.

MULTIPLE CHOICE QUESTIONS

1. An overloaded operator is a user defined function that operates on:
   (a) data (b) operators
   (c) objects (d) classes
2. Operator overloading is a form of:
   (a) polymorphism (b) inheritance
   (c) containership (d) generosity
3. An overloaded unary operator takes ________ arguments.
   (a) one (b) two
   (c) three (d) zero
4. We cannot create any ________ operator by using operator overloading
   (a) new (b) unary (c) binary
5. An overloaded operator cannot have _______ arguments
   (a) multiple (b) default (c) pointer

ANSWERS

1. (c) **2.** (a) **3.** (d) **4.** (a) **5.** (b)

EXERCISES

1. What is meant by overloading an operator? What is the purpose behind it?
2. Modify Example 1 such that it overloads the '–' operator for subtraction of one length object from another.
3. Write a complete program that uses overloaded operator '>' to compare the marks of two student objects (Chapter 4).
4. Modify Question 3 (the above question) so as to obtain a merit list of *N* students of a class on the basis of marks secured by the students.
5. Write a complete program that uses an overloaded operator function for arithmetic assignment operator '*=' to add two length objects.
6. Write a program that uses the overloaded operator '– –' to decrement an object of length type.
7. What are the operators that cannot be overloaded?
8. List the rules for operator overloading.

FILE HANDLING IN C++

10

10.1 FILE CONCEPTS

We know that every program or sub-program consists of two major components: algorithm and data structures. The algorithm takes care of the rules and procedures required for solving the problem and the data structures contain the data. The data is manipulated by the procedures for achieving the goals of the program as shown in Fig. 10.1.

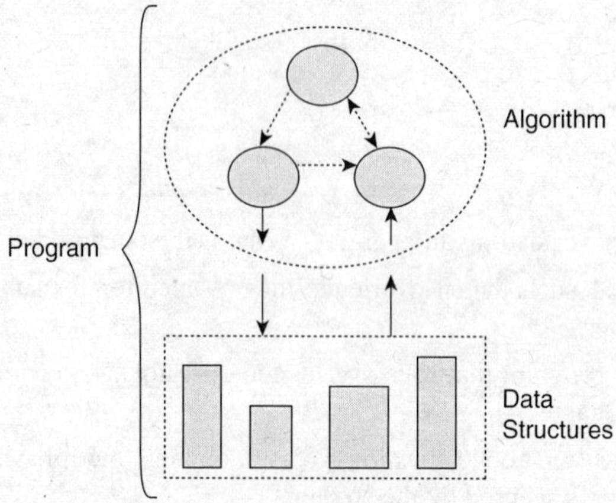

Figure 10.1 *The structure of a program or sub-program*

In object-oriented programming (OOP), an object is central to the ideology. The object has two components: states and behaviours. The states and behaviours model the data and procedures, respectively. Each behaviour is implemented as a subprogram having arrangement similar to that in Fig. 10.1.

A data structure is volatile by nature in the sense that its contents are lost as soon as the execution of the program is over. Similarly, an object also loses its states after the program is over. If we want to permanently store our data or want to create persistent objects then it becomes necessary to store the same in a special data structure called file. The file can be stored on a second storage media such as hard disk. In fact, vary large data is always stored in a file.

Now, any thing stored on a permanent storage such as hard disk is called a file. For example, MBR (master boot record), FAT (file allocation table), partition table, programs, data files, etc. are examples of files.

Let us consider the information recorded in Fig. 10.2.

001	Ajay	50
002	Ram	67
003	John	70
004	Hasan	69

Figure 10.2 *Information about students*

Each entry into the table shown in Fig. 10.2 is a set of three data items: Roll number, Name and Marks. The first entry states that the Roll number and total marks of a student named as Ajay are 001 and 50, respectively. Similarly the second entry relates to a student named as Ram whose Roll number is 002 and total marks equal to 70. Each entry of the table is also known as a record of a student. The term *record* can be defined as *a set of related data items of a particular entity such as a person, machine, place, or operation. An individual data item within a record is known as a* field. When a field assumes unique values then it is called a *key-field*. For example, 'Roll' is the key-field in the record of the student as shown in Fig. 10.3.

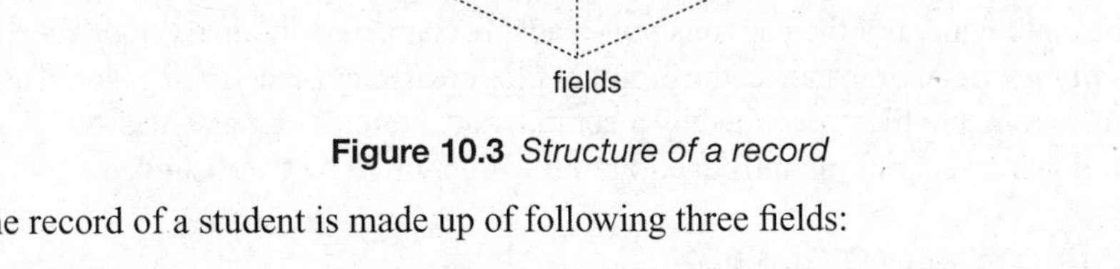

Figure 10.3 *Structure of a record*

Thus, the record of a student is made up of following three fields:

1. Roll number
2. Name
3. Marks

Let us assume that a particular class has 30 students. Now, the entire information of the class consisting of 30 records is referred to as a file. The arrangement of records in the file is shown in Fig. 10.4.

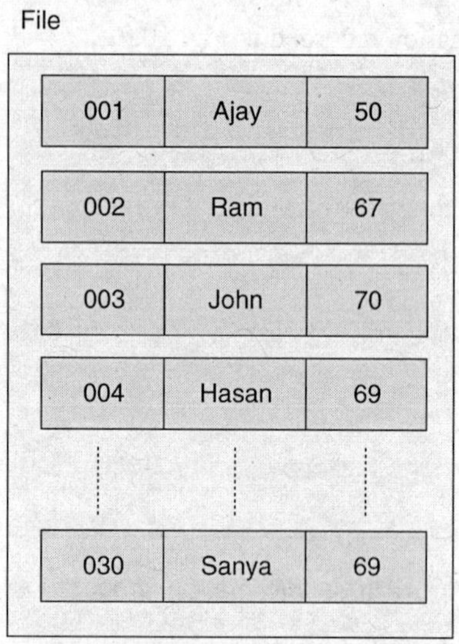

Figure 10.4 *File: collection of records*

A *file* can be precisely defined as *a logical collection of records where each record consists of a number of items known as fields*. The records in a file can be arranged in the following three ways:

1. *Ascending/descending order*: the records in the file can be arranged according to ascending or descending order of a key field. For example, the records in the file of Fig. 10.4 are in ascending order of its Roll field.
2. *Alphabetical order*: if the key field is of alphabetic type then the records are arranged in alphabetical order.
3. *Chronological order*: in this type of order, the records are stored in the order of their occurrence, i.e. arranged according to dates or events. If the key-field is a date, i.e. date of birth, date of joining, etc. then this type of arrangement is used.

When the data of a file is stored in the form of readable and printable characters then the file is known as a **text file**. It is a special type of file that does not contain records but only characters. On the other hand, if a file contains non-readable characters in binary code then the file is called as a **binary file**. For instance, the program files created by an editor are stored as text files whereas the executable files generated by a compiler are stored as binary files.

In the following sections, an introduction to files supported by C++ is given.

10.2 FILES AND STREAMS

In C++, a stream is a data flow from a source to a sink. The sources and sinks can be any of the input/output (I/O) devices or files. For input and output, there are two different streams called input stream and output stream as shown in Fig. 1.2. We have already used the following unformatted I/O streams in our previous programs:

Stream	Description
cin	Standard input stream
cout	Standard output stream
cerr	Standard error stream

The standard source and sink are keyboard and monitor screen, respectively. These unformatted streams are initialized whenever the header file <iostream.h> is included in a program. However, we need to use the operators '<<' and '>>' to implement these streams.

The important stream classes required for file I/O are ifstream, ofstream and fstream. A brief discussion on these streams is given below:

ifstream: It is the input file stream class. Its member function open( ) associates the stream with a specified file in an input mode. For example, if it is desired to open a file called "xyz. dat" for input then the following statements can be used.

```
ifstream myfile;
myfile.open ("xyz.dat");
```

The above declaration means creating an input stream called myfile and associating it with the file called "xyz.dat". In addition to open(), ifstream class inherits the following functions from istream class.

(i) get( ); (ii) getline( ); (iii) read( ); (iv) seekg( ); (iv) tellg( )

ofstream: It is the output file stream class. Its member function open( ) associates the stream with a specified file in an output mode. For example, if it is desired to open a file called "abc. dat" for output then the following statement can be used:

```
ofstream yourfile;
yourfile.open ("abc.dat");
```

The above declaration means creating an output stream called yourfile and associating it with the file called "abc.dat". In addition to open(), ofstream inherits the following functions from ostream class

(i) put( ); (ii) write( ); (iii) seekp( );, (iv) tellp( )

fstream: It supports files for simultaneous input and output. It is derived from ifstream, ofstream and iostream classes. The functions associated with this stream are:

1. open: This associates the stream with a specified file.
2. close: It closes the stream.
3. close all: It closes all the opened streams.
4. seekg: Sets current 'get' position in a stream.
5. seekp : Sets current 'put' position in a stream.

6. tellg: Returns the current 'get' position in a stream.
7. tellp: Returns the current 'put' position in a stream.

The header file 'fstream.h' contains all the class declarations required for file I/O. Even 'iostream.h' is included in 'fstream.h' and therefore, 'fstream.h' should be included in a program that manipulates files.

10.3 OPENING AND CLOSING A FILE (TEXT FILES)

A file can be opened in C++ by two methods:

1. By using the constructor of the stream class to be used.
2. By using the open( ) function of the stream class to be used.

The first method is simple to start with. Let us consider a situation wherein we desire to open a file called "message.dat" containing the following text:

"When you feel angry, keep your mouth shut.
Don't talk and your anger will be fifty percent gone.
Drink some cold water and it will be seventy five
percent gone. Get out of the house and take a walk,
and it will be one hundred percent gone."

We will open this file by using the default constructor of the ofstream class by the following statement:

```
ofstream myfile ("message.dat");
```

The above declaration means open an output stream called myfile and initialize it with the name "message.dat". The "message.dat" is the name of the file lying on the hard disk. However, in the program it will be known as myfile. Thus, whatever is written in myfile stream in the program, will actually be written into the file "message.dat". Since a simple text is to be written into the file, we can use the operator << to write the data. The following program creates the required file:

```
//This program creates a file called "Message.dat"
#include <fstream.h> // Required for file I/O
  main()
  {
    ofstream myfile ("message.dat");
    if (!myfile)
      { // check if the file is opened or not
          cout << "\n Cannot open this file .." ;
          return 1;
      }
   myfile << "\n When you feel angry, keep your mouth shut.\n";
   myfile << "Don't talk and your anger will be fifty percent gone.\n";
   myfile << "Drink some cold water and it will be seventy five\n";
   myfile << "percent gone. Get out of the house and take a walk\n";
```

```
    myfile << "and it will be one hundred percent gone.";
     myfile.close(); //close the file
    return 0;
  }
```

It may be noted from the above program that the stream myfile has been used inside the program instead of 'cout' stream to write the text in the file with the help of the operator '<<'. Moreover, a function close( ) has been used to close the file at the end of the program.

The desired file called "message.dat" has been created by the above program in the current directory. Let us open the file in a text editor (say notepad) to verify the contents. The snapshot of notepad is given in Fig. 10.5:

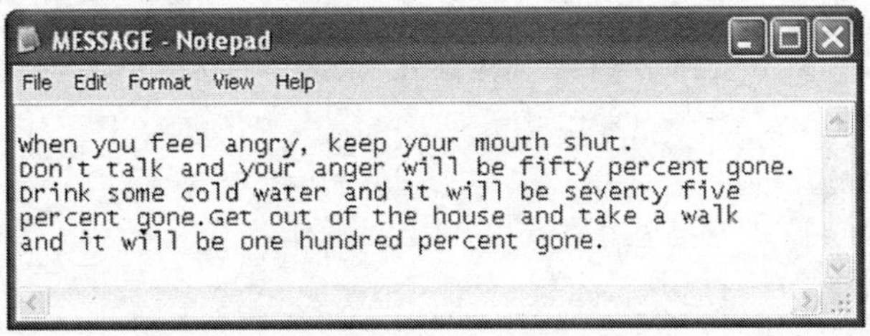

Figure 10.5 *The contents of 'message.dat'*

It may be observed that not only the above program has created the desired file: 'message.dat' but also it contains the correct contents.

We can open the created file for input by using the default constructor of the ifstream class by the following statement:

```
ifstream yourfile ("message.dat");
```

The above declaration means: open an input stream called yourfile and initialize it with the name "message.dat". Thus, the file "message.dat" will be known as yourfile in the program. Since it is a simple text file, we can use the operator '>>' to read the data from the file. However, there is a limitation of the operator '>>' in reading a string containing blanks or white space characters. The operator '>>' stops the input at the occurrence of first white space in the input string. Thus, we can read a word at time from the text file by the '>>' operator.

However, for reading entire lines of text, C++ provides get( ) and getline( ) functions as input member functions of the ifstream class. It also provides a put( ) function as output member function of the ofstream class. These functions are discussed in the following sections.

10.3.1 Function get( )

This function is similar to operator '>>' except that it includes white space characters or blanks in the input string. However, it stops at '\n', the new line character. This function can be used in one of the following variations:

1. get (ch) (i)
2. get (ch, n) (ii)

The first variation of get( ) reads a character at a time from the stream whereas the second variation reads a string of characters of length $n - 1$. In fact, it reads $n - 1$ number of characters for a specified size n.

Let us now write a program that reads the file "message.dat" for us. We will use function get( ) to read a line at a time from the file in a variable called row and repeat this task as many times as there are text lines in the file. The program is given below:

```
// This program reads a file called Message.dat

#include <fstream.h>
#include <conio.h>

main()
{
        ifstream yourfile ("message.dat"); // Open file for input
  char row[80],ch;
  int i;
  clrscr();
  if (!yourfile)
      {
          cout << "Cannot open file .. ";
            return 1;
          }
      for (i = 1;i <= 6;i++)
      {
          yourfile.get(row,80); // Read a line from the file
          yourfile.get(ch); // Read '\n'
          cout << row << "\n"; // Display the line on the screen
      }
      yourfile.close();
      return 0;
}
```

Note: While reading a line the get( ) function stops at '\n'. Therefore, in the above program an extra get( ) has been used in the form of yourfile.get(ch) to read the end of line, i.e. '\n'.

The output of the above program is given below:

```
When you feel angry,keep your mouth shut.
Don't talk and your anger will be fifty percent gone.
Drink some cold water and it will be seventy five
percent gone.Get out of the house and take a walk
and it will be one hundred percent gone.
```

It may be noted that the above program has not only opened the file "message.dat" but also read the text of the file and displayed on the computer screen.

10.3.2 Function getline( )

The format of the function getline( ) is shown below:

```
getline (ch, N)
```

This function reads a line of characters that terminates with '\n', i.e. a new line character. It reads the characters from a line till it encounters a '\n' or $N - 1$ characters are read, where N is the specified length of the character to be read from the file.

A modified program that uses getline( ) function to read the file "Message.dat" is given below:

```
// This program reads a file called Message.dat from the current directory
// It illustrates the usage of getline() function

 #include <fstream.h>
 #include <conio.h>
 main()
 {
   ifstream yourfile("message.dat"); // open the file in input mode char
row[80];
     int i;
     clrscr();
     if (!yourfile)
          {
               cout << "Cannot open file .. ";
               return 1;
          }
     for (i = 1;i <= 6;i++)
     {
          yourfile.getline(row,80); // Read a line from the file
          cout << row <<  "\n"; // Display it
     }
     yourfile.close();
     return 0;
}
```

The getline( ) and get( ) functions have another variation, wherein their argument list can contain a third argument as shown in the following format:

1. getline(ch, n, c)
2. get(ch, n, c)

The third argument 'c' is known as the terminating character. The default terminating character is '\n', i.e. the new line character.

Example 1. *Modify the above program to read a line from the file "message.dat", terminated by the alphabet 'k'.*

Solution: The required program is given below:

```
// This program illustrates the usage of terminating character
// in the argument of getline function()

#include <fstream.h>
#include <conio.h>
     main()
  {
   ifstream yourfile ("message.dat"); // Open a file for input
   char row[80];
   int i;
   clrscr();
   if (!yourfile)
    {
     cout << "Cannot open file .. ";
     return 1;
    }
   yourfile.getline(row,80,'k'); // Read a line from file terminated by
'k' // terminated by 'l'
   cout << row; // display the line
   yourfile.close();
   return 0;
  }
```

The output of this modified program is given below:

```
When you feel angry,
```

Kindly note that the stream yourfile has read the characters from beginning of the line till it encountered the character "k".

However, it is worth noting that the above programs work only with a particular file called "message.dat". It is quite an inflexible arrangement whereas in a real life situation, we would like these programs to work with any user specified text file.

The desired flexibility can be brought by the following two simple steps:

1. Read the name of file to be opened at run time in a variable of type char.
2. Open the stream in a desired mode and associate the stream with the variable that contains the name of the file to be opened.

The following example opens a file for which the user supplies the name at run time.

Example 2. *Write a program that prompts the user to enter the name of the file to be opened (say "message.dat"). It associates the file name with the output stream (say yourfile) and displays its contents.*

Solution: The required program that reads the name of the file, to be opened, at run time is given below:

```
// This program reads a file
// It illustrates the usage of variable file name

#include <fstream.h>
#include <conio.h>
  main()
   {
       char fname[15]; // variable to store filename
       char row[80];
       int i;
       clrscr();
       cout <<"\nEnter the name of the file to be opened :";
       cin >> fname;
       ifstream yourfile(fname);
       if (!yourfile)
       {
           cout << "\n Cannot open file .. ";
           return 1;
       }
    cout << "\nThe contents of 'message.dat' are...\n\n";
    for (i = 1;i <= 6;i++)
         {
       yourfile.getline(row,80);
                 cout << row << "\n";
       }
       yourfile.close();
       return 0;
   }
```

The output of the program is given below:

```
Enter the name of the file to be opened :message. dat
The contents of 'message.dat' are...

When you feel angry ,keep your mouth shut.
Don't talk and your anger will be fifty percent gone.
Drink some cold water and it will be seventy five
percent gone.Get out of the house and take a walk
and it will be one hundred percent gone.
```

It may be noted that the program has now prompted the user to enter the name of the file to be read. The advantage is that the program has become flexible, i.e. the user can give name of any of the existing files at run time.

Though opening of a file through a constructor is an easy method but the following points should be kept in mind while opening the files:

1. Only one file can be connected to a stream.
2. A file opened in any mode (input or output) must be closed by the function close( ).
3. If a file is opened for output then a new file would be created if no file with the same name already exists otherwise the contents of the existing file will be deleted.

10.3.3 Function put( )

This function writes a single character at a time to the output stream. For example, the following statement will write the character content of character variable 'ch' into the stream called testfile.

```
testfile.put (ch);
```

Example 3. *Write a program that writes the following piece of text in a user defined file (say "thought.dat".). Verify the creation of the file by opening the same in output mode and printing its contents on the screen.*

"True education is that destroys narrow-mindedness"

Solution: We would use the function 'put()' to write the above given text of 47 characters into a user specified file. The required program is given below:

```
//This program illustrates the usage of Put() function
//In this program we will write a line of text in a file
//character by character

#include <fstream.h>
#include <conio.h>
void main()
 {
  char fname[15];
  char text[] = "True education is that destroys narrow-mindedness";
  char line[80];
  int i;
  clrscr();
  cout << "Enter the name of the file to be opened : ";
  cin >> fname;
  ofstream afile(fname);
  for (i = 0;i < 48;i++)
   afile.put(text[i]); // Write a character into the file
  afile.put('\n'); // write end-of-line character
  afile.close();
            // Open the file in Input Mode
  ifstream xfile(fname);
   cout << "\nThe line read from the file is  : ";
```

```
    xfile.getline(line,80); // Read a line from the file
    cout << "\n" << line; // Display it
    xfile.close();
  }
```

The above program writes the text "*True education is that destroys narrow-mindedness*" character by character into a file whose name is provided by the user at run time. The program reads the line from the file and displays it on the screen. The output of the program is given below:

```
Enter the name of the file to be opened : throught.dat

The line read from the file is  :
True education is that destroys narrow-mindedness
```

10.4 OPENING THE FILES BY USING FUNCTION OPEN( )

A file can also be opened in a program by a function called open( ). However, we must specify the stream to be associated with the file. For example a file called "test.dat" can be opened for output by the following set of statements:

```
ofstream newfile;                    (i)
newfile.open ("test.dat");           (ii)
```

The statement (i) declares the stream newfile to be of type ofstream, i.e. output stream. The statement (ii) assigns the file stream to the file called "test.dat". Thus, in the program the file "test.dat" would be known as newfile. The major advantage of this method is that more than one files can be opened at a time in a program.

Example 4. *Write a program that creates a text file called 'copy.dat' which is an exact copy of a given textfile called 'thought.dat'.*

Solution: We will open two streams orgFile and copyFile in input and output streams, respectively. The physical files 'thought.dat' and 'copy.dat' would be assigned to orgFile and copyFile, respectively. The get() and put() functions would be used to copy the contents of orgFile to copyFile. The required program is given below:

```
//This program creates an exact copy of a text file

#include <fstream.h>
#include <conio.h>
 main()
   {
      char orgFile[15],copyFile[15];
      char ch;
```

```
        clrscr();
        cout << "\n Enter the input file name : ";
        cin >> orgFile;
        ifstream orgfile;
        orgfile.open(orgFile);
        if (!orgfile)
         {
               cout << "\nCannot Open Input file .";
               return 1;
         }
        cout << "\n Enter the output file name : ";
        cin >> copyFile;
        ofstream docfile;
        docfile.open(copyFile);
        if (!docfile)
         {
               cout << "\n Cannot Open Input file .";
               return 1;
         }
        while (orgfile)
        {
               orgfile.get(ch);
               docfile.put(ch);
         }
        orgfile.close();
        docfile.close();
        return 0;
    }
```

In order to verify the effectiveness of the above program, let us open the 'copy.dat' in notepad. The snapshot of the notepad is given below:

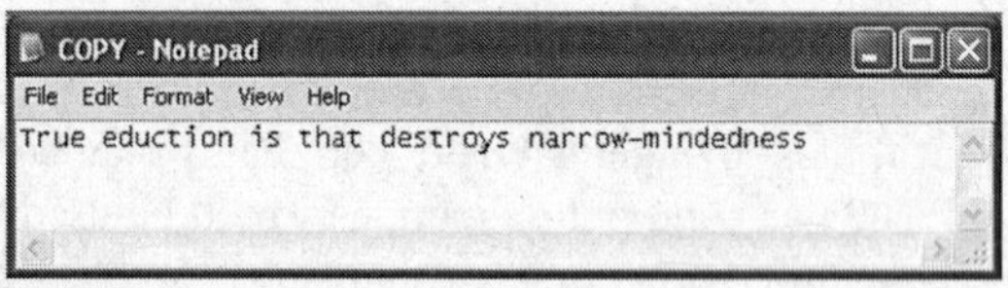

It may noted that the above program has created an exact copy of the 'thought.dat' into a new file called as 'copy.dat'.

10.5 READING AND WRITING BLOCKS AND OBJECTS (BINARY FILES)

In the previous sections, we have used text files. Let us now write binary files which are more versatile and popular among programmers. The major advantage of such files is that they require less memory space for storage of data. Moreover, these files can be used to read or write structured data such as structures, class objects, etc.

For binary files, the functions read() and write() are used to read and write objects, respectively. Blocks of data can also be read or written by these functions. The general form of read( ) function is given below:

```
<name> . read ((char *) & <block>, size);
```

where <name> is the name of the input stream; <block> is the name of the block to be read from the stream; size is the size of the block which can be obtained by a function called size of( ).

The general form of write( ) function is given below:

<name> . write ((char *) & <block>, size);

where <name> is the name of the output stream; <block> is the name of the block to be written into the stream; size is the size of the block.

Note: The type cast (i.e. (char *)) is necessary in the read( ) and write( ) functions.

Let us write the record given below in a file called "Test.dat".

OfficerData

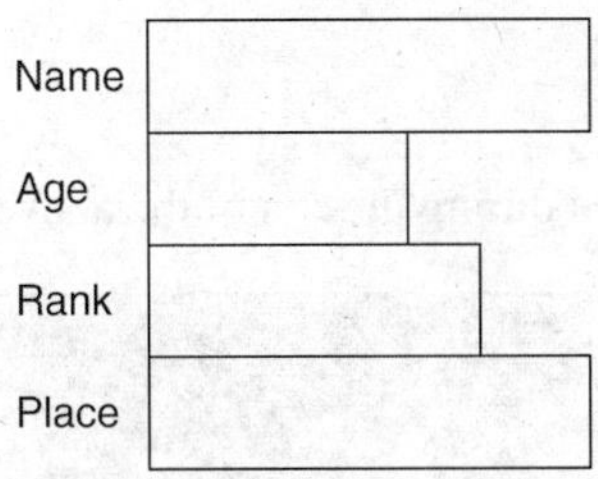

The steps required to do this task are:

1. Create a structure called officer-data.
2. Initialize a structure variable with the given data or read it from the keyboard.
3. Open an output stream (say ofile).
4. Associate the stream ofile with the file "Test.dat".
5. Obtain the size of the structure by the function size of ( ).
6. Write the structure into the file by write( ) function.

The above given steps are implemented in the program given below:

```
// This program writes a block of data into a file

#include <fstream.h>
#include <conio.h>
#include <stdio.h>
void main()
```

```
{
  struct officerData // Declare structure
   {
       char name[15];
       int age;
       char rank[5];
       char place[10];
     };
  int size;
  char fileName[15]; // Initialize the structure variable orec
  officerData offRec;
  cout <<"\n Enter the record of an officer";
  cout <<"\n Name:"; gets(offRec.name); fflush (stdin);
  cout <<"\n Age:"; cin >> offRec.age;
  cout <<"\n Rank:"; gets(offRec.rank);fflush (stdin);
  cout <<"\n Place:"; gets(offRec.place);fflush (stdin);
  cout <<"\n Enter the name of the File to be opened: ";
  gets(fileName);
  ofstream ofile;
  ofile.open(fileName); // open the file for output
  size=sizeof(officer_data); // Compute the size of structure
  ofile.write((char *) &offRec, size); // Write into the file
  ofile.close();

  }
```

The following data was submitted during the run of the above program

```
Enter the record of an officer
Name:Dr. J.P. Gupta
Age:58
Rank:VC
place:Noida
 Enter the name of the File to be opened: test.dat
```

A program that reads the block of data from the file called "Test.dat" and displays it as given below:

```
// This program reads a block of data from a file

#include <fstream.h>
#include <conio.h>
#include <stdio.h>
void main()
 {
    struct officer_data // Declare structure
       {
  char name[15];
  int age;
```

```
char rank[5];
char place[10];
    };
int size;
char fileName[15];
officer_data offRec; // Declare structure variable orec
clrscr();
cout << "\nEnter the name of the file to be opened :";
gets(fileName); fflush(stdin);
ifstream infile;
infile.open(fileName); // Open the File for input
size=sizeof(officer_data); // Compute size of the structure

infile.read((char *) &offRec, size); // Read the structure
cout << "The officer data is :";
cout << "\n Name = " << offRec.name;
cout << "\n Age = " << offRec.age;
cout << "\n Rank = " << offRec.rank;
cout << "\n Place = " << offRec.place;
infile.close();
  }
```

The output of above program is given below:

```
Enter the name of the file to be opened :test.dat
The officer data is :
Name = Dr. J.P Gupta:

Age = 58

Rank = VC

place = Noida
```

It may be noted that the record of the officer was correctly written and read by the above two programs.

Example 5. *Write a program which creates a file containing the records of officers working in a University. The name of the file is provided by the user.*

Solution: The required program is given below:

```
// This program writes a block of data into a file

#include <fstream.h>
#include <conio.h>
#include <stdio.h>
void main()
{
  struct officerData // Declare structure
```

```
   {
     char name[20];
     int age;
     char rank[5];
     char place[10];
    };
 int size, N;
 char fileName[15]; // Initialize the structure variable orec
 officerData offRec;
 cout << "\n Enter the name of the File to be opened: ";
 gets(fileName);
 cout << "\n Enter the number of officers :";
 cin >> N;
 ofstream ofile;

 ofile.open(fileName); // open the file for output
 size = sizeof(officerData); // Compute the size of structure
 cout << "\n Enter the record of  officers one by one";
 for (int i = 1; i <= N; i++)
 {
  cout << "\n Name:"; gets(offRec.name); fflush (stdin);
  cout <<"\n Age:"; cin >> offRec.age;
  cout <<"\n Rank:"; gets(offRec.rank);fflush (stdin);
  cout <<"\n Place:"; gets(offRec.place);fflush (stdin);
  ofile.write((char *) &offRec, size); // Write record into the file
 }
 ofile.close();

 }
```

Example 6. *Write a program which reads a file containing the records of officers working in a University. The name of the file is provided by the user. The records of the officers are displayed in the following format:*

S. NO.	Name	Age	Rank	Place

Solution: The required program is given below:

```
// This program reads block of data into from a file

#include <fstream.h>
#include <conio.h>
#include <stdio.h>
```

```
void main()
{
  struct officerData // Declare structure
   {
       char name[20];
       int age;
       char rank[5];
       char place[10];
     };
  int size, N;
  char fileName[15]; // Initialize the structure variable orec
  officerData offRec;
  cout << "\n Enter the name of the File to be opened: ";
  gets(fileName);
  cout << "\n Enter the number of officers :";
  cin >> N;
  ifstream ofile;

  ofile.open(fileName); // open the file for output
  size = sizeof(officerData); // Compute the size of structure
  cout << "\n\t\t Officer Data";
  cout << "\nS.No.\tName\t\tAge\tRank\tPlace";
  cout << "\n________________________________________";

  for (int i = 1; i <= N; i++)
  {
    ofile.read((char *) &offRec, size); // Read a record into the file
    cout << "\n" << i << " " << offRec.name << "\t" << offRec.age <<
"\t";
    cout << offRec.rank << "\t" << offRec.place;
  }
  ofile.close();
}
```

A sample output of the program is given below:

```
Enter the name of the File to be opend: officer.dat

Enter the number of officers :3

                    Officer Data
 S.No.   Name             Age        Rank       Place
 ----------------------------------------------------------
 1       Dr. J.P. Gupta     58        VC         Noida
 2       Dr. Qasim Rafiq    54        Prof       Aligarh
 3       Dr. Rajendra Sahu  50        Prof       Hyderabad
```

10.5.1 Storing Objects in Files

Normally the contents of an object are lost as soon as the object goes out of scope or the program execution is over. If the information contained in the object is very important then we must try to save it on auxiliary storage such as hard disk so that it can be reused as and when required. In fact, similar to records, objects can also be written into and instantiated from a file. The objects which remember their data and information are called as **persistent objects**.

Thus, a persistent object exists in two forms: in the primary memory, i.e. RAM and the secondary memory such as hard-disk. The RAM-copy of the object represents the current state of the object for that moment, the disk copy of the object represents the old state of the object.

The program can make changes to the object in the primary memory and before going out of scope, the object is written onto the disk in a file. The following example is using the student object for the purpose of illustrating the above discussed concept.

Example 7. *Consider the class called student of Example 1 of Chapter 4 which models the following states and behaviours of a student:*

States

Name
Roll
Marks
Grade

Behaviours

Read_data()
Display_grade()
Compute_grade()

Perform the following operations

1. *Create an object of student type and reads its data.*
2. *Write the object onto a file (say "student.dat").*
3. *Read the object from the file.*
4. *Display the data onto the screen.*

Solution: The required program is given below:

```
// This program illustrates the creation of persistent objects

# include <fstream.h>
# include <stdio.h>

class student {
private:
  char name[20];
  int roll;
```

```
  int marks;
  char grade;
  void compute_grade();
public:
  void read_data();
  void display_grade();
  };

      // Function to read data of a student
  void student :: read_data()
   {
    cout << "\n Enter Name:";
    cin >> name;
    cout << "\n Enter Roll:";
    cin >> roll;
    cout << "\n Enter Marks:";
    cin >> marks;

    compute_grade(); // compute the grade
    }
      // Function to display grade
 void student:: display_grade()
     {
      cout << "\n Name:" << name;
      cout << "\n Roll:" << roll;
      cout << "\n Grade:" <<grade;
     }

    // Function to compute grade
  void student :: compute_grade()
      {
        if (marks >= 80) grade = 'A';
        else
       if (marks >= 70) grade ='B';
       else
         if (marks >= 60) grade = 'C';
         else
           if (marks >= 50) grade = 'D';
           else
             grade = 'E';
      }

 void main()
 {
  int size = sizeof (student);
  student sOb1,sOb2;
  sOb1.read_data();
  char fname[15];
  cout << "\n Enter the name of the file for output:";
```

```
   gets(fname);
   ofstream outfile;
   outfile.open(fname);
   outfile.write((char *) & sOb1, size); // Write Object1 onto file
   outfile.close();
   cout << "\n Enter the name of the file input:";
   gets(fname);
   ifstream infile;
   infile.open(fname);
   infile.read((char *) & sOb2, size); // Read Object2 from the file
   infile.close();
   sOb2.display_grade();
}
```

A sample output of the program is given below:

```
Enter Name:Akshay
Enter Roll:101
Enter Marks:98
Enter the name of the file for output:student.dat
Enter the name of the file input:student.dat
Name:Akshay
Roll:101
Grade:A
```

It may be noted that the student data was supplied for the object 'sOb1'. Its grade was computed and it was stored into a file called "student.dat". The stored object was read in another object called 'sOb2' from the file. From the output, it is verified that the contents have remained intact.

From above, it may be appreciated that this arrangement can be used to store objects on files for their usage at later stage.

Example 8. *Write a program which opens a file whose name is provided by the user (say "studFile.dat"). The program writes N (say 5) number of objects of student types into the file.*

Solution: The required program is given below:

```
// This program writes N number of student objects into a file

# include <fstream.h>
# include <stdio.h>

class student {
```

```
private:
  char name[20];
  int roll;
  int marks;
  char grade;
  void compute_grade();
public:
  void read_data();
  void display_grade();
  };

     // Function to read data of a student
  void student :: read_data()
   {
    cout << "\n Enter Name:";
    cin >> name;
    cout << "\n Enter Roll:";
    cin >> roll;
    cout << "\n Enter Marks:";
    cin >> marks;

    compute_grade(); // compute the grade
   }
     // Function to display grade
 void student :: display_grade()
     {
      cout << "\n Name:" << name;
      cout << "\n Roll:" << roll;
      cout << "\n Grade:" <<grade;
     }

   // Function to compute grade
  void student :: compute_grade()
      {
       if (marks >= 80) grade = 'A';
       else
       if (marks >= 70 ) grade ='B';
       else
         if (marks >= 60) grade = 'C';
         else
           if (marks >= 50) grade = 'D';
           else
             grade = 'E';
       }

 void main()
 {
  int i, N;
  int size = sizeof (student);
```

```
student sOb1;
char fname[15];
cout << "\n Enter the name of the file for output:";
gets(fname);
ofstream outfile;
outfile.open(fname);
cout << "\n Enter the number of objects to be written into the file:";
cin >> N;
for (i = 1; i <= N; i++)
  {
    sOb1.read_data();
    outfile.write((char *) & sOb1, size); // Write Object onto file
  }
outfile.close();
}
```

Note: In this section, only an introduction to persistent objects is being given. A little more effort is required to make those objects persistent which are objects of derived classes and are having pointers.

10.6 DETECTING END OF FILE

As far as files are concerned, till now we have been reading or writing a certain number of characters or objects. While reading a file, a situation can arise when we do not know the number of objects to be read from the file, i.e. we do not know where the file is going to end? A simple method of detecting **end of file** (eof) is by testing the stream in a while loop as shown below:

```
while (<stream>)
  {
     :
  }
```

The condition <stream> will evaluate to 1 as long as the end of file is not reached and it will return 0 as soon as end of file is detected. In simple words, we can say that the while loop will terminate as soon as the eof of <stream> is reached. Consider the following program segment

```
 :
ifstream xfile;
   xfile.open (fname)
 :
while (xfile)
{
 :
}
```

The while loop in this program executes till eof of xfile is reached. The following example illustrates the usage of detection of eof.

Example 9. *Write a program which opens a file created in Example 8 ("studFile.dat"). The program reads the objects from the file till the end of the file.*

Solution: The required program is given below:

```
// This program writes N number of student objects into a file

# include <fstream.h>
# include <stdio.h>

class student {
private:
  char name[20];
  int roll;
  int marks;
  char grade;
  void compute_grade();
public:
  void read_data();
  void display_grade();
  };

      // Function to read data of a student
  void student :: read_data()
   {
    cout << "\n Enter Name:";
    cin >> name;
    cout << "\n Enter Roll:";
    cin >> roll;
    cout << "\n Enter Marks:";
    cin >> marks;

    compute_grade(); // compute the grade
    }
      // Function to display grade
 void student :: display_grade()
     {
       cout << "\n"<< roll << "\t";
       cout << name << "\t" << marks << "\t";
       cout << grade;
     }

    // Function to compute grade
  void student :: compute_grade()
      {
```

```
        if (marks >= 80) grade = 'A';
        else
          if (marks >= 70 ) grade ='B';
          else
          if (marks >= 60) grade = 'C';
        else
           if (marks >= 50) grade = 'D';
           else
             grade = 'E';
      }
  void main()
  {
   int size = sizeof (student);
   student sOb;

   char fname[15];
   cout << "\n Enter the name of the file for input:";
   gets(fname);
   ifstream infile;
   infile.open(fname);
   cout << "\n The Student data";
   cout << "\nRoll\tName\tMarks\tGrade";
   cout << "\n___________________________________";

   while (infile) // till the end of the file
     {
       infile.read((char *) & sOb, size); // Read an Object from file
       sOb.display_grade();
      }
   infile.close();
   }
```

The output is given below:

```
Enter the name of the file for input:studfile.dat
The student data
 Roll   Name     Marks  Grade
  101   Ram        98     A
  102   Sham       86     A
  103   John       89     A
  104   Hasan      90     A
  105   Issac      88     A
  105   Issac      88     A
```

The end of file can also be detected by a function called 'eof()'. This function returns a non-zero value when it detects the end of file else it returns a zero. An example of usage is given in the following program segment:

```
while ( !xfile.eof() )
{
  :
}
```

Example 10. *Modify the function main() of Example 9 such that it uses the function 'eof()' for detecting the end of the file.*

Solution: The required modified function main() is given below:

```
void main()
 {
  int size = sizeof (student);
  student sOb;

  char fname[15];
  cout << "\n Enter the name of the file for input:";
  gets(fname);
  ifstream infile;
  infile.open(fname);
  cout << "\n The Student data";
  cout << "\n Roll\tName\tMarks\tGrade";
  cout << "\n_____________________________";

  while (!infile.eof())
     {
      infile.read((char *) & sOb, size); // Read an Object from file
      sOb.display_grade();
     }
  infile.close();
 }
```

Example 11. *Write an interactive menu driven program that creates a text file (say "input.dat") and then displays its contents. The program also creates another text file (say "output.dat") as copy of the former. However, while copying it converts all the characters into their equivalent uppercase characters.*

Solution: We will use toupper() function to convert the characters read from the original file. The required program is given below:

```
#include <fstream.h>
```

```
#include <stdio.h>
#include <conio.h>
#include <ctype.h>
  void main()
   {
   char fname[15];
   char row [80];
   cout <<   "\n Enter the name of the file to be created : ";
   gets(fname);
   ofstream myfile (fname);
   char ch;
   while (1)
     {
      cout << "\n Enter a line of text :";
      gets (row);
      myfile << row << "\n";
      cout << "\n want to continue ? Y/N";
      cin >> ch;
      if ((ch == 'N') || (ch == 'n'))
        break;
    }
   myfile.close();
                              // convert each line to upper case
    clrscr();                 // and copy into new file
    ofstream tempfile ("output.dat");
    cout <<"\n The input file is...\n";
    ifstream newfile (fname);
      while (newfile)
      {
       newfile.get(ch);
       cout << ch; // write on the display screen
       if (ch !='\n')
       ch = toupper (ch);
       tempfile.put(ch); // write in the target file
      }
      newfile.close();
      tempfile.close();

                        // Display the new file
   cout << "\n The output file is ....\n";
   ifstream yourfile ("output.dat");
    while ( !yourfile.eof() )
      {
       yourfile.getline (row,80);
       cout << row << "\n";
      }
   yourfile.close();
  }
```

The output is given below:

```
 The input file is...
Who is a friend? who is an enemy?
There is no permanent friend but when
You say "no sorry", fifty percent of this friendship
is gone! so who is friend and who is an enemy

 The output file is....
WHO IS A FRIEND? WHO IS AN ENEMY?
THERE IS NO PERMANENT FRIEND BUT WHEN
YOU SAY "NO SORRY", FIFTY PERCENT OF THIS FRIENDSHIP
IS GONE! SO WHO IS FRIEND AND WHO IS AN ENEMY
```

10.7 SUMMARY

Any thing stored on a permanent storage is called a *file*. A set of related data items is known as a record. The smallest unit of a record is called a *field*. A *key field* is used to uniquely identify a record. A file is a logical collection of records. In a serial file, the records are stored in the order of their arrival without considering the key field. On the other hand, in a sequential file, the records are written in a particular order of the key field. The key field is also known as a *primary key*. 'ifstream' and 'ofstream' are input and output streams, respectively. The objects that remember their data and information are called *persistent* objects. The function *eof()* returns 0 when it detects the end of file. An opened file must be closed after its usage.

MULTIPLE CHOICE QUESTIONS

1. A program consists of two major components: algorithm and
   (a) logic (b) code
   (c) data structures (d) output
2. An object has two components: states and
   (a) abstraction (b) behaviours
   (c) encapsulation (d) variables
3. Any thing stored on a permanent storage is called a:
   (a) file (b) data
   (c) information (d) object
4. A set of related data items of a particular entity is called a:
   (a) record (b) file
   (c) data (d) field
5. A field having a unique value is called:
   (a) main field (b) local field
   (c) global field (d) key field

6. A logical collection of records is called a:
   (a) pile (b) group
   (c) file (d) class
7. The stream that supports both input output is called:
   (a) ifstream (b) fstream
   (c) ofstream (d) iostream
8. A file can be opened by a ______ constructor
   (a) copy (b) default
9. The functions read() and write() are used to read() and write()
   (a) data (b) file
   (c) objects (d) information
10. The RAM copy of the object represents its:
    (a) current sate (b) old state

ANSWERS

1. c **2.** b **3.** a **4.** a **5.** d **6.** c **7.** b **8.** b **9.** c **10.** a

EXERCISES

1. Define the terms: field, record and file.
2. In how many ways the records can be arranged in a file?
3. Write an explanatory note on the relationship between files and streams.
4. What are the different methods of opening a file? Explain in brief.
5. Differentiate between get() and getline() functions of ifstream class.
6. How the end of file can be detected? Explain in brief.
7. Write a program which counts the number of records in a given file.
8. Give suitable declarations for the file containing components where each component consists of the following information.

   name: 20 characters

   empId: integer type

   netSal: float type
9. Write a program which creates an exact copy of a given file called Ofile in the form of a new file called Nfile. Choose appropriate component type for this problem.
10. Write a program which counts the number of times a given alphabet appears in a text file.
11. Write a program which searches a given file for a record equal to an input value of empId. The component record structure of the file is as given in Question 8.
12. Write a program which reads a text file called document and generates a table of frequency count of alphabets appearing in the text. The output should be displayed in the following form

Document

Alphabet	Count

13. A product record is given below.

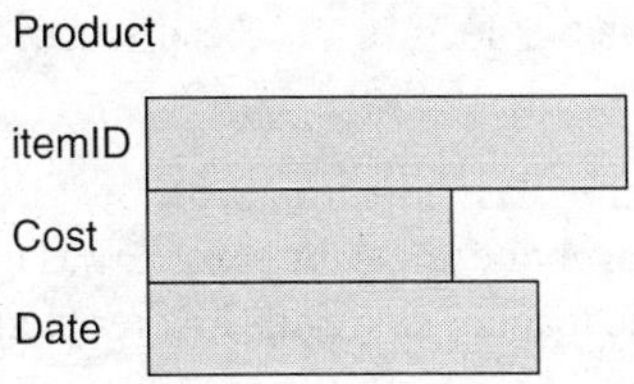

Choose appropriate data types for the fields. Write a program which reads a file of such records and prints them in the following format.

Product

itemID	Cost	Date

14. Assuming that a text file named 'book', already contains some text written into it, write a function named noVowel (), that reads the file 'book' and creates a new file named newBook, which shall contain only those words from the file 'book' which don't start with an upper case vowel, i.e. with 'A', 'E', 'I', 'O', 'U'. For example if the file 'Book' contains: "One and Only One". Then the file 'newBook' shall contain: "and".
15. What is eof? Explain its utility.
16. Write an interactive menu driven C++ program that creates a text file (say myDoc) and then display the file. Create another text file (say lowDoc) by converting each line of the 'myDoc' file into a lowercase string. Display the contents of 'lowDoc' file.
17. Write an interactive menu driven C++ program that creates a text file (say myDoc) and then displays the file. Create another text file (say revDoc) by reversing each line of the 'myDoc' file. Display the contents of 'revDoc' file.

EXCEPTION HANDLING 11

11.1 INTRODUCTION

When a teacher is in a class, his/her lecture can be disrupted by either of the following two events:

1. Somebody from outside the class *interrupts* the lecture by knocking on the door. This event is an *asynchronous* event because the teacher has nothing to do with this disruption. At his/her convenience, the teacher suspends his/her lecture and listens to what the visitor has to say.

   This is a situation similar to a device interrupting the CPU for seeking a particular service. The CPU suspends the execution of the current program, saves its context, and jumps to an interrupt service routine.

   There is no specific time for the interrupt to occur. The CPU need not handle the interrupt immediately but only when it is ready to handle it.

2. On the other hand, a student may ask a question from the teacher for clarification on the topic being discussed in the class. Now this type of disruption is called an *exception*. It is a *synchronous* event because the question is in response to the discussions being done by the teacher. The teacher also expects the question from the students.

   This is a similar situation wherein a program generates a run time error leading to abnormal program termination. A careful programmer can avoid this eventuality by predicting such exceptions and taking suitable measures within the program to handle them.

   On every run of the program, the exception will occur at precisely the same instruction of the code. The program cannot run further until the exception is handled.

11.2 TRADITIONAL ERROR HANDLING

In non-object oriented programming, many traditional error handling techniques are used by the programmers to catch and handle errors generated by programs. A broad level error-handling pseudo code is given below:

```
while (not end of program)
 {
      perform a task
      if (error )
          then handle the error
      else
          perform the rest of the work
 }
```

Example 1. *Write a program that reads a list of N non-negative integer values and finds the largest number from the list. If an input number is a negative value then it displays the following message and exits the program.*

Solution: The required program is given below:

```
// This program illustrates a traditional error handling technique
// It reads a list of non-negative integers and finds the largest
// among them. It exits the program on encounter of a negative integer

# include <iostream.h>
# include <process.h>

 void main()
   {
    int num, N, large, i;
    cout <<"\n Enter the size of the list : ";
    cin >> N;
    large = -1; // initialize large to an out of range value
    cout << "\n Enter the list one by one\n";
       for (i = 1; i <= N; i++)
       {
         cin >> num;
         if (num < 0)
         {
          cout << "\n Wrong input"; // error has occurred
          exit (0); // exit the program
         }
       else
       if (num > large)
       large = num;
      }
       cout << "\n The largest = " << large;
   }
```

Sample outputs are given below:

Run 1

```
  Enter the size of the list  : 5
  Enter the list one by one
11
6
-7
  Wrong input
```

Run 2

```
  Enter the size of the list  : 5
  Enter the list one by one
```

```
11
6
7
76
51
  The largest  = 76
```

It may be noted that an extra piece of code has been written to handle the error in the input of the program. In fact, we will have to write such error handling codes as many times as the demand of the program. The situation becomes even more severe when an error occurs in a function which has been called by another function. The error necessarily propagates back to the calling function as shown in Fig. 11.1.

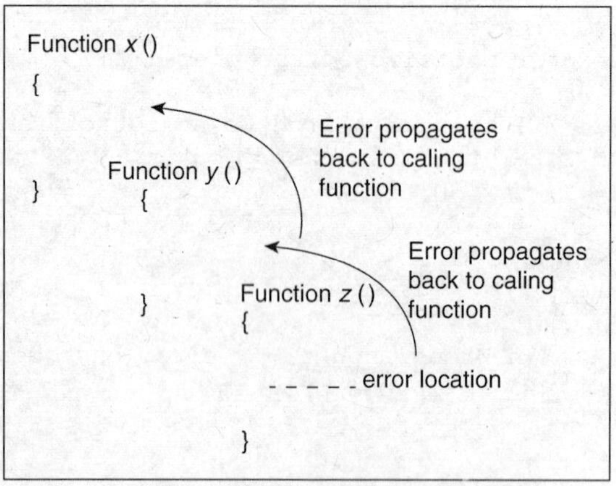

Figure 11.1 *The propagation of error*

In some programs, especially the large one, it may so happen that *we may write more lines of code to handle the errors than the actual code of the program.*

A better way of traditional error handling is possible with a special function called 'atexit()' included in 'stdlib.h'. It works as follows:

1. Write the error handling code as a separate function (say errorHandler()).
2. Pass the name of the error handling function (i.e. errorHandler) as an argument to the special function 'atexit()' as shown below:

```
atexit (errorhandler);
```

Now the name of the error handling function has been registered with 'atexit()'. So as soon as an exit() function is called in the program, the control is passed to 'atexit()' function which in its turn passes the control to its registered function (i.e. 'errorhandler()' in this case).

A modified program of Example 1 is given below. It uses very simple, rather a trivial, error handling function called 'dispMessage()' which is registered with function 'atexit()'. At the exit of the program, the function dsipMessage() is automatically called. A variable 'flag' has been used to find whether it is a normal exit or abnormal exit. In case of abnormal exit, the message "wrong input" is displayed.

```
// This program illustrates a better traditional error handling technique
// It reads a list of non-negative integers and finds the largest
// among them. It exits the program on encounter of a negative integer
// The exit() function called atexit() function

# include <iostream.h>
# include <process.h>
# include <stdlib.h>

  int flag;
 void main()
    {
    int num, N, large, i;

    int readNum();
    void dispMessage();

    atexit (dispMessage); // call the error handling function

    cout << "\n Enter the size of the list : ";
    cin >> N;
    large = -1; // initialize large to an out of range value
    cout << "\n Enter the list one by one \n";
       for (i = 1; i <= N; i++)
       {
         num = readNum();

         if (num > large)
         large = num;
       }
       flag = 1; // normal exit
       cout << "\n The largest = " << large;
     }
int readNum()
  {
    int num;
    cin >> num;
     if (num < 0)
       {flag = 0; // abnormal exit
          exit (1);
       }
    return num;
  }
void  dispMessage() // error handling function
  {
    if (flag == 0)
     cout << "\n Wrong input \n";
  }
```

It may be noted that the program has become more elegant in the sense that the error handling code has been separated from the logic of the program. However, the programmer has to write every bit of the code.

Sample outputs of the program are given below:

Run 1

```
   Enter the size of the list  : 5
   Enter the list one by one
4
5
-2
   Wrong input
```

Run 2

```
   Enter the size of the list  : 5
   Enter the list one by one
34
2
67
8
1
   The largest = 67
```

Nevertheless, the drawbacks of traditional error handling techniques are:

1. The program and error-handling code are intermixed.
2. The program becomes less readable and therefore difficult to maintain
3. Most of the large programs contain more than 50–60% of the error handling code.
4. The 'atexit()' function helps to some extent but the error handling code runs for both normal and abnormal exits which the programmer has to properly keep track of.

C++ provides a built-in support for handling exceptions which is discussed in detail in the following sections.

11.3 EXCEPTION HANDLING IN C++

C++ exception handling mechanism uses three components: *try*, *throw*, and *catch*. It works as follows:

1. The exception is monitored in a try block.
2. When an exception occurs, the try block throws the exception.
3. The thrown exception is caught by the catch block.
4. Once the exception has been thrown, the remaining code after throw statement is not executed, i.e. the control does not go back to try block.

The general arrangement of try–throw–catch is given in Fig. 11.2.

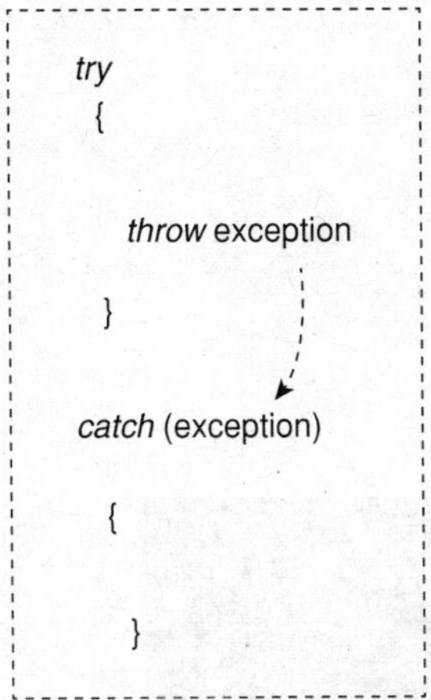

Figure 11.2 *Try–throw–catch arrangement*

Let us now rewrite the program of Example 1 to demonstrate the working of try–throw–catch arrangement. The try block throws a 'message' which is caught by the catch block. The modified program is given below:

```
// This program illustrates the usage of try-throw-catch arrangement

# include <iostream.h>
# include <string.h>
 void main()
   {
    char message[] = "Wrong input";
    int num, N, large, i;
    cout <<"\n Enter the size of the list : ";
    cin >> N;
    large = -1; // initialize large to an out of range value
    cout << "\n Enter the list one by one \n";
       for (i = 1; i <=N; i++)
       {
      cin >> num;
      try
       {
        if (num < 0) // The exception
         {
             cout << "\n Wrong input \n";
             throw message                        // Throw the exception
         }
      else
      if (num > large)
```

```
        large = num;
      }
    catch (char message[]) // Catch the exception
        {
         cout << "\n" << message;
        }
     }
     cout << "\n The largest = " << large;
    }
```

The sample output is given below:

Run 1

```
  Enter the size of the list  : 5
  Enter the list one by one
5
4
-7
  Wrong input_
```

Run 2

```
  Enter the size of the list  : 5
  Enter the list one by one
12
3
45
6
8
  The largest = 45
```

It may be noted that the arrangement is working very well.

Note: The exception handling is not supported by some compilers. This program has been tested on '*Borland C++ 4.5 version*'.

Example 2. *Write a program that reads two numbers X and Y. It uses a function divide() to compute X/Y. This function checks for Y and if it is equal to 0 then the function throws an exception otherwise returns X/Y.*

Solution: The required program is given below:

```
// This program throws an exception for divide by zero exception

# include <iostream.h>
# include <string.h>
```

```
float divide (float X, float Y)
  {
    if (Y == 0) // The exception detected
      throw "divide by zero"; // Throw the exception
     else
       return (X/Y);
   }
 void main ()
  {
    float val1, val2, result;
    cout << "\n Enter two values";
    cin >> val1 >> val2;
    try {result = divide (val1, val2); // Try block
    cout << "\n The result = " << result;
    }
        catch (char message[])
       {
         cout << "\n" <<  message; // display message
       }
  }
```

Sample outputs are given below:

```
 Enter two values 34.2 16.4
 The result = 2.08537

 Enter two values 45.2 0
divided by zero
```

It may be noted that:

1. The statements that cause exceptions must be included in the try block or inside a function called from within the try block.
2. The try block should also contain the statements that must be skipped in case of anexception.
3. The catch handler must be written immediately after a try block.
4. The parameter type of catch handler must match the exception thrown by the try block.
5. The program continues to execute after dealing with the exception. This is in contrast to the traditional error handling techniques wherein the program terminates.

11.3.1 Multiple Throw Statements and Multiple Catch Blocks

A try block can have as many throw statements as the number of exceptions handled in that block. If the messages thrown by the various throw statements are of the same type then only one catch block is required to handle them otherwise we may require as many catch blocks as required to catch the different types of exceptions thrown by the try block.

Example 3. *Write a program that throws exceptions for out of range input values of various components of a valid date of 21st century having the following structure:*

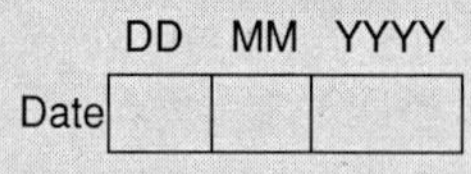

Solution: We will use multiple throw statements in a try block. The required program is given below:

```
// This program illustrates the usage of multiple throw statements

# include <iostream.h>

struct date {
 int dd;
 int mm;
 int yyyy;
 };

date readDate()
{
  date dateVar;
  cout << "\n Enter month";
  cin >> dateVar.mm;
  if (dateVar.mm < 1 || dateVar.mm > 12)
           throw '1';
  cout << "\n Enter Day";
  cin >> dateVar.dd;

  if (dateVar.mm == 2 && (dateVar.dd < 1 || dateVar.dd > 28))
           throw 1;

  if (dateVar.mm == 4 || dateVar.mm == 6 || dateVar.mm == 9 ||
dateVar.mm == 11)
       { if (dateVar.dd < 1 || dateVar.dd > 30)
           throw 1;
    }
  else
       if (dateVar.dd < 1 || dateVar.dd > 31)
           throw 1;
  cout << "\n Enter year (yyyy)" ;
  cin >> dateVar.yyyy;

  if (dateVar.yyyy < 2000 || dateVar.yyyy > 2999)
           throw "1.0";
```

```
  return dateVar;
 }
 void main()
  {
    date myDate;
 try
  {
   myDate = readDate();
   cout << "\n The valid date is :" << myDate.dd <<" / " << myDate.mm ;
             cout << " / " << myDate.yyyy;
  }
  catch (char ch)
    {
       cout << "\n wrong month";
    }
  catch (int i)
    {
      cout << "\n wrong day";
    }
  catch (char text[])
    {
       cout << "\n wrong year";
    }
}
```

Sample output is given below:

```
Run 1
          Enter month13
          wrong month
Run 2
          Enter month2
          Enter Day31
          wrong Day
Run 3
          Enter month5
          Enter Day15
          Enter year (yyyy)1990
          wrong year
Run 4
          Enter month5
          Enter Day15
          Enter year (yyyy)2013
          The valid date is :15/5/2013
```

It may noted that we have used three catch blocks to catch the various throw statements used in the program.

It may be further noted that in all the above programs, we have displayed simple messages to inform about the happening of an error or exception, which is probably not the aim. In fact we should provide a remedial action in terms of either asking the user to enter fresh data or by loading appropriate values into the variables.

Example 4. *Write a program that reads a list of numbers in an array called List[] of N integers. It asks from the user for the size of the list. If the size entered by the user is found to be more than N then the program throws the following exception:*

"The size of the list is out of bound"

However, the program recovers from the exception and sets the size of the list equal to the maximum size of the array, i.e. N and proceeds to find the smallest of the list.

Solution: The required program is given below:

```
// This program illustrates as to how to recover from an
exception

# include <iostream.h>

void main()
  {
  int const N =5;
  int List[N], i;
  int size, smallest;

  try
    {
      cout << "\n Enter the size of the list to be read :" ;
      cin >> size;
      if (size > N)
         throw "The size of the list is out of bound";
    }

  catch (char message[])
    {
       cout << "\n" << message;
       size = N; // recover from error
       cout << " - The size is set to " << N;
     }

  cout << "\n Enter the elements one by one \n";

  for (i = 0; i < N; i++)
   {
      cin >> List[i];
```

```
  }
 smallest = List[0];

 for (i = 1; i < N; i++)
  {
    if (smallest > List[i])
       smallest = List[i];
  }
 cout << "\n The smallest = " << smallest;
 }
```

A sample output is given below:

```
 Enter the size of the list to be read : 12
The size of the list is out of bound - The sizeis set to 5
Enter the elements one by one
12
3
45
6
7
 The smallest = 3
```

It may be noted that the above program has not only caught the error but also recovered from it. This is a major step towards creating robust programs.

11.3.2 Throwing Objects

A structure or an object can also be thrown by a 'throw' statement. This may be required in a situation where the object or the structure has errors.

Consider Example 3 wherein many throw statements have been used to 'throw' many exceptions all relating to the structure called 'date'. While on the contrary, it was possible to send whole of the structure by a single throw statement. A modified program that throws the entire structure is given below. It uses a variable called 'flag' to monitor the input given by the user. If any of the component of 'dateVar' is provided wrong input, the 'flag' is set to 1.

Similarly, a variable called 'setVar' is being used to monitor the occurring of an exception.

```
// This program uses a single throw statement to throw a structure

# include <iostream.h>

struct date {
 int dd;
 int mm;
 int yyyy;
 };
```

```
date readDate()
{
  int flag = 0;
  date dateVar;
  cout << "\n Enter month : ";
  cin >> dateVar.mm;
  if (dateVar.mm < 1 || dateVar.mm > 12)

          flag =1;
  cout << "\n Enter Day : ";
  cin >> dateVar.dd;

  if (dateVar.mm == 2 && (dateVar.dd < 1 || dateVar.dd > 28))
          flag = 1;
  if (dateVar.mm == 4 || dateVar.mm == 6 || dateVar.mm == 9 || dateVar.
  mm == 11)
   {if (dateVar.dd < 1 || dateVar.dd > 30)
            flag = 1;
   }
  else
   if (dateVar.dd < 1 || dateVar.dd > 31)
      flag = 1;
  cout << "\n Enter year (yyyy): " ;
  cin >> dateVar.yyyy;
  if (dateVar.yyyy < 2000 || dateVar.yyyy > 2999 )
      flag = 1;
  if (flag ==1) throw dateVar; // Throw the structure

  return dateVar; // valid date
 }
 void main()
  {
    int setDate = 0;
    date myDate;

   try
    {
       myDate = readDate();

    }
catch (date dateVar)
    {
      cout << "\n the date is wrong, it is being set to 1.1.2013";
      dateVar.dd = 1;
      dateVar.mm = 1;
      dateVar.yyyy = 2013;
      myDate = dateVar;
      setDate =1;
    }
if (setDate == 0)
```

```
    cout << "\n The date is valid:";
else
    cout << "\n The modified date is :";
    cout << myDate.dd <<" / " << myDate.mm << " / " << myDate.yyyy;
}
```

A sample output of this program is given below:

```
Run 1
        Enter month 13
        Enter Day : 2
        Enter year (yyyy): 1998
        The data is wrong, it is being set to 1.1.2013
        The modified data is :1/1/2013
Run 2
        Enter month : 12
        Enter Day : 31
        Enter year (yyyy): 2012
        The data is valid:31/12/2012
```

Similar to the structures, objects also can be thrown from a try block as illustrated by the following example wherein the data about a student object is read. If the data provided by the user is not within the range then the object is thrown for a catch block to handle. The '*this*' pointer can be used to throw the object.

Example 5. *Write a program that reads the data of an object of student class (Chapter 4) with following members:*

States

Name
Roll
Marks
Grade

Behaviours

Read_data()
Display_grade()
Compute_grade()

The data is validated for following range of values:

100 < Roll <= 200
0 < Marks < = 100

If the data is found out of range then the object is thrown. The catch block sends back the control to the while loop of try block with the help of a continue statement. The user is made to enter fresh data. After the correct data is received, the grade is computed. Thereafter, the data of the student is displayed.

Solution: The required program is given below:

```
// This program illustrates the method of throwing an object from a
try block

# include <iostream.h>
# include <conio.h>

class student {
private:
  char name[20];
  int roll;
  int marks;
  char grade;
  void compute_grade();
public:
  void read_data();
  void display_grade();
  };

  // Function to read data of a student
  void student :: read_data()
   {
    cout <<"\n Enter Name:";
    cin >> name;
    cout << "\n Enter Roll:";
    cin >> roll;
    cout << "\n Enter Marks:";
    cin >> marks;
    if ( roll <=100 || roll > 200 || marks <= 0 || marks > 100)
        throw this; // Throw object
    compute_grade(); // compute the grade
    }
   void student :: display_grade()
      {
        cout << "\n Name:" << name;
        cout << "\n Roll:" << roll;
        cout << "\n Grade:" <<grade;
      }
    void student :: compute_grade()
      {
        if (marks >= 80) grade = 'A';
        else
          if (marks >= 70) grade = 'B';
          else
             if (marks >= 60) grade = 'C';
             else
               if (marks >= 50) grade = 'D';
```

```
            else
               grade = 'E';
   }
void main()
   {
int choice;
student studOb;
do
   {
      int flag = 0;
      //clrscr();
      cout << "\n Menu";
      cout << "\n";
      cout << "\n Read data\t 1";
      cout << "\n";
      cout << "\n Display grade \t 2";
      cout << "\n";
      cout << "\n Quit \t \t 3";
      cout <<"\n";
      cout <<"\n Enter your choice:";
      cin >> choice;
switch (choice)
  {
    case 1 : while (! flag)
             {
             try
             {
             studOb.read_data();
             flag = 1;
             }
             catch (student *Ob) // Receive a pointer to the object
                {
                    cout << "\n In catch";
                    cout << "\n Enter Data again";
                    continue; // Continue the while loop
                }
             }
             break;
      case 2 : studOb.display_grade();
      }
      getch();
  }
  while (choice != 3);
  }
```

A sample output is given below:

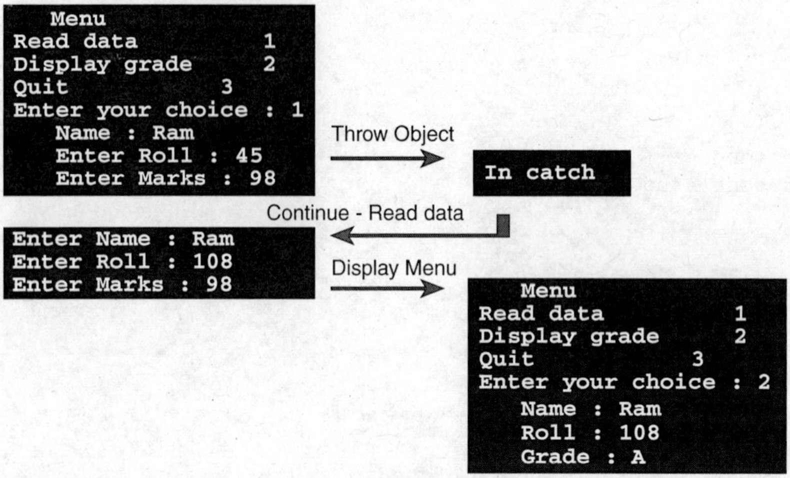

When multiple throw statements in a try block throw same type of data then it maps to a single catch block. Therefore, it becomes difficult to resolve them in the sense that from the received data, it becomes difficult to identify its originating exception or error. In such a situation, the programmer can create a separate *exception class* and place all the bad data and the related messages into an object of this class. Thereafter, a single throw statement is used to throw the object. Within the receiving catch block, the various data items are extracted from the object and accordingly acted upon.

This try–throw–arrangement must be used very carefully. For instance, if no catch block were provided for an exception thrown by a try block then the program would abnormally terminate giving the following message:

```
Abnormal Program Termination
```

A resource taken from the system has to be returned back to the system after its usage. But while using the resource if an exception is thrown before the statement that returns the resource back to the system then the resource becomes unavailable.

From above, it can be concluded that "*An exception indicates an exceptional situation or behaviour in a function or program.*" The situations of usage of 'Exception Handling' are listed below:

1. Identify the exception and repair the same. If necessary recall the code or function in which the exception occurred.
2. If the problem cannot be handled then terminate the program
3. If the problem has been fixed in the catch block and no more action is required then proceed with rest of the work.
4. If the problem could not be fixed or was fixed partially then you may re-throw exception the same or a different exception to correct the error.

Nevertheless, it is necessary that the exception handling code must be separated from the normal code of the program.

11.4 SUMMARY

An interrupt is an asynchronous event. The exception is a synchronous event. The exceptions can be predicted. In normal programming, extra piece of code is written to handle the occurrence of a possible error. The program and error handling code are intermixed. 'atexit()' is a special function for traditional error handling. Exception handling mechanism in C++ has three components: try, throw, and catch. The exception is monitored in 'try' block, thrown by 'throw' block and caught by the 'catch' block. The program does not terminate after the exception is handled. A try block can have multiple throw statements. Good exception handling renders a robust program. In special circumstances, a programmer can use an exception class.

MULTIPLE CHOICE QUESTIONS

1. An exception is a _________ event
   (a) normal (b) asynchronous
   (c) serial (d) synchronous
2. An exception occur at the _______ instruction of the code.
   (a) same (b) different
3. Exception handling mechanism uses three components: try, throw, and:
   (a) get (b) catch
   (c) slip (d) drag
4. When an exception occurs, the try block throws the:
   (a) code (b) message
   (c) exception (d) error
5. The exception is monitored in a:
   (a) try block (b) catch block
   (c) main function
6. The catch handler must be written immediately after a
   (a) main() (b) try block
7. A program terminates abnormally if there is no ___ block for a thrown exception
   (a) try (b) main()
   (c) catch

ANSWERS

1. d **2.** a **3.** b **4.** c **5.** a **6.** b **7.** c

EXERCISES

1. Differentiate between an interrupt and an exception.
2. Write a short note on traditional error handling.

3. Explain the working of 'atexit()' function with the help of an example.
4. What is an exception handler and what are its components?
5. Discuss try, throw and catch with the help of examples.
6. How do you catch the exception? Give example.
7. Why an exception is re-thrown?
8. Create a class called 'employee' with following fields:

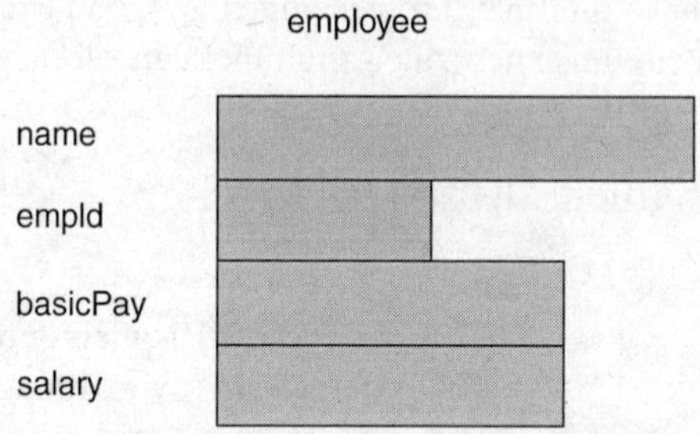

The data fields name, empId, basicPay and salary are of type string, string, float and float respectively. Include a readData() function that displays appropriate messages and accepts the data items of the employee object. It throws an exception if the basicPay is less than Rs. 5000 and greater than Rs. 80,000. Include another function compSal() that computes the salary of the employee on the basis of a formula chosen by your self. A third function dispData() may also be included that displays the data of an employee object.

INTRODUCTION TO UML

12

12.1 INTRODUCTION TO UML

In order to understand a complex problem or system, we need to represent it in a simple way called 'model'. For example, when a large apartment building in a housing society is built, first its plan is drawn by the architect on a paper and then a small prototype is prepared. When all the stake holders (builder, clients, etc.) agree on the plan and the looks of the prototype, the project gets approved for construction. The prototype is nothing but the model of the proposed building. Similarly, when software is to be constructed, its model needs to be prepared.

A model can be precisely defined as *a hypothetical description of a complex entity or process, constructed to understand a problem or system.*

Once the model is in place, it can be modified for improvement or approved for final construction. However, we need to have necessary tools for the construction of a model. For software modeling, a language is required that can express the various components and the relationship among them. For instance, in object oriented software construction, we need to specify and depict pictorially the components like classes, objects, relationships, hierarchies, etc.

A number of object oriented languages have been proposed by proponents like Rumbaugh, Booch, Jacobson, Coad-Yourdon, etc. Each had its own symbols and specifications for expressing object-oriented programming (OOP) components. In 1994, an effort was started to unify all the methodologies to form a Unified Modeling Language (UML). In 1997, UML 1.0 was offered to the user as a standard OOP modeling language.

UML can be precisely defined as "*a language that models the structural, architectural, and behavioral features of a system*".

Some important UML diagrams are given below:

1. Class diagram
2. Use-case diagram
3. Behavioral diagrams
   a. Interaction diagrams
      i. Sequence diagram
      ii. Collaboration diagram
   b. State chart diagram

c. Activity diagram

4. Implementation diagrams

   a. Component diagram

   b. Deplayment diagram

A model can be of following two types:

Static model: A representation of a system at a specific time at rest. It shows the states and parameters of a system at that particular instance in time, e.g. class diagrams.

Dynamic model: This model depicts the dynamism of the system in terms of its behaviors over a period of time. In fact it is the collection of procedures that govern the overall behaviour of the system, e.g. UML interaction diagrams.

12.2 CLASS DIAGRAMS (STATIC)

A class symbolizes a specific feature of the system. It can be represented by a rectangle having three sections: name, states (attributes) and behaviours (operations) as shown in Fig. 12.1. Where an attribute defines the range of values a state can take, an operation represents the implementation of a service or behaviour of the object that the class represents. The access specifiers can be assigned to various members of the class by prefixing the symbols: – (private), + (public), and # (protected).

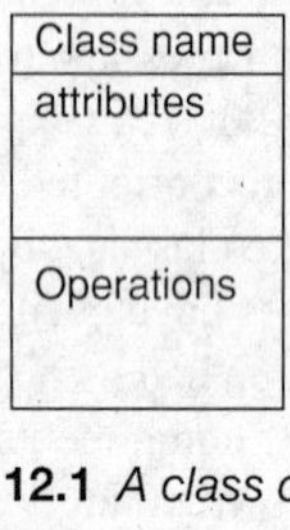

Figure 12.1 *A class diagram*

Depending upon requirement, the class diagram can be as short as shown in Fig. 12.2(a) or as detailed as shown in Fig. 12.2(b).

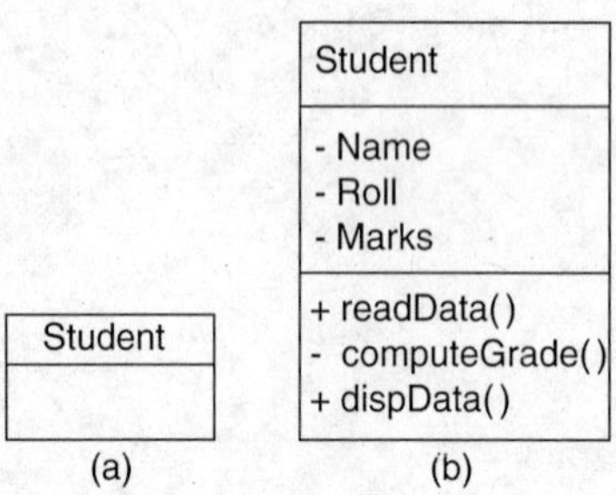

Figure 12.2 *(a, b) Class diagrams*

An object is represented by a similar diagram but its name is qualified by its corresponding class name. An object called 'studOb' of type 'student' class is shown in Fig. 12.3.

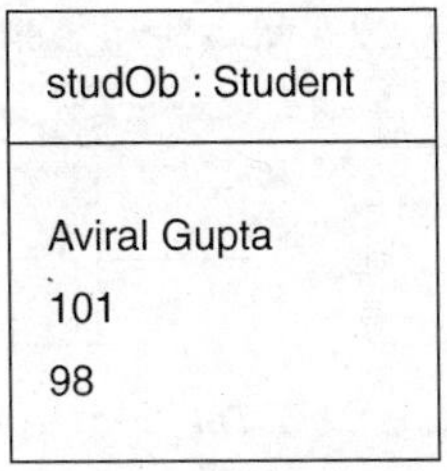

Figure 12.3 *An object*

It may noted that the object contains the actual data in contrast to a class which has only attributes names. The reason is simple that class is a compile time entity and the objects are instances of the class created at run time. Therefore, the objects get the memory for storing the data for its states. An *object diagram* is an instance of the class diagram.

12.2.1 Relationships Among Classes

The various relationships that exist between classes are composition, generalizations and dependencies. A brief discussion on each of them is given below:

Composition: An object can be composed of components bound by two types of relationships: association and aggregation. Both represent a 'has-a' relationship.

Association: A loose relationship between two objects in which both the objects are visible. For instance, a computer *has a* mouse. Similarly, a teacher has students to teach. Or other way round, a student has a teacher to be taught by. This type of association is shown by a simple line or link between the participating classes as shown in Fig. 12.4.

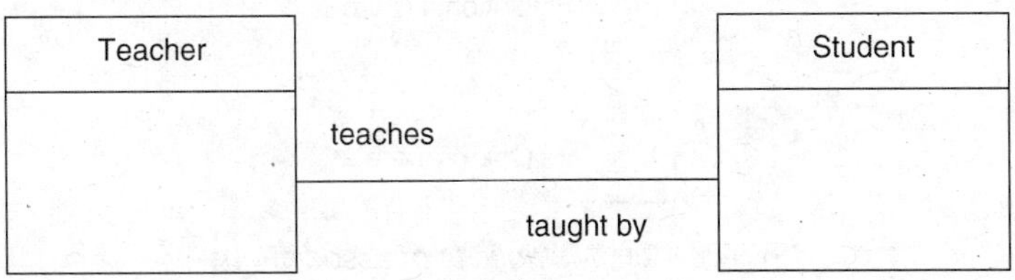

Figure 12.4 *An association*

This type of relationship is flexible in the sense that different teachers can be associated with different students or vice-versa. As discussed earlier in the book, an association is implemented in C++ as a pointer of one class embedded in other class. For example, the class teacher would contain a pointer of student's type.

Aggregation: A tight relationship between two objects wherein only one object is visible. In fact one object acts as a container of other object and therefore only the container remains visible.

For example, a car has an engine. Now we see only the car object and not the engine object. Similarly, CPU is an aggregation of three objects: ALU, CU and registers.

The aggregation is represented by a link with an open diamond at the container class end. Consider the aggregation shown in Fig. 12.5 wherein it is shown that a University has department.

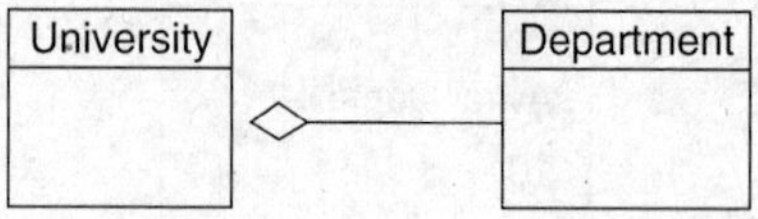

Figure 12.5 *The aggregation*

The aggregation is modeled as containership in C++. For the aggregation shown in Fig. 12.5, the University class would contain an object of department type.

It may be noted that both association and aggregation are 'has-a' relationships. Both have their own advantages. The association provides flexibility in relationship. For example, an optical mouse can be very easily replaced by a wireless mouse in a computer system. On the other hand, the aggregation is an inflexible but more secured relationship. For instance, engine object is very much secured within the car object.

Multiplicity of association can be shown by appropriately annotating the association links as shown in Fig. 12.6.

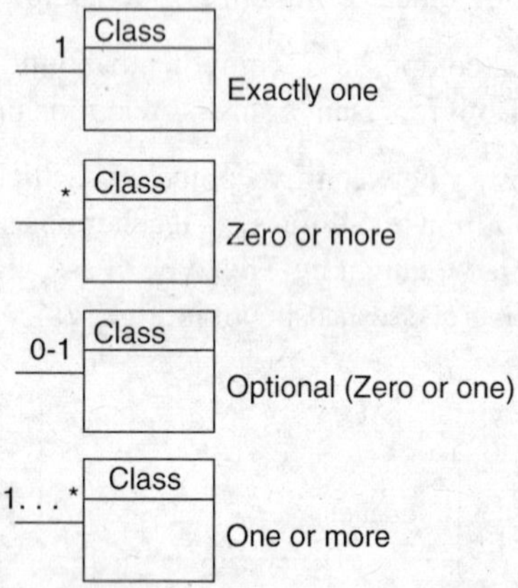

Figure 12.6 *Multiplicity of associations*

Thus the relationship that the University has many departments can be represented by the diagram shown in Fig. 12.7.

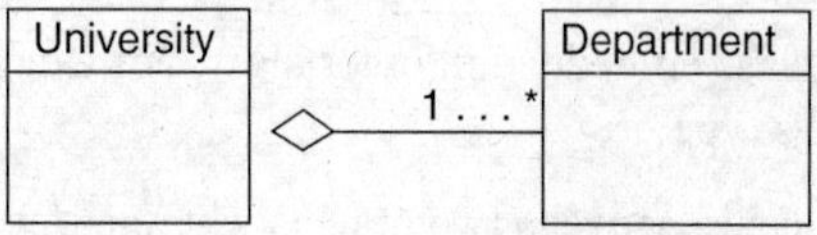

Figure 12.7 *One to many relationship*

Generalization: In this OOP strategy, common elements are identified among the different classes. It follows two approaches: 'top down' and 'bottom up'. In top down approach, we create specialized classes from existing classes. On the other hand, in bottom up approach, from different classes, a super class is created. In both the cases a hierarchy of classes is created with the help of inheritance leading to 'a kind of' (ako) relationship. Inheritance is represented by a solid line starting from the derived class with an arrow like triangle pointing to the base class, i.e. the apex of the triangle point to the base class a shown in Fig. 12.8.

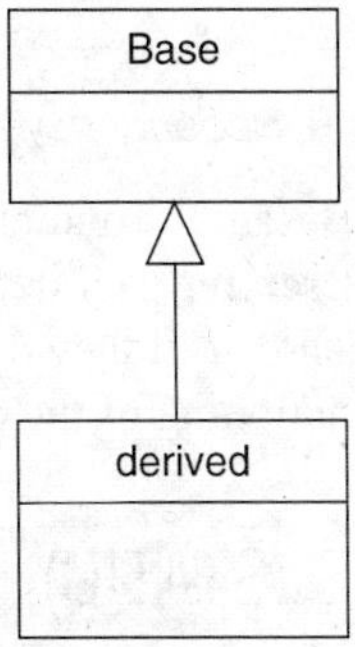

Figure 12.8 *Inheritance (generalization)*

Consider the hierarchy given in Fig. 12.9. From top to down, it can be said that an 'infrared mouse' is a kind of 'wireless mouse' which itself is a kind of 'mouse'. In bottom up approach, we can say that wireless mouse is a generalization of 'infrared mouse' and 'radio frequency mouse'.

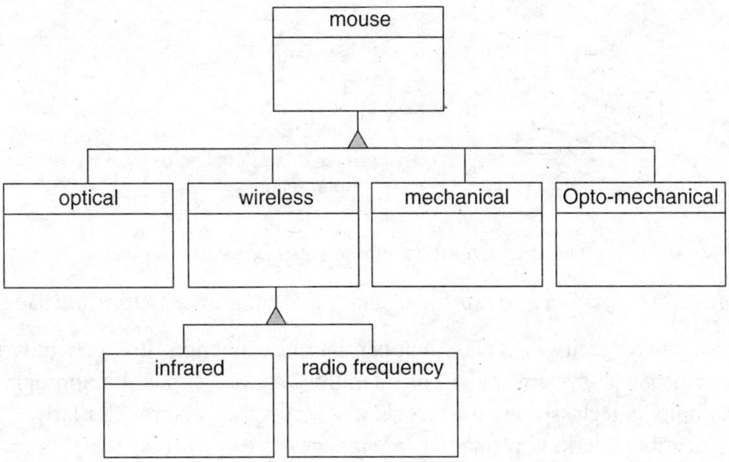

Figure 12.9 *Hierarchy of classes*

Dependency: It is a special relationship between two classes where one class depends upon other class. This relationship is shown as a *dashed directed line* from dependent class to the class on which it depends. Consider the relationship shown in Fig. 12.10.

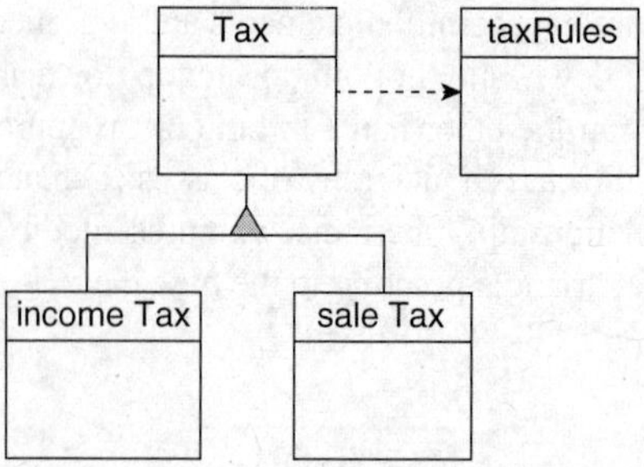

Figure 12.10 *Dependency relationship*

In fact dependency is a relationship of usage of one class by another. For instance, the 'Tax' class is using the 'taxRules' class. Therefore, it is dependent upon 'taxRules' class. On the other hand, two classes are called '*orthogonal*' if they do not depend on each other. If a class is modified then it has no effect on the functioning of the other class.

12.3 USE CASE DIAGRAMS (STATIC)

A system has a boundary surrounded by an environment. The system has some objectives which are achieved through functions or classes called *use cases*. Some entities of the environment called as 'actors' interact with the system as shown in Fig. 12.11.

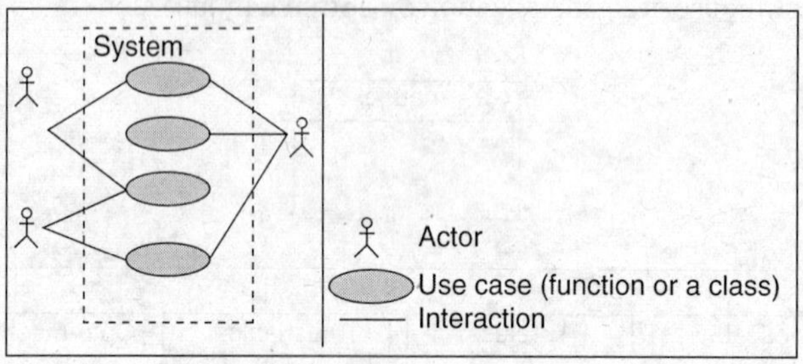

Figure 12.11 *A use case diagram*

A use case diagram is a graph that represents interactions between actors and use cases. where:

1. An '*actor*' is an entity or a class that can initiate an action. It is generally not a part of the system or sub-system under consideration. An actor must be appropriately named. For example, in a classroom, the teacher and student are actors. Similarly in a library, the library member, clerk, librarian, etc. are all actors.
2. A *use case* is a class or a function that provides a service to the system. It describes the interaction between an actor and the system. Each use case realizes the aim of an actor. The name of the use case should be so chosen that it properly represents the functionality of the system.
3. An edge is a path of communication from an actor to a use case or vice-versa.

Therefore, the following need to be identified before a use case is drawn:

1. Actors.
2. Use cases defining what is to be done, i.e. functionality.
3. Relationships between actors and use cases.

For example, consider the use case diagram of the book issue scenario of a library given in Fig. 12.12. It consists of two actors: member and library clerk. The use cases are 'request a book', 'search book', and 'issue book'.

It may be noted that the name of a use case indicates about the service it provides and collectively all the use cases realize the objectives of the system.

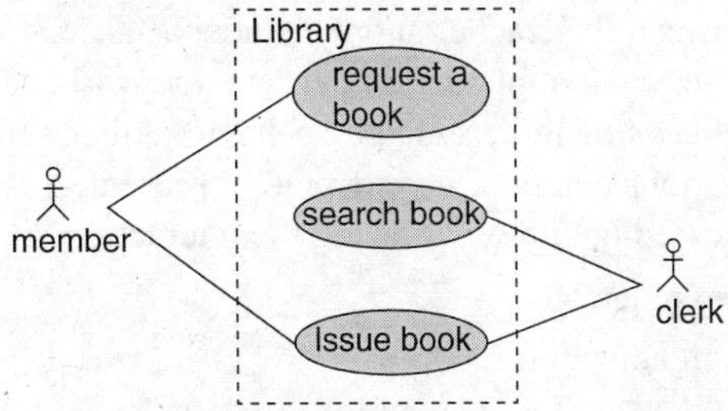

Figure 12.12 *Use case diagram of book issue scenario*

Similarly, a classroom scenario consists of two actors: 'teacher' and 'student' and the possible use cases are: 'write on black board', 'deliver lecture', 'ask question', 'answer question' and 'jot down'. The use case diagram for this scenario is given in Fig. 12.13.

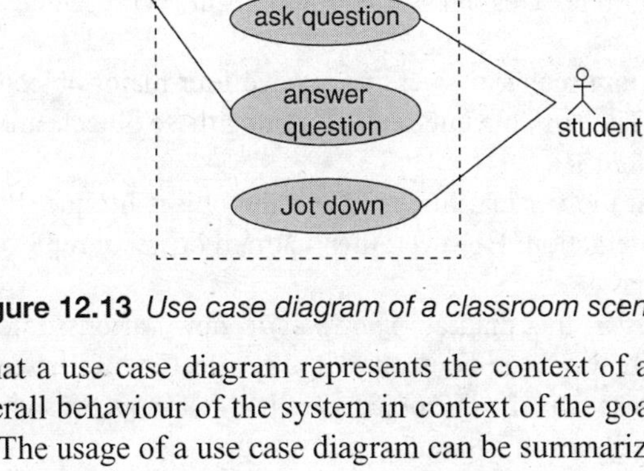

Figure 12.13 *Use case diagram of a classroom scenario*

In fact, we can say that a use case diagram represents the context of a system. It helps us in understanding the overall behaviour of the system in context of the goals of the actors associated with the system. The usage of a use case diagram can be summarized as given below:

1. Gather system requirements.
2. Identify factors that influence the system. The factors can be either internal or external.
3. Draft a broader view of the system.
4. Represent the interaction among the actors and the use cases.

12.4 BEHAVIORAL DIAGRAMS (DYNAMIC)

The world around us is dynamic in the sense that it is continuously evolving. After nightlong sleep, whether we wake up or not, the sun rises, the birds chirp, people go to their offices and so on. While driving, the vehicles around us move with different speeds. In a classroom, lots of interactions take place between the teacher and the students. All these examples show that the world is characterized by action and interaction between the world actors. This behavior of the world or a part of the world can be represented by behavioral diagrams.

Interactions between various actors of a system are represented using interaction diagrams. The following steps are carried out before drawing the interaction diagrams:

1. Identify participating objects.
2. Find out the object organization.
3. Identify messages that take place between the objects.
4. Determine the sequence of messages.

A brief discussion on interaction diagrams is given in the following section.

12.4.1 Interaction Diagrams

An interaction diagram helps us in capturing the behavior of a 'use case' scenario. There are two types of interaction diagrams: sequence diagrams and collaborations diagram.

Sequence diagram: this diagram shows the interaction between various objects in terms of a time sequence. Each object has a lifeline and the messages it exchanges with other objects are arranged in the order of their occurrence.

In a sequence diagram, objects are placed in horizontal dimension. The lifeline of each object is depicted by a vertical line. Messages or interactions are represented as horizontal arrows as shown in Fig. 12.14.

Consider the classroom scenario wherein we have four major objects: teacher, black board, student and notebook. The possible interactions among these objects are shown in the sequence diagram given in Fig. 12.15.

It may be noted that the vertical line is called the object lifeline. It represents the object's existence during the interaction. However, this diagram does not represent associations among the participating objects.

Collaboration diagram: this diagram shows as to how various objects work together in a particular context to achieve desired outcome. It is a collection of vertices and arcs representing objects and messages respectively. The objects are laid out in an organized manner and the arcs are labeled with the messages they send to each other.

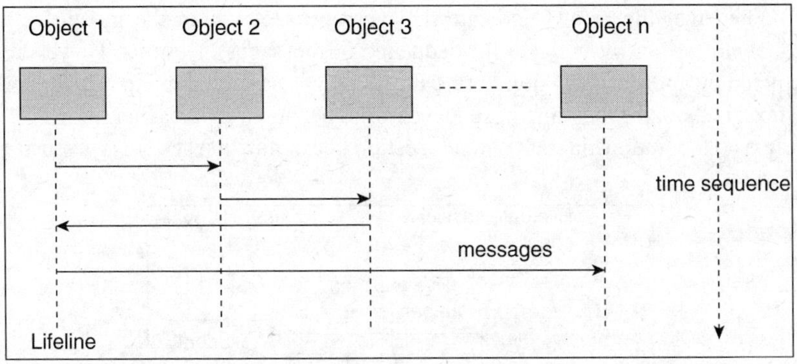

Figure 12.14 *A sequence diagram*

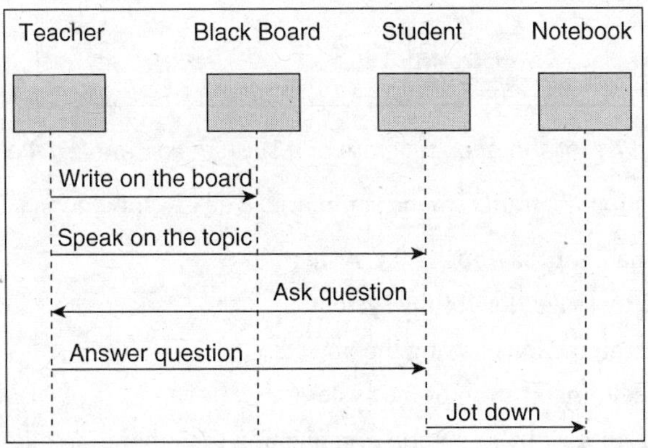

Figure 12.15 *Sequence diagram of a classroom scenario*

The collaboration diagram for classroom scenario is shown in Fig. 12.16.

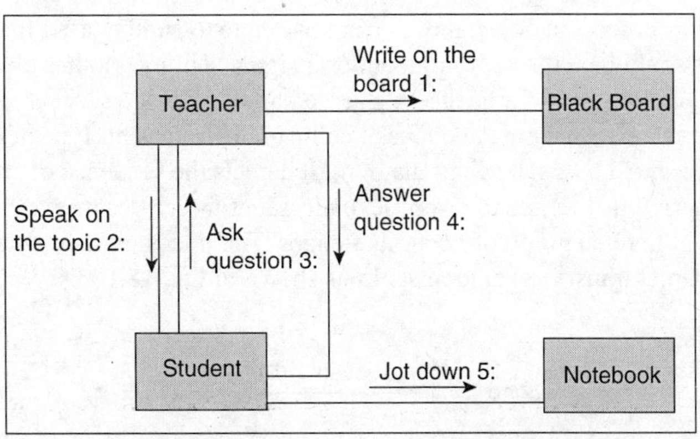

Figure 12.16 *A classroom scenario*

It may be noted that the arrows indicate the message sent within the given use case. This diagram does not primarily indicate the sequence of messages or events. However, sequence can be depicted by appropriately numbering the messages as shown in Fig. 12.16. For instance, 'Ask question' is the third message in sequence from a student to a teacher.

Similarly, a collaboration diagram of a sub-section of examination system is given in Fig. 12.17.

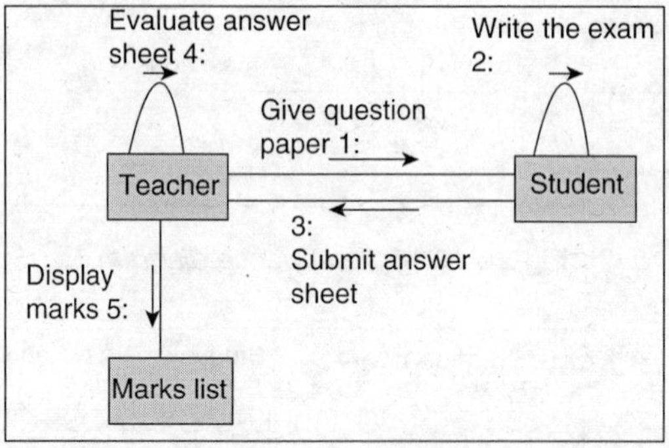

Figure 12.17 *Collaboration diagram of a sub-section of examination system*

The usage of interaction diagrams can be summarized as given below:

1. Model the dynamic behaviour of the system.
2. Represent the message flow of the system.
3. Represent the interactions among the objects.
4. Show the object organization of the system.
5. Show the control flow by structural organization (collaboration diagram).
6. Show the control flow by time sequence (sequence diagram).

12.4.2 State Chart Diagrams

In a dynamic environment, an object moves from one state to another after the occurrence of an event. The event could be a message, timeout or a signal sent by another object. For example, when the object on the front of a queue gets served and leaves the serving window, the server gives a signal to the object next in the queue to come to the front. This type of dynamic behavior of objects is represented by a state chart diagram. It depicts the sequence of states that an object passes through during its lifetime in response to messages it receives from other objects. A state chart diagram is a directed graph of nodes and edges. The nodes represent states of the objects and the arrows depict transitions among states as shown in Fig. 12.18.

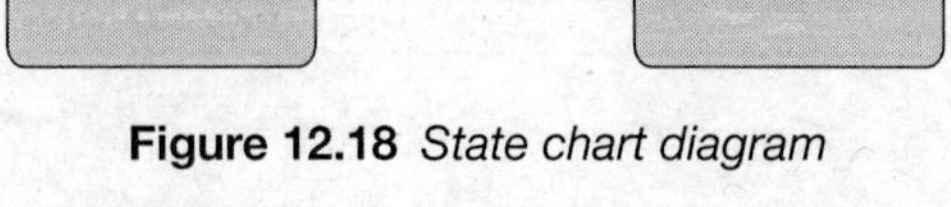

Figure 12.18 *State chart diagram*

Therefore, the following needs to be identified before drawing the state chart diagram:

1. Identify the objects.
2. Identify the states.
3. Identify the transitions and the related events.

Consider the state chart diagram shown in Fig. 12.19. It illustrates that initially the teacher object is in 'wait' state. It polls the status of the students. If the students are present then the teacher goes to 'teach' state else the teacher goes back to the 'wait' state. The teacher goes to 'stop' state from 'teach' state as soon as the bell rings.

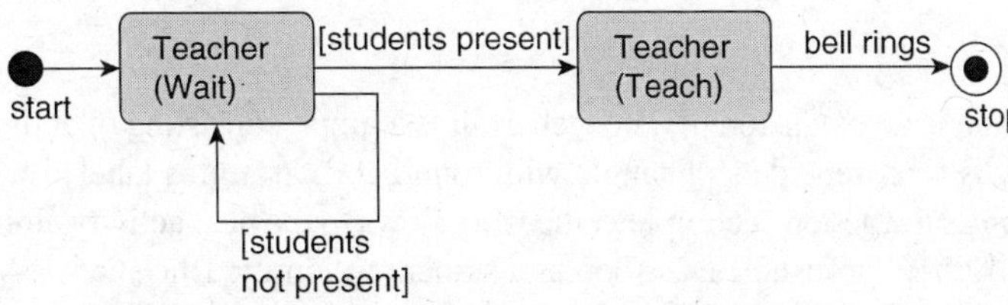

Figure 12.19 *State chart showing states and transitions*

It may be noted that the conditions that govern the transitions have been placed between the square brackets. The start state is represented by a solid ball whereas the stop state is shown by a solid ball within a circle. It may further be noted that a state chart represents a reactive system wherein the participating objects react to external or internal events. Therefore the objects are also called as *reactive objects*.

If it is needed to branch to many states depending upon different values of conditions then we can use a *choice point* (a circle) as a junction from where the bifurcation begins. A condition is also called a *guard*.

Let us now modify the state chart of Fig. 12.19 to include the guard that the teacher goes to the stop state after waiting for 10 minutes for the students. The modified state chart is given in Fig. 12.20.

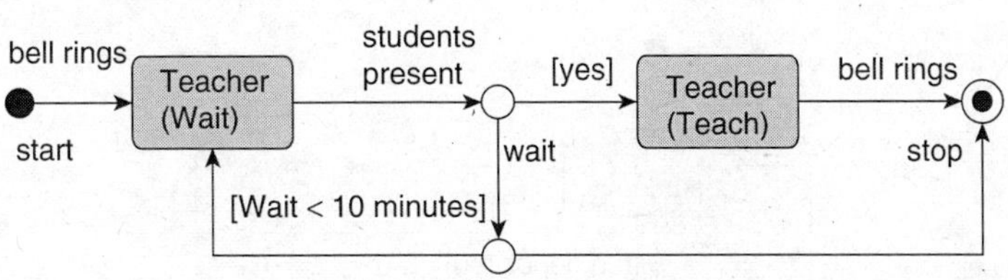

Figure 12.20 *Modified state chart diagram*

The usage of state chart diagrams can be summarized as given below:

1. To represent the states of objects.
2. To represent a reactive system.
3. To represent the events responsible for transitions of objects from one state to another.

12.4.3 Activity Diagrams

An internal action of an object at a particular state is called an activity. Therefore, the activity diagram represents a flow of work inside a use case, an algorithm, a protocol or between objects. The workflow itself is represented as a series of actions. The workflow can be sequential, branched or parallel.

The following needs are to be identified before drawing the activity diagram:

1. Activities
2. Association
3. Conditions
4. Constraints

An activity diagram is an extension of a flow chart. It is a graph consisting of activities and transitions. An activity is represented as rectangle with round corners and is labeled with the action it performs. As soon as the action is complete, the work flows to the next activity along the transition as shown in Fig. 12.21. For instance, as soon as a student is admitted, he/she is assigned a course.

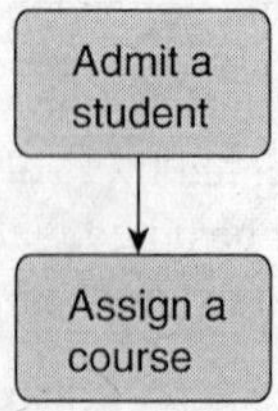

Figure 12.21 *An activity diagram*

An activity can have more than one out going transition. When the workflow follows a transition the internal action of the activity is stopped. The outgoing transitions are resolved through suitable conditions. Let us extend the activity diagram of 12.21 so that the course is only assigned after the fee is deposited by the student. The modified activity diagram is shown in Fig. 12.22.

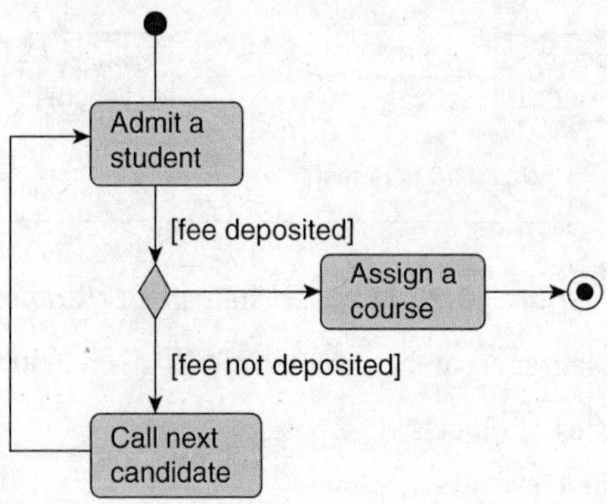

Figure 12.22 *Modified activity diagram*

Let us carry on further to extend the activity diagram by including the activity of calling candidates from the list of candidates till the number of admitted students is equal to 30. The further modified activity diagram is given in Fig. 12.23.

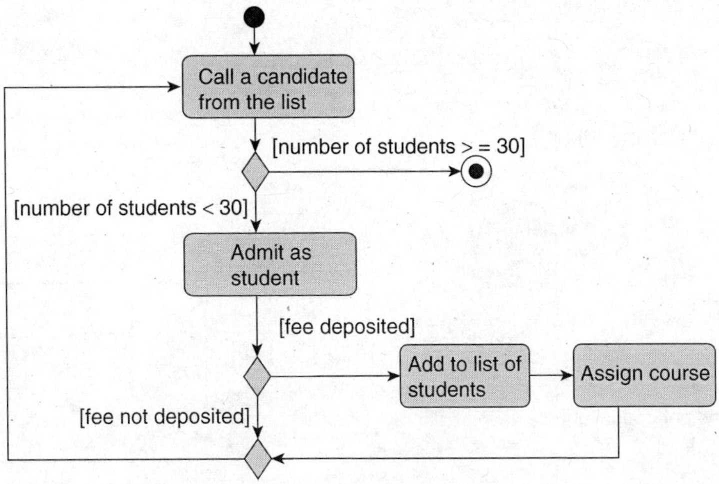

Figure 12.23 *Activity diagram of admitting 30 students for a course*

Concurrent activities can also be depicted by using fork–join construct of UML as shown in Fig. 12.24. At 'Fork' the workflow splits into more than one workflow and at 'Join' all the threads of workflows join to form a single workflow.

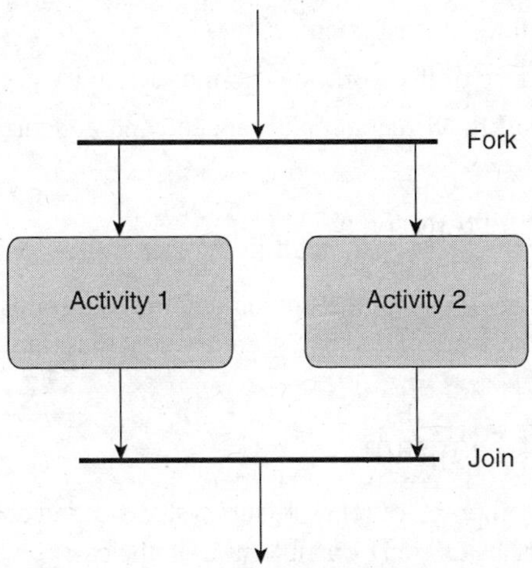

Figure 12.24 *Fork- and join-construct for concurrent activities*

For example, after a student has been admitted, the course and hostel can be assigned concurrently as shown in Fig. 12.25.

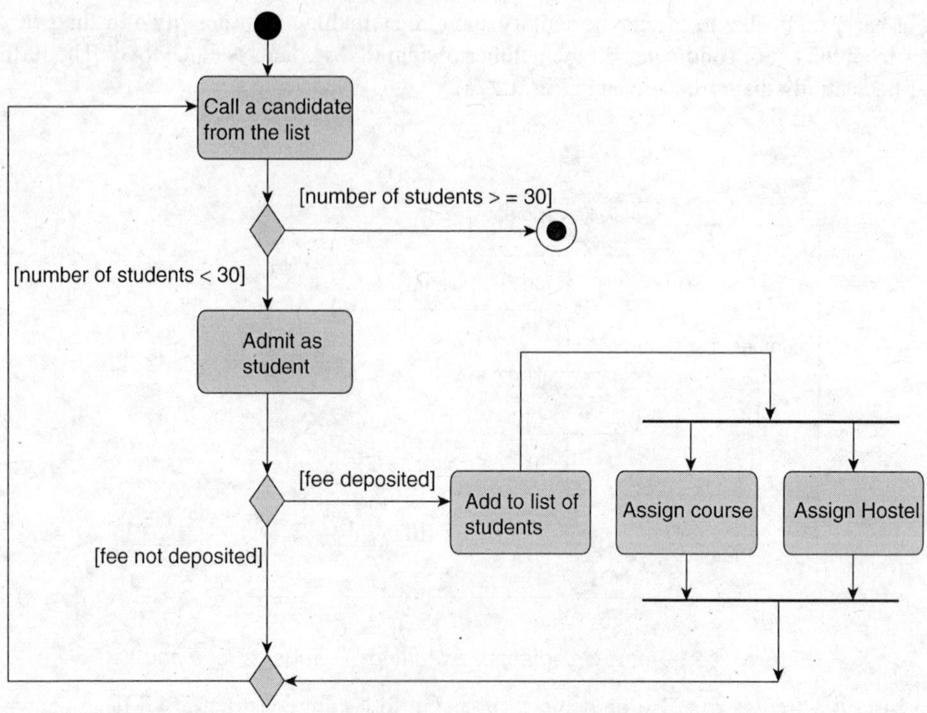

Figure 12.25 *Activity diagram depicting concurrent activities*

The usage of activity diagrams can be summarized as given below:

1. Represent the workflow of the system.
2. Represent the sequence of the workflow from one activity to another.
3. Show the type of workflow: sequential, branched and concurrent.

12.5 IMPLEMENTATION DIAGRAMS

From the name itself, it is obvious that the implementation diagrams represent the implementation aspects of a system. These are of two types: component diagrams and deployment diagrams.

12.5.1 Component Diagram

We know that a system is composed of reusable sub-systems called components. Each component implements a particular service offered by an interface. In the component diagram, the components are connected with each other either by the dependency relationship or the composition relationship.

For instance, a student gets registered with a university through an interface. The interface communicates with the registration module. The registration module stores the registration information in a student database as shown in Fig. 12.26.

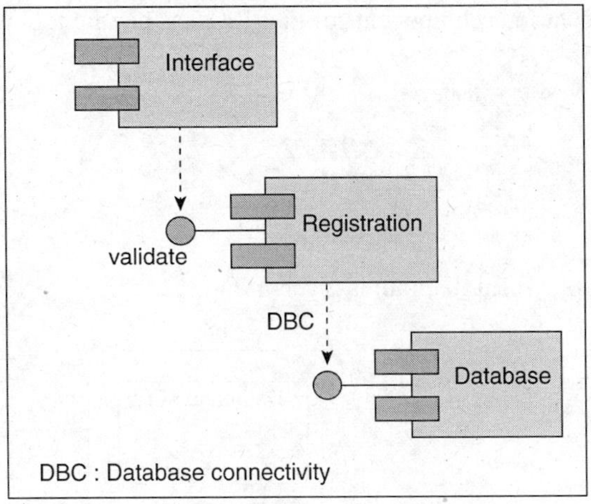

Figure 12.26 *Component diagram*

Thus, it can be said that "a component diagram represents the components of a system and the relationship among them at an instance of time". In fact the main purposes of drawing a component diagram are:

1. Plan and name the components that are going to be the executable parts of the system.
2. Represent the organization of components in the system visually.

12.5.2 Deployment Diagram

As the name suggests, a deployment diagram *represents the topology of components in terms of their deployment on different nodes.* The nodes in general are computational hardware components like client and server machines, modems, monitors, etc. Therefore, in addition to software components, we need to identify nodes and their relationships. A software component runs on a particular node. Therefore, a node necessarily contains the instance of that component as shown in Fig. 12.27.

It may be noted that the node is named as a 'client m/c', i.e. client machine. An instance of 'interface' component is deployed on this node for execution.

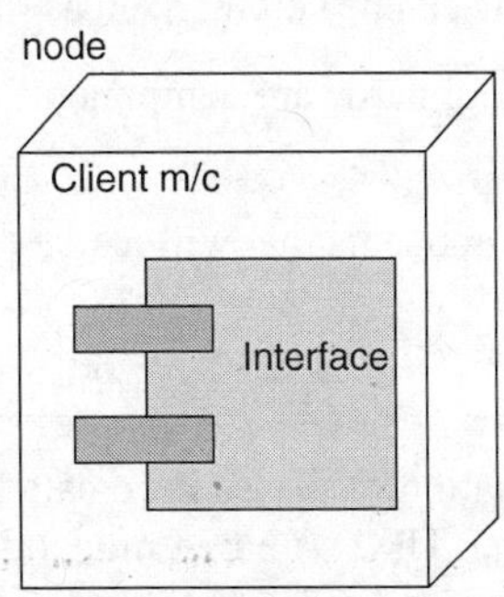

Figure 12.27 *A node containing the instance of 'interface' component*

Let us now deploy the various components of Fig. 12.26 as per the following choice:

Component	Node
Interface	client m/c
Registration	web server
Database	Database server

The corresponding deployment diagram is given in Fig. 12.28.

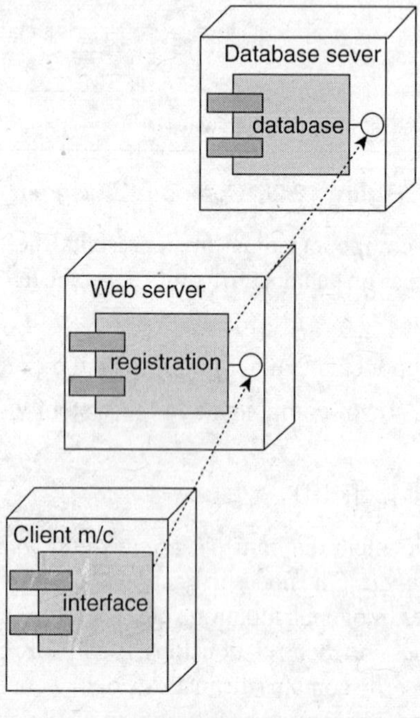

Figure 12.28 *A deployment diagram*

The usage of deployment diagrams can be summarized as given below:

1. To illustrate the distribution of hardware components called nodes.
2. To specify the topology of the nodes.
3. To identify the software components that will reside on the these nodes.

12.6 SUMMARY

A model is a simplified representation of a system, created for the purpose of understanding the system. For software modeling, UML (unified modeling language) is used. A model can be static or dynamic. A class represents a specific feature of a system. An object is also represented by a rectangle but its name is qualified by its class name. A composition represents a 'has-a' relationship. Association is modeled as a pointer from one class to another. Aggregation is modeled as containership. Top down approach identifies specialization in classes. Bottom up approach creates super classes. Inheritance models 'ako' relationship. Dependency is the relationship of usage of one class by another. An actor is a class that initiates some action. A use case diagram represents the context of a system. An object moves from one state to another after the occurrence of an event. A state chart represents a reactive system. An activity can have more than one outgoing transition. Implementation diagrams are of two types: component and deployment.

MULTIPLE CHOICE QUESTIONS

1. A static model represents a system at:
   (a) motion (b) rest
2. A class is represented as a ________ in UML.
   (a) circle (b) ellipse
   (c) rectangle (d) triangle
3. An attribute defines a range of values for a:
   (a) state (b) object
   (c) class (d) function
4. An object diagram is ______ of a class diagram.
   (a) a copy (b) opposite
   (c) instance
5. An association is _________ relationship.
   (a) loose (b) tight
   (c) secured
6. In containership only the _______ is visible.
   (a) relationship (b) link
   (c) contained object (d) container
7. The aggregation is represented by a link with an open ______ at the container class end.
   (a) circle (b) ellipse
   (c) arrow (d) diamond
8. Orthogonal classes do not ________ each other.
   (a) depend on (b) touch
   (c) inherit (d) associate with
9. A use case is a class or a function that provides a ______ to the system.
   (a) link (b) state
   (c) service (d) name
10. Messages in a sequence diagram are arranged in the order of their:
    (a) placement (b) occurrence
11. Interaction diagrams model the ______ behaviour of the system.
    (a) primary (b) static
    (c) dynamic (d) optimal

12. In a state chart diagram, an arrow represents a:
    (a) transition (b) state
    (c) event (d) object
13. An internal action of an object at a particular state is called:
    (a) impulse (b) provocation
    (c) activity (d) reaction
14. An activity diagram is an extension of a:
    (a) class diagram (b) object diagram
    (c) sequence diagram (d) flowchart
15. A deployment diagram represents the __________ of components.
    (a) interaction (b) ordering
    (c) topology (d) relationship

ANSWERS

1. b	**2.** c	**3.** a	**4.** c	**5.** a	**6.** d	**7.** d	**8.** a	**9.** c
10. b	**11.** c	**12.** a	**13.** c	**14.** d	**15.** c			

EXERCISES

1. What is a model? Differentiate between static and dynamic models.
2. What is UML? Explain in brief.
3. How a class is represented in UML?
4. How member access specifiers are represented in a UML class diagram?
5. What is an object diagram?
6. How aggregation, association and inheritance are represented in a UML class diagram?
7. Draw the use case diagram of a Super Bazaar billing window scenario wherein the customers get the bill for the items purchased by them and making the payment in cash.
8. Draw the use case diagram of an examination room scenario?
9. Give the equivalent sequence diagram of the use case developed for examination room scenario.
10. Draw the use case for an ATM machine wherein a customer withdraws cash by presenting the ATM card to the machine.
11. Give the state chart diagram for the use case diagram developed for ATM machine.
12. Differentiate between a sequence and collaboration diagrams.
13. Give the activity diagram for use case developed for Super Bazaar billing window in Question 7.
14. Explain component diagrams with the help of examples.
15. Explain deployment diagrams with the help of examples.

POLYMORPHISM: A REVIEW

13

13.1 POLYMORPHISM

We have already introduced ourselves with 'polymorphism' in Section 5.1 wherein it was defined as an entity or object having two or more forms. In object-oriented programming (OOP), functions and operators can be overloaded to achieve polymorphic behaviour.

Polymorphic functions have one name with different implementations. If the functions belong to different classes then a message (say 'close') can be interpreted differently by different objects resulting in different responses as shown in Fig. 13.1.

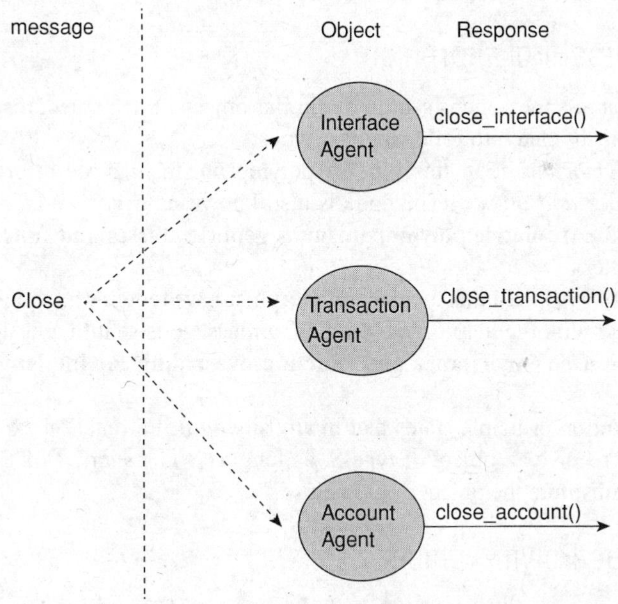

Figure 13.1 *Polymorphic behaviour of objects*

13.2 TAXONOMY OF POLYMORPHISM

Cardelli and Wegner gave the taxonomy of the polymorphism wherein it was primarily divided into two categories called **Universal** and **Ad Hoc** polymorphism as shown in Fig. 13.2.

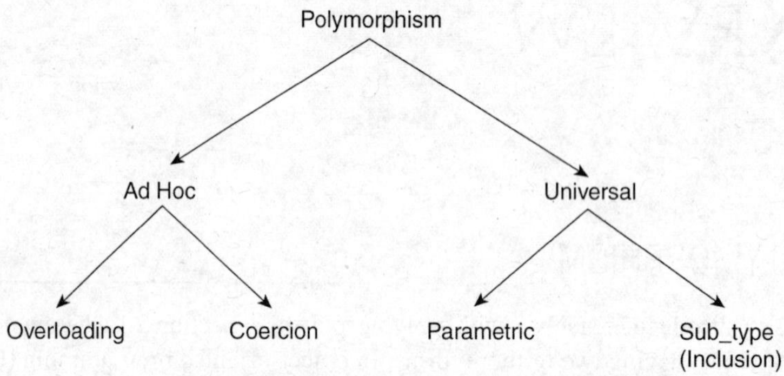

Figure 13.2 *Taxonomy of polymorphism*

The Universal polymorphism is further divided into two categories: parametric and sub_type polymorphism. Similarly the Ad Hoc polymorphism is divided into two categories: overloading and coercion polymorphism.

13.2.1 Universal Polymorphism

In this polymorphism, a message is sent to dissimilar objects. Each object responds differently to the message. It is divided into following two types.

Parametric polymorphism: In this type of polymorphism, *a piece of code is shared for variety of data types and objects*. The code is also known as *generic code*. In our book, **we have implemented parametric polymorphism as generic classes and functions using C++ templates** in Chapter 8.

Sub_type polymorphism: In this type of polymorphism, we redefine a function of a base class in derived class and with the help of late binding, a message is sent to a designated object. In our book, **we have used inheritance and function overriding for implementing sub_type polymorphism**.

Liskov's substitution principle states that in any situation if a function expects an object of type T, it can also receive an object of type S, as long as S is a *subtype* of T, i.e. an object of derived type can substitute the object of base class.

13.2.2 Ad Hoc Polymorphism

In this polymorphism, same name refers to a finite number of objects or programming entities. It is divided into following two types.

Overloading: The capacity to use same name to denote a group of functions or operations is called overloading. In our book, **we have implemented overloading in the form of function overloading and operator overloading**.

Coercion: In this polymorphism, same syntax is used to combine operands of different types. It is a semantic operation that helps avoiding a type error. Consider the statements given below:

```
int val = 50;
float rate = 100;
double total = val * rate;
```

It may be noted that in the last statement, C++ compiler automatically converts 'val' into float and the result of expression 'val * rate' into double before loading its outcome to the variable 'total'. These implicit type conversions are termed as *coercion*.

However, we can also explicitly convert a data type into another by prefixing the data with the desired type as shown below:

```
double val, rate;
rate = (double) 100; (explicit type conversion from int to double)
```

It may be noted that the value '100' has been prefixed by 'double' to force the compiler to convert the value into double type. This activity of explicitly converting one data type into another is called as *type casting*.

Thus, we can say that *coercion* is carried out by default by the compiler and the *typecasting* is forced by the programmer.

APPENDIX
TURBO C++ KEYWORDS

The turbo C++ keywords are listed below:

asm	_cs	far	long	register	switch
auto	default	float	_near	return	template
break	do	for	near	_saveregs	this
case	double	friend	new	_seg	typedef
catch	_ds	goto	opeator	short	union
_cdecl	else	huge	_pascal	signed	unsigned
cdecl	enum	if	pascal	sizeof	virtual
char	_es	inline	private	_ss	void
class	_export	int	protected	static	volatile
const	extern	interrupt	public	struct	while
continue	_far	_loadds			

INDEX

U

V

W